D1573171

THE CLINICIAN'S GUIDE TO THE BEHAVIOR ASSESSMENT SYSTEM FOR CHILDREN (BASC)

THE **CLINICIAN'S GUIDE** TO

THE BEHAVIOR ASSESSMENT SYSTEM for CHILDREN

CECIL R. REYNOLDS
RANDY W. KAMPHAUS

THE GUILFORD PRESS
New York   London

© 2002 The Guilford Press
A Division of Guilford Publications, Inc.
72 Spring Street, New York, NY 10012
www.guilford.com

Printed in the United States of America

This book is printed on acid-free paper.

Last digit is print number: 9   8   7   6   5   4   3   2   1

Library of Congress Cataloging-in-Publication Data

Reynolds, Cecil R., 1952–
   The clinician's guide to the behavior assessment system for children /
Cecil R. Reynolds, Randy W. Kamphaus.
      p. cm.
Includes bibliographical references and index.
   ISBN 1-57230-772-2
   1. Behavior Assessment System for Children.   I. Kamphaus, Randy W.
II. Title.
RJ503.7.B42 R49 2002
618.92′89075—dc21

                                                        2002005511

The Behavior Assessment System for Children (BASC), created by Cecil R. Reynolds
and Randy W. Kamphaus, is a publication of American Guidance Service, Inc.
Copyright 1992 American Guidance Service, Inc.

About the Authors

Cecil R. Reynolds, PhD, ABPN, ABPP, is currently a Professor of Educational Psychology, Professor of Neuroscience, and Distinguished Research Scholar at Texas A & M University. Prior to joining the Texas A & M University faculty in 1981, Dr. Reynolds was a faculty member at the University of Nebraska–Lincoln, where he served as Associate Director and Acting Director of the Buros Institute of Mental Measurement, after writing the grants and proposals to move the Institute to Nebraska following the death of its founder, Oscar Buros. His primary research interests are in all aspects of psychological assessment, with particular emphasis on assessment of memory, emotional, and affective states and traits, and issues of cultural bias in testing. He is the author of more than 300 scholarly publications and author or editor of 34 books, including *Clinical Applications of Continuous Performance Tests, Handbook of School Psychology*, the *Encyclopedia of Special Education*, and the *Handbook of Clinical Child Neuropsychology*. He is the author of several widely used tests of personality and behavior, including the Behavior Assessment System for Children, the Revised Children's Manifest Anxiety Scale, and the Adult Manifest Anxiety Scale. He is also senior author of the Test of Memory and Learning, the Clinical Assessment Scales for the Elderly, the Comprehensive Trail Making Test, and the Developmental Test of Visual Perception—Adolescent and Adult Version, and coauthor of several computerized test interpretation systems. He has a clinical practice in Bastrop, Texas.

Dr. Reynolds holds a diplomate in Clinical Neuropsychology from the American Board of Professional Neuropsychology, of which he is also a past president. He is a diplomate in School Psychology of the American Board of Professional Psychology, and is a diplomate of the American Board of Forensic Examiners. He is a past president of the National Academy of Neuropsychology, American Psychological Association Divisions 5 (Evaluation, Measurement, and Statistics), and 40 (Clinical Neuropsychology). He is a Fellow of APA Divisions 1, 5, 15, 16, and 40 and of the American Psychological Society. Dr. Reynolds is Editor in Chief of *Archives of Clinical Neuro-*

psychology (since 1990), and serves on the editorial boards of 11 other journals in the field. Dr. Reynolds has received multiple national awards recognizing him for excellence in research, including the Lightner Witmer Award and the early career awards from APA Divisions 5 and 15. He is a corecipient of the Society for the Psychological Study of Social Issues Robert Chin Award and a MENSA best research article award. In 1999, Dr. Reynolds received the Senior Scientist Award from APA Division 16 (School Psychology). In 2000, he received the National Academy of Neuropsychology's Distinguished Neuropsychologist Award, the Academy's highest award for research accomplishments. His service to the profession and to society has been recognized as well through the University of North Carolina at Wilmington 50th Anniversary Razor Walker Award for Service to the Youth of America. In 2001 he became the first member of the National Academy of Neuropsychology to receive the Distinguished Service Award and the Distinguished Clinical Neuropsychologist Award.

Randy W. Kamphaus, PhD, is Department Head and Professor of Educational Psychology at the University of Georgia. In addition to classroom work, he has served in roles such as the Director of Training for the doctoral program in School Psychology, the Director of the School Psychology Clinic, and as the Faculty Administrator for Research in the College of Education.

A focus on issues related to clinical assessment has led Dr. Kamphaus to pursue research in classification methods, differential diagnosis, test development, and learning disability and ADHD assessment. He has served as principal investigator, coinvestigator, or consultant on several federally funded research projects dealing with early intervention and prevention, child classification methods, prevalency of ADHD and conduct disorder in Latin America, and violence prevention in schools.

As a licensed psychologist and a Fellow of the American Psychological Association, he has contributed extensively to his profession, and he is past president of APA's Division of School Psychology. Dr. Kamphaus has also authored or co-authored five books, two psychological tests, more than 40 scientific journal articles and more than 20 book chapters. He also participates in scholarship in the field through work as an editorial board member, test reviewer, and serves as a frequent guest lecturer and speaker.

Preface

We have been surprised, gratified, and flattered by the acceptance of the Behavior Assessment System for Children (BASC) by our colleagues in schools, clinics, hospitals, and private offices throughout the United States and Canada. The BASC has also received a warm reception in other neighboring countries and is used often in Latin America. The decision to devote 7 years of our lives (1985–1992) to developing the BASC was born largely out of the need we experienced in our own practices in evaluating children referred to us for a variety of emotional, behavioral, and learning problems. Since the publication of the BASC in 1992, we have received requests for a more detailed interpretive manual. We resisted writing a speculative work on clinical applications of the BASC, determined to wait until research was available by individuals other than ourselves and until there was a body of clinical experience as well. Over the last year, a critical mass became available to us in both arenas.

We have been fortunate enough to see the BASC come of age in the research literature as it is cited frequently in leading journals in several fields. We have also seen it adopted and applied in a number of large, longitudinal research projects, both federally and privately funded, that are now coming to fruition. At the same time, as we have offered well over 200 training workshops on using the BASC, we have learned and benefited from the clinical experience our colleagues have shared with us in these settings.

Correspondence as well as the vigorous interchanges occurring at *www.bascforum.com*, the American Guidance Service interactive web page devoted to the BASC, continued to educate us and led us to the development of this project.

We have written this text primarily as a guide for clinicians to use as they apply the BASC to the difficult, day-to-day assessment problems they face with children and adolescents. Although we review most of the published literature on the BASC, our research reviews are not exhaustive but are rather focused on the clinical questions at hand. We begin with a description of the BASC and enough overview of its development that the novice user can benefit from the remainder of the text. (This coverage is not, however, a substitute for a careful reading of the BASC manual.) We then note more specific applications of the BASC and its various components. Summary tables of interpretation are provided to give more guidance to those who interpret the individual subscales of the BASC. Applications of each of the BASC components are reviewed in detail throughout the text. Authentic case examples are provided from our files and those of school and clinical psychologists in several settings. Specialized applications, such as the use of the Student Observation System in functional behavioral assessment, are discussed throughout the work, as appropriate; specialized applications of the core standardized components of the BASC—the various rating scales and self-report scales— also are reviewed throughout and emphasized in Chapter 7. A new BASC content scale for application with brain-injured children and adolescents is presented with normative data in Chapter 7. Interviews with BASC users in various settings are interspersed, where appropriate (edited for grammar and style, not content). They are not likely a representative sample of BASC users.

We believe that clinicians will find the greatest use for this work, but we have also noted areas of need in the research literature in each chapter. Those seeking to use the BASC in clinical research, basic science, or dissertation research are encouraged to contact us as well as the American Guidance Service, publishers of the BASC. We are always happy to answer questions about the BASC and its applications and to share knowledge of ongoing research projects.

We owe a special debt of thanks to all the BASC users who have shared their experiences, insights, and knowledge with us. Without their input and their encouragement to develop this volume, we could not have completed this work. The American Guidance Service provided special support to us in preparing this volume, especially Dr. Mark Daniel, answering questions we posed and analyzing data from the BASC standardization sample in ways that were helpful to us. The ongoing support of a publisher following the presentation of a work such as the BASC cannot be overstated in the successful adoption and use of any measurement device.

Our graduate students and alumni who made important contributions include Dr. A. Shayne Abelkop, Carolyn Brennan, Dr. Nancy Lett, Dr. Spomenka Calic-Newman, Cheryl Hendry, Kim Blaker, Ellen Rowe, Dr. Martha Petoskey, Anna Kroncke, Erin Dowdy, Amanda Dix, Mauricio Garcia, Anne Pierce Winsor, Karen Musgrove, Jennifer Thorpe, Marcia Heringa, and colleagues such as Dr. A. Michele Lease influenced our thinking. We are especially grateful to the staff of The Guilford Press for their patience with us, and to Sharon Panulla and Chris Jennison, in particular. The volume took far longer to prepare than we estimated and we appreciate their staying the course.

To our mentor, Alan S. Kaufman, we continue to owe a debt of thanks for the preparation he provided us as his students and the model of scholarship and humanity he unfailingly presents to us as we move through our careers.

CRR would like to express his priceless debt to Julia, once again, for all of her support in ways too diverse and meaningful to describe, not only in the preparation of this work but in all aspects of his life. RWK wishes to express his gratitude to Norma for her devotion and companionship through the years of arduous labor that resulted in the BASC and such follow-up projects as this volume.

We issue an open invitation to those who use the BASC and those who consider using it, to continue to share with us their impressions, experiences, knowledge, and data concerning the BASC. We promise to use this feedback wisely in any revision of the BASC and in developing additional assessment tools that we hope will assist clinicians in the habilitation of the development of the children and adolescents whom we all serve.

CECIL R. REYNOLDS, PHD
RANDY W. KAMPHAUS, PHD

Contents

THE CLINICIAN'S GUIDE TO THE BEHAVIOR ASSESSMENT SYSTEM FOR CHILDREN (BASC)

CHAPTER 1

Overview of Components
and Uses

Dr. James, you are not alone in having invested many hours in research producing uninterpretable results because of unreliable measures. In fact I would go so far as to say that difficulty in measuring the phenomena of interest in the behavioral sciences goes a long way toward explaining why we live in a world so technologically advanced and so behaviorally primitive.

—STRAYHORN (1993, p. 1301)

Our overriding purpose for developing the *Behavior Assessment System for Children* (BASC; Reynolds & Kamphaus, 1992) is largely consistent with Strayhorn's view, quoted above. We wanted to improve the quality of the assessment technology available for assessing child behavior. In this volume we strive to improve child assessment technology by providing guidance in BASC usage that is based in measurement science, common sense, and accumulated experience—with the flaws of each dimension fully recognized.

The BASC is a multimethod, multidimensional approach to evaluating the behavior and self-perceptions of children ages 2 years 6 months to 18 years, and includes its new variant, the BASC ADHD Monitor (Kamphaus & Reynolds, 1998)[1]. The original BASC is *multimethod* in that it has five components, which may be used individually or in any combination:

- The *Teacher and Parent Rating Scales (PRS and TRS)*, separate instruments that elicit descriptions of the child's observable behavior at home, in the community, and at school

---

[1]Portions of this chapter are reprinted with permission or adapted from Reynolds and Kamphaus (1992) and Kamphaus and Reynolds (1998).

1

- The *Self-Report of Personality (SRP)*, which the child uses to describe his or her emotions and self-perceptions
- The *Structured Developmental History (SDH)*, which is used to collect biographical, demographic, historical, and developmental information from parents or other primary caregivers, and which can serve as the basis for a parent interview
- The *Student Observation System (SOS)*, a form for recording and classifying directly observed classroom behavior

These components compile different sources of information and use different methods, a factor important to assessing generalizability of results and validation in diagnosis. The SRP provides a view of how the child experiences his or her behavior, feelings, attitudes, and cognitions. The PRS and TRS provide impressionistic, holistic summaries of behavior as seen through the eyes of behavioral experts specific to the child in question. The SDH supplies a context for the presenting problem and a format for a structured interview as an additional method of assessment. The SOS provides direct observation and counting of behavior, believed by many to be the sine qua non of behavioral assessment (e.g., see Ramsay, Reynolds, & Kamphaus, 2002, Ch. 1, for a review).

The BASC is *multidimensional* in that it measures numerous dimensions of behavior and personality, including positive (adaptive) and negative (clinical) dimensions including internalizing and externalizing problems. The inclusion of positive dimensions of behavior is an important component of the BASC that, among other characteristics, differentiates it from other behavior rating scales and systems. The absence of positive behavioral dimensions was a significant limitation of preceding behavior rating scales, remedied by the BASC (e.g., see Kratochwill, Sheridan, Carlson, & Laseck, 1999). The BASC also assesses overt and covert behavior along with attitudes, feelings, and cognitions as well as certain affective states—for example, anxiety, depressed mood, and attributional states—giving a range of dimensions heretofore unavailable except via the use of many different scales, developed over the span of many years, and/or with disparate samples.

TEACHER RATING SCALES

The TRS has three forms with items applicable to three age groups: preschool (2½–5), child (6–11), and adolescent (12–18). The forms contain descriptors of behaviors that the respondent rates on a 4-point scale of frequency, ranging from *never* to *almost always*. The TRS takes 10–20 minutes to complete, although teachers who are familiar with the scale seldom require more than 10 minutes.

The TRS assesses clinical problems in the broad domains (composites) of externalizing problems, internalizing problems, and school problems and measures adaptive skills. Table 1.1 shows the composites and scales for all levels of the TRS. The slight differences between levels are due to developmental changes in the behavioral manifestations of child problems. Composites and scales with the same name contain the same conceptual content at all age levels, even though specific items change across age. Children do not show their problems the same way at all developmental levels. In addition to individual scale and composite scores, the TRS provides a broad composite rating, the Behavioral Symptoms Index (BSI), which assesses the overall level of problematic behaviors.

TABLE 1.1. Composites and Scales in the TRS and PRS

Composite and Scales	Teacher Rating Scales			Parent Rating Scales		
	Preschool	Child	Adolescent	Preschool	Child	Adolescent
Externalizing Problems	*	*	*	*	*	*
Aggression	*	*	*	*	*	*
Hyperactivity	*	*	*	*	*	*
Conduct Problems		*	*		*	*
Internalizing Problems	*	*	*	*	*	*
Anxiety	*	*	*	*	*	*
Depression	*	*	*	*	*	*
Somatization	*	*	*	*	*	*
School Problems		*	*			
Attention Problems	*	*	*	*	*	*
Learning Problems		*	*			
Other Problems						
Atypicality	*	*	*	*	*	*
Withdrawal	*	*	*	*	*	*
Adaptive Skills	*	*	*	*	*	*
Adaptability	*	*	*		*	*
Leadership	*	*	*	*	*	*
Social Skills	*	*	*	*	*	*
Study Skills		*	*			
Behavioral Symptoms Index	*	*	*	*	*	*

Note. Italicized scales compose the Behavioral Symptoms Index. From Reynolds and Kamphaus (1992). Reprinted by permission.

A recent study found that children's teachers from the previous year can provide accurate ratings of the child at the beginning of the new year with the new teacher. Hoover, Braver, Wolchik, and Sandler (2000) found that teacher ratings on the Teacher–Child Rating Scale (T-CRS; Hightower, 1986) were very similar for a group of 240 elementary-grade children who were part of a divorce intervention study. They concluded:

> However, neither the previous teachers' nor the current teachers' fall ratings were significantly different from the spring teachers' pretest ratings. Thus, school psychologists may elect to obtain ratings from either the previous or current teacher early in the fall of a new academic year. (p. 2)

We cite this study because it supports our perception that these findings are likely to hold true for many teacher ratings. We prefer, however, to obtain ratings from the current teacher as soon as possible in the new school year.

The TRS can be interpreted in relation to national age norms (general, female, or male) and to clinical norms. In addition, selected critical items can be interpreted individually. The TRS includes a validity check in the form of an F ("fake bad") index designed to detect an excessively negative response set in the teacher completing the rating. The BASC software programs also yield a patterning validity index that assesses deviant patterns such as alternating between choices on a consistent basis. This validity index is usually of little applicability; teachers and parents have little incentive to complete a rating carelessly. The consistency index produced by the software is of greater value in that it detects agreement among highly similar items. By doing so, this index assesses more subtle response biases and detects rater unreliability.

PARENT RATING SCALES

The PRS is a comprehensive measure of a child's adaptive and problematic behaviors in community and home settings. It uses the same four-choice response format as the TRS and also takes 10–20 minutes to complete.

As indicated in Table 1.1, the PRS has three forms at three age levels: preschool, child, and adolescent. The age levels of the PRS are similar in content and structure. Table 1.2 lists the scale definitions of the PRS.

The PRS assesses almost all of the clinical and adaptive behavioral domains that the TRS measures. However, the PRS does not have a School Problems composite, nor does it include the two TRS scales that are best observed by teachers (Learning Problems and Study Skills).

The PRS offers the same norm groups as the TRS: national age norms (general, female, and male) and clinical norms. Like the TRS, the PRS includes *F*, patterning, and consistency indexes, as checks on the validity of the parent ratings, and critical items that may signify behaviors that should be interpreted individually.

TABLE 1.2. TRS and PRS Definitions

Scale	Definition
Adaptability	The ability to adapt readily to changes in the environment
Anxiety	The tendency to be nervous, fearful, or worried about real or imagined problems
Aggression	The tendency to act in a hostile manner (either verbally or physically) that is threatening to others
Attention Problems	The tendency to be easily distracted and unable to concentrate more than momentarily
Atypicality	The tendency to behave in ways that are immature, considered "odd," or commonly associated with psychosis (such as experiencing visual or auditory hallucinations)
Conduct Problems	The tendency to engage in antisocial and rule-breaking behavior, including destroying property
Depression	Feelings of unhappiness, sadness, and stress that may result in neurovegetative symptoms and the inability to carry out everyday activities and/or may bring on thoughts of suicide
Hyperactivity	The tendency to be overly active, rush through work or activities, and act without thinking
Leadership	The skills associated with accomplishing academic, social, or community goals, including, in particular, the ability to work well with others
Learning Problems	The presence of academic difficulties, particularly in understanding or completing schoolwork
Social Skills	The skills necessary for interacting successfully with peers and adults in home, school, and community settings
Somatization	The tendency to be overly sensitive to and complain about relatively minor physical problems and discomforts
Study Skills	The skills that are conducive to strong academic performance, including organizational skills and good study habits
Withdrawal	The tendency to evade others to avoid social contact

Note. From Reynolds and Kamphaus (1992). Reprinted by permission.

SELF-REPORT OF PERSONALITY

The SRP is an omnibus personality inventory consisting of statements to which the child or adolescent responds as either *true* or *false*. It takes 20–30 minutes to complete and has forms at two age levels: child (8–11) and adolescent (12–18). These levels overlap considerably in scales, structure, and individual items. Both levels have identical composite scores: School Maladjustment, Clinical Maladjustment, Personal Adjustment, and an overall composite score, the Emotional Symptoms Index (ESI). The child level (SRP–C) has 12 scales and the adolescent level (SRP–A) has 14 scales, all grouped in composites (see Table 1.3). Unlike the BSI, the ESI has both negative (clinical) and positive (adaptive) scales whose scoring has been reversed, because these are the scales that load highest on a general psychopathology factor.

    Like the rating scales, the SRP can be interpreted in relation to national age norms (general, female, and male) and to clinical norms. Special indexes are incorporated to assess the validity of the child's responses: the patterning and consistency indexes, *F* index, *L* ("fake good") index for the SRP–A only, and the *V* index designed to detect invalid responses due to poor reading

TABLE 1.3. Composites and Scales in the SRP

Composite and Scales	Child	Adolescent
Clinical Maladjustment	*	*
Anxiety	*	*
Atypicality	*	*
Locus of Control	*	*
Social Stress	*	*
Somatization	*	*
School Maladjustment	*	*
Attitude to School	*	*
Attitude to Teachers	*	*
Sensation Seeking		*
Other Problems		
Depression	*	*
Sense of Inadequacy	*	*
Personal Adjustment	*	*
Relations with Parents	*	*
Interpersonal Relations	*	*
Self-Esteem	*	*
Self-Reliance	*	*
Emotional Symptoms Index	*	*

*Note.*Italicized scales compose the Emotional Symptoms Index. From Reynolds and Kamphaus (1992). Reprinted by permission.

TABLE 1.4. Student SRP Scale Definitions

Scale	Definition
Anxiety	Feelings of nervousness, worry, and fear; the tendency to be overwhelmed by problems
Attitude to School	Feelings of alienation, hostility, and dissatisfaction regarding school
Attitude to Teachers	Feelings of resentment and dislike of teachers; beliefs that teachers are unfair, uncaring, or overly demanding
Atypicality	The tendency toward gross mood swings, bizarre thoughts, subjective experiences, or obsessive–compulsive thoughts and behaviors often considered "odd"
Depression	Feelings of unhappiness, sadness, and dejection; a belief that nothing goes right
Interpersonal Relations	The perception of having good social relationships and friendships with peers
Locus of Control	The belief that rewards and punishments are controlled by external events or other people
Relations with Parents	A positive regard toward parents and a feeling of being esteemed by them
Self-Esteem	Feelings of self-esteem, self-respect, and self-acceptance
Self-Reliance	Confidence in one's ability to solve problems; a belief in one's personal dependability and decisiveness
Sensation Seeking	The tendency to take risks, to like noise, and to seek excitement
Sense of Inadequacy	Perceptions of being unsuccessful in school, unable to achieve one's goals, and generally inadequate
Social Stress	Feelings of stress and tension in personal relationships; a feeling of being excluded from social activities
Somatization	The tendency to be overly sensitive to, experience, or complain about relatively minor physical problems and discomforts

Note. From Reynolds and Kamphaus (1992). Reprinted by permission.

comprehension, failure to follow directions, refusal to respond seriously to the task, or poor contact with reality. Table 1.4 lists scale definitions of the SRP.

STRUCTURED DEVELOPMENTAL HISTORY

The SDH is an extensive history and background survey that may be completed by a clinician during an interview with a parent or guardian, or may be completed as a questionnaire by a parent, either at home or in the school or clinic.

The purpose of the SDH is to elicit information crucial to the diagnostic and treatment process. Many developmental events and medical or related problems in the family have an impact on children's behavior. The SDH structures the gathering of the child and family history, both social and medical. Because it is comprehensive, the SDH is an asset to any child evaluation, whether or not other BASC components are used.

STUDENT OBSERVATION SYSTEM

The SOS is a form for recording a direct observation of the classroom behavior of a child. The SOS uses the technique of momentary time sampling (i.e., systematic coding during 3-second intervals spaced 30 seconds apart over a 15-minute period) to record a wide range of children's behaviors, whether positive (such as teacher–student interaction) or negative (such as inappropriate movement or inattention).

The SOS can be used in regular and special education classes, as part of the initial assessment and diagnostic process. It can also be used repeatedly to evaluate the effectiveness of educational, behavioral, psychopharmacological, or other treatments over time.

FORMS

The TRS, PRS, and SRP forms come in two formats: hand-scoring or computer entry. The hand-scoring forms are printed in a convenient self-scoring format, which facilitates rapid scoring (requiring about 5 minutes each, after practice) without using templates or keys. Each form includes a profile of scale and composite scores. The computer entry forms, which are simpler one-part forms, are designed to allow the user to key item responses into a microcomputer in about 5 minutes.

COMPUTER SOFTWARE

A microcomputer program, BASC Plus, is available that offers online administration of the TRS, PRS, and SRP and computer scoring of a completed computer-scored or hand-scored form. The manual for BASC Plus explains how to use the program to administer, score, and report the TRS, PRS, and

8

SRP. It includes additional interpretive text and a listing of target behaviors not available on other computer programs.

The BASC Enhanced ASSIST program offers users a simpler computer program that produces all possible scores, a graphical display of results, and item responses, but does not allow online administration.

NORMATIVE SAMPLES

General Norms

General norms are based on a large national sample that is representative of the population of U.S. children with regard to sex, race/ethnicity, clinical or special education classifications, and parent education (for the PRS). These norms are subdivided by age, which allows for comparisons between the child under assessment and the general population of children that age. These norms (combining females and males) are the preferred norms, and they are recommended for general use.

Several of scales in the TRS, PRS, and SRP show gender differences. Males tend to obtain higher raw scores on scales of Aggression, Conduct Problems, Hyperactivity, Attention Problems, and Learning Problems in the TRS and PRS, and on the Sensation Seeking, Attitude to School, Attitude to Teachers, and Self-Esteem scales in the SRP. Females tend to score higher than males on scales of Social Skills, Study Skills, Leadership, and Depression in the TRS and PRS, and on the Anxiety and Interpersonal Relations scales of the SRP. These differences in scores likely reflect real differences between males and females in the incidence of the indicated behavioral or emotional problems or strengths in adaptive skills.

A common set of norms must be used for both males and females in order for these gender differences to surface in the normative scores. The general combined-sex norms serve this purpose. General norms answer the question, how commonly does this level of rated or self-reported behavior occur in the general population at this age? Using general norms, for example, more males than females show high T scores on Aggression, and more females than males have high T scores on Social Skills. The combined gender or general norms preserve observed gender differences in the shape and level of the raw score distributions. The general norms should be used if one believes that boys and girls are different in regard to various behavioral characteristics (i.e., observed differences are not due to psychometric artifacts). For example, girls score higher than boys on the SRP Anxiety scale (a common finding in research on anxiety; e.g., see Reynolds & Richmond, 1985). In determining which set of norms to use, clinicians must answer the question, "Are girls more anxious than boys, or are they simply more willing to admit to symptoms of anxiety?" If the former is true, the general norms would be more appropriate, but in the latter case, the gender-specific norms would be the correct choice. Reynolds and Kamphaus (1992) recommend the use of the general norms—a decision with which we continue to concur—but the individual clinician may disagree and opt for the other norms. The option allows clinicians more latitude than typically occurs on behavioral and self-report scales.

Female Norms and Male Norms

These norms are based on subsets of the general norm sample; each is representative of the general population of children of that age and gender. The effect of using these separate-sex norms is to eliminate differences between males and females in the distribution of T scores or percentiles. For example, although raw score ratings on the Aggression scale tend to be higher for males than females, use of separate-sex norms removes this difference and produces distributions of normative scores that are the same for both genders.

An Illustration of the General versus Same-Sex Norms

In the abstract, the different applications of these norms can be difficult to understand. To some it may seem counterintuitive that the use of combined gender norms *preserves* gender differences in scaled scores (T scores in the BASC) and that same-sex norms *equalizes* the two genders. Table 1.5 provides illustrative data from the norms table for the PRS–A Anxiety scale for 13- to 14-year-olds. This scale shows a consistent, albeit small, trend for girls to score higher than boys. If girls as a group are, in fact, generally more anxious than boys, it is appropriate to present this difference.

Consider a raw score of 13 on the Anxiety scale in Table 1.5. Comparing boys only to boys, a male with this raw score earns a T score of 72; comparing girls only to girls, a female earns a T score of 69. When we combine the two groups so that each child's anxiety score is compared to all other children, both earn a T score of 70. The T score of the female is adjusted upward and the T score of the male downward. If we had used the Aggression scale as our example, the reverse pattern would occur: The combined gender versus general norms would adjust male scores upward and female scores downward.

TABLE 1.5. Example of Male, Female, and Combined Norms on the BASC PRS-A Anxiety Scale, Ages 13–14

Raw score	Males only *T* score	Females only *T* score	Combined gender *T* score
30	120	117	118
29	119	114	116
28	116	111	113
27	114	108	110
26	111	106	107
25	108	103	104
24	105	100	101
23	102	97	99
22	99	94	96
21	96	91	93
20	93	89	90
19	90	86	87
18	87	83	84
17	84	80	82
16	81	77	79
15	78	75	76
14	75	72	73
13	72	69	70
12	69	66	67
11	66	63	65
10	64	61	62
9	61	58	59
8	58	55	56
7	55	52	53
6	52	49	50
5	49	47	48
4	46	44	45
3	43	41	42
2	40	38	39
1	37	35	36
0	34	33	33
Raw Score Mean/*SD*	5.4/3.4	6.2/3.6	5.8/3.5

Most often, the group with the highest mean raw score undergoes an upward adjustment in the scaled score when moving from homogeneous to more heterogeneous norms tables; conversely, the group with the lowest mean raw score undergoes a downward adjustment at most raw score points.

As noted above, the deciding factor in determining which set of tables to use lies in the examiner's view of reality. If boys are believed to be innately more aggressive than girls, then combined versus general norms should be applied. If it is believed that the higher mean raw scores for boys on Aggression scales are due to some sort of systematic error or measurement bias,

11

INTERVIEW 1.1

Robert A. Byrne, PhD, ABPP
Lieutenant Colonel, U.S. Army
Director, USMA Center for Personal Development

How do you use the BASC in your practice, research, and/or training?

I use the PRS, TRS, and SRP scales with every child I evaluate. All BASCs are completed and scored prior to conducting the evaluation. Shortly before conducting a clinical interview with the parents and child, I review all BASC data, complemented by additional data I request (e.g., a comprehensive medical history questionnaire completed by the parent(s), school records and testing, Parenting Stress Index, etc). These data allow me to develop a tentative master problem list (i.e., internalizing vs. externalizing problems, critical items, etc).

Also, a review of the BASC validity scales gives me a sense about the respondent (e.g., a parent who is overreporting problems), from which I may develop preliminary hypotheses (e.g., problems with attachment). The consistency between respondents and/or settings of the BASC ratings also helps me determine if the problem is localized to one setting, pervasive across settings, or more circumscribed (e.g., parent–child problem). With this analysis, I can focus my clinical interview with greater specificity when I meet with the parent(s) and child. This is in stark contrast to my previous method of conducting a lengthy and comprehensive standardized interview with all clients. When I write up the results of an evaluation, I always include an organized summary of the BASC results and reference these results in support of my diagnostic impressions. Perhaps more importantly, in conducting interpretive interviews with parents and teachers, I frequently display BASC profiles in partial support of these impressions (e.g., support or lack of support for an ADHD diagnosis vs. a parent–child problem).

I often reference the BASC during the teacher inservice programs I conduct on the management of disruptive behaviors. I explain both the broad and more narrowly defined bands of behavior and emotional problems and emphasize the importance of collecting data from a variety of sources and settings over time to more thoroughly understand a child's problem(s). I also emphasize the BASC's strong psychometric foundations and properties—it is a state-of-the-art instrument that greatly enhances the quality of practice—as well as its compatibility with IDEA's assessment requirements. Finally, I consistently urge my colleagues (e.g., psychologists, pediatricians, child psychiatrists, and special educators) to consider using it in their practice.

(continued)

INTERVIEW 1.1 *(continued)*

Please identify some of the outcomes of these activities (e.g., patient care and scientific findings).

Generally, I feel that the overall quality of my evaluations has increased considerably. Also, as I mentioned above, I am much more efficient and focused at the outset of a clinical interview. Finally, my clients and consultees appear to feel a greater level of confidence in my impressions as well—which I attribute, in large part, to the comprehensive information provided by the BASC.

Can you identify any particular strengths or weaknesses of the BASC that others should consider in their work?

Strengths

Extremely well conceptualized, developed, standardized, and normed. I'd go to court with it—anywhere, anytime.

Easily interpretable printouts.

The innovation of validity scales for a child behavior rating scale is long overdue, not to mention extremely useful in clinical settings.

The availability of critical items helps ensure that I do not fail to adequately address/assess important, albeit sometimes unmentioned, concerns, that I might otherwise fail to cover in my more narrowly focused interview.

Weakness

No place for narrative comments by the respondent. The one thing I miss about the CBCL is its first page that provided for narrative comments by parents and teachers. I find this information to be qualitatively useful and wonder if might be considered a BASC revision.

Neutral

Intraindividual score comparisons have never been that helpful.

Do you have any other remarks regarding the BASC?

I think the BASC represents a significant milestone in the psychometric assessment of emotional and behavioral problems in children. All child and school psychologists should make it a primary tool in their assessments.

then the use of same-sex norms is corrective. The latter is highly unlikely (e.g., see Reynolds, Lowe, & Saenz, 1999; Brown, Reynolds, & Whitaker, 1999). Our view of the literature suggests that boys and girls are, in fact, different on some dimensions of behavior. For these reasons we urge the use of the combined or general norms on the BASC. However, recognizing that professionals should be allowed to make their own choices, we provide both options in the BASC manual (Reynolds & Kamphaus, 1992) and in all versions of the BASC computer scoring programs.

INDEXES OF VALIDITY AND RESPONSE SET

Several indexes are provided to help the BASC user judge the quality of a completed form. Validity may be threatened by several factors, including failure to pay attention to item content, carelessness, an attempt to portray a child in a highly negative or positive light, lack of motivation to respond truthfully, or poor comprehension of the items. Information on the development of these indexes and the setting of cutoff scores is provided in Reynolds and Kamphaus (1992).

F Index

The F index, included in all of the BASC rating-scale and self-report forms, is a measure of the respondent's tendency to be excessively negative about the child's behaviors or self-perceptions and emotions. The F scale was developed using traditional psychometric methods associated with Infrequency scales (e.g., see Reynolds, 2001a).

On the PRS and TRS, the F index is scored by counting the number of times the respondent answered *almost always* to a description of negative behavior, or *never* to a description of positive behavior. Because responses on the SRP are limited to *true* and *false*, items selected for that F index are either extremely negative items to which the child responded *true* or positive items to which the response was *false*. Items selected for these scales have a low probability of co-occurrence; that is, they are seldom endorsed in concert with one another.

The TRS, PRS, and SRP record forms show what levels of F index scores are high enough to warrant concern. Detailed guidance for interpreting the F index is given in Reynolds and Kamphaus (1992). Applications of the F index to forensic problems are discussed in Chapter 7 of this book.

L Index

The *L* index, included in the adolescent level of the SRP, measures an adolescent's tendency to give an extremely positive picture of him- or herself—what could be called "faking good." The index consists of items that are unrealistically positive (such as, "I like everyone I meet") or mildly self-critical, which most people would endorse (such as, "I sometimes get mad"). Individuals scoring high on this scale may be giving what they believe to be the most socially desirable responses, or possibly they are psychologically naive (relative to their peers) in their denials of common, everyday problems and concerns. The SRP–A record form shows which *L* scores warrant concern.

V Index

Each level of the SRP includes a *V* index made up of five or six nonsensical or highly implausible statements (such as, "Superman is a real person"). The *V* index serves as a basic check on the validity of the SRP scores in general. If a respondent marks two or more of these statements as *true*, the respondent's score may be invalid.

USER QUALIFICATIONS

We are often asked about user qualifications (we addressed this issue at the time of initial publication; Reynolds & Kamphaus, 1992). With the support of our publisher, we designated the BASC as a so-called "Level C" product. We receive so many questions about this issue for good reason: The BASC has become extremely popular. For this reason we will provide further guidance regarding this issue.

We developed the BASC with the expectation that psychologists would be the most frequent users of the scales. The inclusion of clinical scales on depression, atypicality, and hyperactivity is consistent with a long history of psychometric assessment of these and numerous other dimensions of behavioral and clinical syndromes. Furthermore, we anticipated some transfer of training from use of other instruments such as the MMPI and those that established the popularity of the *T*-score metrics. We also believe that psychologists licensed by state or provincial boards or certified by departments of education typically have the training specified by the Level C criteria.

The qualifications to use the BASC, however, will never be as clear as

INTERVIEW 1.2

Gail S. Matazow, PhD
Clinical Neuropsychologist
Alberta Hospital Edmonton
and Neuropsychology Consulting Services

I use the BASC in my clinical practice and in training activities at the University of Alberta—graduate courses in childhood psychopathology and behavioral diagnosis/intervention. I have found the BASC to be particularly useful in highlighting areas of concern. Specifically:

1. Depression/suicide: Elevations on scales of depression, sense of inadequacy, and decreased self-reliance suggest possible suicidal ideation. Further evaluation should be sought when this pattern is obtained.

2. Validity scales: Elevations on disruptive behaviors, mood-related or anxiety-related symptoms, and decreased adaptability suggest an inordinately high number of problematic behaviors and/or marked parental distress in managing this child. Further exploration toward a parental "plea for assistance" is warranted.

3. Withdrawal scale/atypicality scale: Elevations are noteworthy for patient population(s) who are socially isolated or when there is indication of social relationship difficulties (e.g., Asperger's).

4. Disruptive behavior disorders: Elevations on scales of attention, hyperactivity, aggression, and conduct disorder suggest further interviewing toward multiple diagnoses of ADHD, oppositional defiant disorder, and/or conduct disorder.

5. The use of parent, teacher, and self-report scales allows the clinician to glean information from multiple raters across multiple settings. This standard has proven invaluable toward accurate diagnosis of behavioral disorders. As suggested, the BASC has continued the tradition (with extremely well-developed norms) of obtaining comprehensive information from a variety of sources in the effort to understand a child's behavioral functioning. The BASC has established the tradition of ensuring that clinical and adaptive behavior functioning is addressed in formulating childhood diagnoses and setting appropriate treatment guidelines.

6. The BASC theoretical basis allows for scales that are cohesive and provide succinct information about problem areas. In other scales that use a factor analytic approach to scale construction, it is necessary to examine item content of the scales to obtain an understanding of the specific areas of deficit. It has

(continued)

INTERVIEW 1.2 *(continued)*

been my experience with the latter approach that a scale may, in fact, incorporate multiple areas of deficiency.

7. *V* index: I have seldom seen an elevation on this scale. The one time that it happened, the mother of the child stated that her son told her that he answered the second half of the scale at random. She was impressed that it was so easily identifiable.

8. Ease of scoring: The setup of the BASC allows for particularly easy scoring.

9. Standardization: It has been my clinical impression that the BASC accurately identifies areas of weakness/clinical impairment. In other words, clinical elevations on the BASC generally correspond with parent or teacher reports regarding areas of behavioral concern.

Please refer to our chapter in Matazow and Kamphaus (in press) for strengths of the BASC. My major complaint of the BASC is the Anxiety scale—particularly for adolescents and secondary students. I find that it is not highly sensitive to identifying anxiety difficulties, due to the high number of items that must be endorsed for clinical significance. If there is suggestion of an anxiety issue, I administer additional measures (e.g., Revised Children's Manifest Anxiety Scale [RCMAS]; Reynolds & Richmond, 1985) because the BASC does not adequately measure these difficulties.

---

those for the MMPI, WISC, or many others because many of these instruments require courses unto themselves and/or have limited uses. The MMPI and WISC, for example, are infrequently used for screening purposes due to their length. Even the WISC, however, is used by non-psychologists such as educational diagnosticians.

The BASC, on the other hand, has many uses beyond that of differential diagnosis. Screening is one application. Screening for attention-deficit/ hyperactivity disorder (ADHD) for example, occurs daily without the assistance of social workers, physicians, counselors, or psychologists. Parents frequently complete ADHD screening scales, or lists of symptoms from the fourth edition of the *Diagnostic and Statistical Manual of Mental Disorders* (DSM)published in the popular press. Teachers, psychologists, counselors, speech pathologists, in some cases trained paraprofessionals (e.g., parents), and others may use the BASC for screening purposes. We suggest that a person with Level C credentials be notified if *any T* scores of 60 or higher are obtained using the general norms so these professionals can review the data to determine whether further diagnostic work or related follow-up are required.

As is the case when using any psychometric device, the user's decision regarding whether or not he or she meets Level C credentials is an ethical one. Just as there are few limitations on who can provide "psychotherapy" or "counseling," there are few legal proscriptions regarding psychometric test use and no regulatory body. Publishers can try to limit sales to those holding Level C credentials, though they are not "required" to do so; in an effort to help all of us practice within the ethical bounds of our competencies, they do so as a service to the profession and the public.

Our second major point is that nonpsychologists can meet Level C credentials. We know of medical schools that offer thorough training in the use of the BASC and the BASC ADHD Monitor to their residents in developmental pediatrics. We also know of groups of pediatricians and social workers who have sought training in developmental psychopathology, psychometrics, and the BASC in order to use the BASC system for differential diagnosis. It is ultimately up to the clinician to determine if he or she meets Level C criteria. Even those who do not meet these criteria may use portions of the BASC for nondiagnostic purposes, such as treatment/program planning and evaluation, administration, research, and screening.

We know of HMOs, agencies, and other health care groups who use the BASC for program evaluation purposes. In these formats the BASC is used by a variety of professionals for reporting purposes. An individual or group of individuals with research expertise and Level C credentials then analyze the results for administrative and program planning.

When asked at various venues about the qualifications issue, we typically respond with two questions:

1. For what purposes are you using the BASC?
2. If you are using it as part of making differential diagnosis or classification decisions, do you meet Level C credentials?

18

CHAPTER 2

Scales

The BASC scales comprise the heart of the instrument's utility. The scales are based on a half century, or more, of psychological and medical science. Constructs such as anxiety and depression, for example, have been the subjects of countless research investigations and theoretical treatises. Consequently, BASC users have considerable evidence upon which to draw inferences related to individual scale scores. In order to elucidate this linkage between scores, science, and theory, each scale is discussed separately in this chapter.

HYPERACTIVITY

The content of the Hyperactivity scale is based on the last two decades of research investigating the core symptom domains of ADHD. This body of research findings was summarized prior to the initiation of the field trials for the DSM-IV (Lahey et al., 1994). In short, numerous factor analytic investigations produced consistent findings.

There appear to be two core symptoms of ADHD, not three. Impulsivity items have been found to be colinear with hyperactivity items of rating scales, rendering derivation of a separate factor (or scale) unwise. The result is that the DSM-IV criteria for ADHD subsume impulsivity symptoms within the hyperactivity domain, just as the BASC does (Kamphaus & Frick, 1996). Is the overlap between the BASC and DSM happenstance or purposeful? It is neither. The BASC Hyperactivity (and impulsivity) and Attention Problems scales are the product of independent research efforts. Their resulting similarity merely reflects the robustness of the finding of two core behavioral domains associated with ADHD.

The BASC Hyperactivity scale also resembles the DSM-IV in that the majority of the behaviors are symptoms of hyperactivity, with fewer impulsivity items. This mixture of items suggests that elevated scores on this scale will reflect hyperactivity problems in most cases. Other interpretive considerations include the following.

1. Hyperactivity problems can exist independently of attention problems. Our prepublication and subsequent research (Kamphaus & Frick, 2002), also supported by the DSM-IV field trial findings, which resulted in the identification of the ADHD subtype, predominantly hyperactive–impulsive type.

2. Hyperactivity problems are more likely to co-occur with aggression and conduct problems. This prediction is based on (a) clinical experience, (b) the known high comorbidity between ADHD combined type and other externalizing findings, and (c) our factor analytic results showing that these three scales produce a factor separate from internalizing, adaptive skills, and the TRS learning problems factor (which includes the Attention Problems scale).

3. A content-based interpretation of this scale may be warranted to determine the relative contributions of hyperactivity and impulsivity problems to the child's daily adjustment at school or at home. Specifically, if problems such as impulsive decision making are noted by referral sources, it may be helpful to consider interpreting impulsivity items separately.

A study by Biederman, Wilens, and Mick (1999) found that a sample of white ADHD boys ($N = 15$) treated with medication were at significantly lower risk for the development of a substance abuse disorder in adolescence than boys with ADHD who were not treated with medication. Specifically, for a sample of boys age 15 years or older, the substance abuse diagnostic rate was 75% for the untreated group, 25% for the treated group, and 18% for a control group without ADHD. These findings, if replicated, may allay the fears of some parents who are considering medication for their child. In addition, such findings show the importance of using scales such as the BASC to identify ADHD and treat it aggressively.

The ratings received on the BASC Hyperactivity scale correlate well with

TABLE 2.1. Hyperactivity Scale Interpretation Guide

T-score range	Qualitative descriptor	Potential interpretation
≥ 80	Extreme	Extremely high levels of activity commonly accompanied by severe impulsivity; very disruptive; diagnosis of ADHD common.
70–79	Clinically significant	Restless and overactive, problems with impulse control, likes attention; ADHD often present.
60–69	Mildly to moderately elevated or at risk	Restless, frequently agitated, overly active, tends to distract others; probably not ADHD unless attention problems also evident.
40–59	Average or typical	Normal levels of activity relative to same age children.
≤ 39	Low to very low	Very low activity levels, sedate, calm, possibly depressed or experiencing psychomotor retardation.

continuous performance test (CPT) results, indicating problems with impulsivity and attention or CPT measures (Entwhistle, Kalinsky, & Toscano, 1997). Thus there is correspondence among very different methods of assessing these constructs that support (1) the use of the BASC in the diagnosis of ADHD, and (2) the pervasive, negative influence of high levels of hyperactivity on behavior and decision making. Table 2.1 summarizes interpretations of the Hyperactivity scale.

AGGRESSION

The item content of the Aggression scale is tipped in favor of verbal aggression (e.g., cursing, threatening). This mixture of content typically beckons the user to review the items that contribute to high scores—a process that is facilitated greatly by using the computer-scoring programs, all of which allow the option of printing the items listed by scale along with the response of the rater. Having done so, clinicians may find it more insightful to draw separate conclusions about verbal and physical aggression.

In some cases, findings on the Aggression scale may mandate further assessment of anger and anger outbursts. High scores on this scale suggest that anger is a potential problem deserving inquiry through qualitative or quantitative means. Clinicians might ask teachers, parents, or examinees about feelings of anger (under what circumstances and to what resolution), their frequency, duration, stimuli, and typical responses. Answers to such questions lead indirectly to intervention planning, wherein treatment providers can target anger stimuli and response in an effort to thwart aggressive behavior.

Clinicians are also reminded that the Aggression scale is part of the externalizing composite and is expected to be a co-occurring problem. Therefore, even if elevated only slightly, perhaps in the at-risk range, aggression problems may warrant treatment. Aggression is one of the least tolerated behavior problems at all age levels. During the development of the BASC, large numbers of teachers and children ($N = 7,500$) were asked to list the behavior of children at school they "hated the most." Aggressive behaviors topped the list for every group. Small elevations on this scale may identify kids who are likely to be rejected or ostracized by more positive peer groups and also by teachers. Reducing aggressive behavior will have the advantage of providing indirect treatment to the offending child by improving his or her all-important peer and teacher interactions. Improved management of aggression symptoms in a child with conduct disorder, for example, may play an important role in assisting adjustment at home and/or school. Table 2.2 summarizes interpretations of the Aggression scale.

TABLE 2.2. Aggression Scale Interpretation Guide

T-score range	Qualitative descriptor	Potential interpretation
≥ 80	Extremely aggressive	Extremely argumentative; often narcissistic and bullying; threatens or hurts others and their property.
70–79	Clinically significant	Angry, argumentative, "sore loser," overly critical of others; feelings of entitlement, brags, cruel, likes to show off.
60–69	Mildly to moderately elevated or at risk	Mildly abrasive bullying type who is critical of others; talks back often and shows tendency toward verbal aggression, disruptive.
40–59	Average	Aggressive usually only if provoked or with others; seldom more aggressive than most at this age; aggressive acts, if present, often are isolated events.
≤ 39	Low to very low	Passive individual, seldom provoked, may even be shy and withdrawn, especially if Withdrawal scale elevated.

CONDUCT PROBLEMS

In many ways the Conduct Problems scale is an "old-fashioned" juvenile delinquency measure in that it includes the traditional items associated with antisocial behavior: stealing, cheating, lying, destruction of property, etc. Thus, the Conduct Problems scale can be interpreted similarly to other scales measuring antisocial behavior, delinquency, and conduct disorder. Caution in using these instruments is warranted, however, because the item content can include an overly varied array of symptomatology. Kamphaus and Frick (1996) reviewed numerous behavior rating scales and self-report inventories and found that many contain construct irrelevant items and shared items between scales.

We have not changed our views on scale construction since we originally conceptualized the BASC scales. We did our best to design scales that measured only one construct that is distinct from others in the battery. The results of the review by Kamphaus and Frick (1996) and the comments of independent external reviewers (Flanagan, 1995; Doyle, Ostrander, Skare, Crosby, & August, 1997), strongly suggest that the BASC differs from other scales in this regard. Consequently, even identically named conduct problem scales may have some, or several, distinctly different items, making direct comparisons to our scale questionable. Table 2.3 summarizes interpretations of the Conduct Problems scale.

TABLE 2.3. Conduct Problems Scale Interpretation Guide

T-score range	Qualitative descriptor	Potential interpretation
≥ 80	Extreme	Narcissistic rule-breaker with high probability of psychopathic features; feels above the rules, steals, often in trouble with authority figures; high risk of substance abuse.
70–79	Clinically significant	Generally enjoys breaking rules and challenging authorities; befriends others who also get into trouble frequently; lies to get out of trouble.
60–69	Mildly to moderately elevated or at risk	Hostile tendencies toward authority figures and breaks rules if no one around; occasionally in trouble with authorities.
40–59	Average or typical	Occasionally challenges authority (usually as limit testing), not characterological.
≤ 39	Low to very low	Conformist, hesitant to challenge others; at very low scores may be submissive or even docile.

INTERVIEW 2.1

Kimberly Adams, PhD
University of Minnesota/Minneapolis Public Schools

How do you use the BASC in your practice, research, and/or training activities?

I've used the BASC primarily in practice and in training activities. In practice, I use the BASC as a tool for psycho-educational assessment, specifically when addressing behavioral concerns and determining eligibility for special education services related to emotional/behavioral disorders (EBD).

During the assessment process, I use the portions of the Structured Developmental History (SDH) most relevant to the referral question. The SDH serves as an extremely thorough tool for interviewing parents regarding their child's developmental history. Although I rarely use the SDH cover to cover, it is a very useful "prompt" to address a variety of domains that may have an impact on the child. In most cases, I use the SDH in an interview format, rather than giving it directly to the parent to complete. This allows for a clearer understanding of the items, clarification of answers given by respondents, and greater flexibility in gathering critical information.

I use the Student Observation System (SOS) occasionally to determine levels of appropriate and problem behaviors in classroom settings. I have typically practiced in settings that have on-going data collection systems in place, which reduced the need for an additional observational tool such as the SOS. However, I have found the SOS to be useful for observing students in mainstream settings where these data collection systems were not in place.

The BASC rating scales are a critical component of my assessment practices for emotional or behavioral difficulties, particularly when I need a normative comparison of a student's emotional or behavioral difficulties. I typically ask for BASC ratings from one or more teachers, parents, and the student, which allows for comparisons across raters and settings, as well as standardized ratings of the child's behavior.

Results are shared with teachers, parents, and students during a team meeting and in a written report. I use a table for presentation of BASC rating scale results to clearly display results, to facilitate comparison across raters (keeping in mind the effects of different raters and different environments), and as a catalyst for further discussion. All results need to be understood in relation to other assessment data about the child. Typically, I report descriptors (e.g., *average, at-risk*) and percentile ranks for all composites, and descriptors only for subscales. I find that the results are rarely surprising; however, they do seem to lead to a

(continued)

INTERVIEW 2.1 *(continued)*

substantive discussion regarding both the child's strengths and areas of need. The rating scales work well in identifying these strengths and areas of need, while the SOS and SDH can be useful in intervention planning.

In training, I typically present the above model as a portion of a multi-method approach to assessing problem behavior. Graduate students are provided classroom instruction on the multiple components of the BASC, and then proceed to use the BASC to assess "practice students" in the local public schools. They are given supervised experience in using and interpreting teacher, parent, and student rating scales; parent interviews; and student observations.

Please identify some of the outcomes of these activities (e.g., patient care, scientific findings).

I use the results of the BASC for several purposes. Primarily, BASC results are used to contribute to the determination of initial or continuing eligibility for special education services. Once eligibility is determined, BASC results, particularly results from the SOS and rating scales, can be used as one tool to evaluate present levels of performance and IEP goals and objectives. However, I feel it is very important to state the specific areas to be addressed, and not just the name of the scale that is elevated. For example, "Reduce Amelia's aggressive behaviors, such as [examples]" and not "Reduce Amelia's aggression score on the BASC."

Additionally, results of the BASC provide several pieces of information that can be helpful in intervention planning. For an initial assessment, BASC rating scale and SOS results can be important baseline information upon which to evaluate the effects of intervention. The SDH provides a wealth of information regarding etiology, course, student and family strengths and needs, and other rich, contextual information.

Can you identify any particular strengths or weaknesses for the BASC that others should consider in their work?

Strengths

The BASC is a technically sound, comprehensive, multi-informant, multi-method system.

All portions of the BASC address both adaptive and problem behaviors.

Items are written at low levels of readability.

Provides "objective" ratings of student behavior.

Flexibility in use of all components.

Ease of computer scoring and easy to read printout.

(continued)

INTERVIEW 2.1 *(continued)*

Weaknesses

No drug/alcohol use section on the SDH.

Difficulty in interpretation of the Atypicality scale.

No peer comparison for the SOS (although you can do this on your own using another SOS form).

Additional Comment

I feel that users of the BASC should be very skilled in interpretation of the BASC, as well as having a strong background in mental health, as the potential for misunderstanding or misuse of the results is high. Additionally, I feel that BASC data can only be understood and interpreted in conjunction with additional data and should never be used in isolation.

Do you have any other remarks regarding the BASC?

I just want to share one of my favorite BASC stories:

"The Validity Scales: It all depends on your Perspective"

I was working in a school for students with the most severe emotional/behavioral disorders (EBD) in Minnesota. A 15 year-old young man, "Jordan" recently moved from out of state to live with his father, who resided in the school district. Jordan had engaged in a series of activities while living in Ohio that brought him into contact with the law. Following his last arrest (grand theft auto), the judge gave him the option of staying in Ohio and going to juvenile detention, or leaving the state, never to return upon penalty of being placed in juvenile detention for the aforementioned crime. Jordan chose to move to Minnesota with his father.

Jordan arrived at the school with an overdue 3-year reassessment. We started an assessment upon his enrollment, which included the BASC rating scales. Since Jordan had approximately first-grade reading skills, I decided to read the BASC Student Self-Report to him, marking his responses on my protocol. Despite sulkily lounging on the chair in my office and offering no eye contact or small talk, Jordan answered every question on the BASC rating scale. As we were completing the ratings scale, we came across the following item: "The local newspaper has a story about me almost every day." (V index). Jordan looked up at me, with a glimmer in his eye and an impish grin on his face, and said, "In Ohio there is."

ANXIETY

We employed many logical and statistical procedures to differentiate the internalizing constructs of the BASC. The first and most crucial step was to develop an item pool distinct from that of the depression and somatization constructs. The result is a scale that is correlated with, but distinct from, the other internalizing scales. As such, the Anxiety scale can show independent elevation as well as comorbidity with depression and related disorders. Anxiety can be a symptom of another disorder (e.g., obsessive–compulsive or somatization disorders), or it can be a distinct, identifiable disorder. Individuals with high anxiety levels may or may not have an anxiety disorder, and careful attention to the history and the complete profile are necessary.

Ascertaining the distinct nature of the anxiety and its physiological symptomatology is important for refining the clinical picture of a child with internalizing symptoms. Interpretive possibilities include the following:

1. An anxiety score elevated in conjunction with the Depression or Somatization scales suggests that independent treatment focused on anxiety symptoms is warranted. This obvious interpretation is highlighted because anxiety problems are highly amenable to treatment (Nathan & Gorman, 2002). For a child with depression or even inattention problems, the successful treatment of anxiety may serve to improve daily adjustment even though other, even primary, clinical problems persist. Moreover, a successful response to the treatment of choice, cognitive–behavioral therapy, may suggest that this same treatment holds promise for other problem domains.

2. A low–normal anxiety score does not necessarily indicate an *absence* of anxiety symptoms. In some cases anxiety problems are indicated by other scales. We encountered a case where teacher and mother produced significant ratings of withdrawal and somatization and no ratings of anxiety problems. These symptoms led to a second interview with the parents, wherein they were asked for details about these problems. As it turned out, the headaches and stomachaches were noted to occur only during the school day. Moreover, the child always chose to play alone at school, never left her mother's company, and had slept with her mother since birth. The eventual diagnosis was separation anxiety disorder, early onset. In this case there were adequate indications of problems to complete the evaluation successfully; in addition, the subtlety of anxiety problems, which often leads to underdiagnosis, is demonstrated (Last, 1993). Table 2.4 summarizes interpretations of the Anxiety scale.

TABLE 2.4. Anxiety Scale Interpretation Guide

T-score range	Qualitative descriptor	Potential interpretation
≥ 80	Extreme	Severely anxious with unproductive thought patterns; may evidence confusion; constantly worried and often agitated.
70–79	Clinically significant	Prone to excessive worry, tension, and hyperresponsivity to stress; ineffective at problem solving, ruminative thought.
60–69	Mildly to moderately elevated or at risk	Motivated but perhaps mildly insecure; mildly anxious but generally conscientious, trustworthy, and psychologically minded.
40–59	Average or typical	Handles stress appropriately, able to "let go," trusting of others.
≤ 39	Low to very low	Highly confident and secure, relative to age.

SOMATIZATION

The Somatization scale is likely to have two high-frequency interpretations. First, scores in the at-risk range or above are indicative of physical symptomatology associated with a health problem. For example, we have seen elevated ratings on this scale that are due to the child's expression of physical complaints associated with diabetes, acute lymphocytic leukemia, muscular dystrophy, juvenile diabetes, and other conditions.

Second, this scale indicates the presence of physical complaints that are attributable to a mental health condition. To this end, we have seen scale elevations indicate the presence of separation anxiety disorder, subsyndromal anxiety problems (e.g., worry about school achievement or family problems), and clinical depression. In fact, it has been suggested that somatic complaints are one of the first signs of depression (Cooper, 1993).

We advise psychologists to check medical history and current health status information in order to determine the proper interpretation of an elevation on this scale. In some cases, a health screening by a medical provider will be necessary to rule out somatic complaints that are secondary to physical health problems. Table 2.5 summarizes interpretations of the Somatization scale.

TABLE 2.5. Somatization Scale Interpretation Guide

T-score range	Qualitative descriptor	Potential interpretation
≥ 80	Extreme	Significant histrionic response to illness and fabrication of symptoms or bizarre symptoms that appear to be real to the individual; preoccupation with illnesses compromises daily living skills in multiple domains; seldom feels healthy.
70–79	Clinically significant	Physical symptoms unexplained by physiological problems; usually subjective, hyperreactive responses to physical changes; lack of treatment compliance common; anxiety problems common.
60–69	Mildly to moderately elevated or at risk	Hyperresponsive and overconcerned about sickness; may worry excessively about health concerns but functions well; health concerns are more an annoyance than an interference with life.
40–59	Average or typical	Evaluates physical complaints realistically and seeks medical help appropriately.
≤ 39	Low to very low	May ignore physical problems and avoid doctor visits unless convinced to go by others; reluctant to adhere to treatment; may not take health concerns as seriously as those in the same age group.

DEPRESSION

The Depression scale "begs the question" as to whether or not there is a general psychopathology *g* factor that is conceptually similar to the well-known general intelligence *g* factor (Kamphaus, 2001). If one believes in such a general psychopathology factor, then the Depression scale is the best measure of this construct. Such a conclusion is consistent with the factor analytic findings for the BASC, which revealed that the Depression scale is associated with *both* the externalizing and internalizing factors (Reynolds & Kamphaus, 1992).

The correlation between the Depression scale and many dimensions of child behavior problems is demonstrated frequently in research findings and clinical experience. The scale's findings are almost certainly associated with the concept/construct of negative affectivity that is prominent in the adult literature on psychopathology. The profiles of clinical samples given in Chapter 5 show that clinical samples of both the externalizing and internalizing variety produce Depression scale elevations in the at-risk range or higher.

In one sense, then, the Depression scale can indicate the overall severity of problems, although the Behavioral Symptoms Index or Emotional Symptoms Index is better designed for this purpose. A more useful interpretation of these factor analytic findings is that depression problems are ubiquitous in referral populations from hospitals, schools, clinics, and other settings. Moreover, this ubiquity suggests that clinicians need to exercise vigilant attention to the possibility of depression problems in child assessment practice. This need for vigilance is validated by the known high prevalency of the disorder and its lack of diagnosis (Kamphaus & Frick, 1996).

There are several possible interpretations of the Depression scale. High scores—we have seen these scores range from a *T* score of 64 (on a self-report of a teenager) upward—frequently indicate the presence of depression that meets or exceeds DSM-IV criteria. Scores in the at-risk range may indicate subsyndromal problems that warrant prophylactic or preventive treatment, or monitoring of symptomatology. Scores of 55 or higher may reveal tendencies toward negative affectivity—simply put, episodic or chronic feelings of sadness or unhappiness.

TABLE 2.6. Depression Scale Interpretation Guide

T-score range	Qualitative descriptor	Potential interpretation
≥ 80	Extreme	Withdrawn, despondent, very sad; likely experiencing a major depressive disorder or an acute reactive disorder; suicidal ideation likely if anxiety and social stress elevated; males and adolescents may show high levels of agitation or even be hyperactive; thought processes may be slowed.
70–79	Clinically significant	Dysphoric mood, frequently in the midst of a major depressive episode or exacerbated dysthymic condition; may be sad, tired, and pessimistic; psychopharmacotherapy often indicated with scores above 70.
60–69	Mildly to moderately elevated or at risk	Mildly to moderately depressed, possibly dysthymic; anhedonic, discouraged, with a tendency toward external locus of control.
40–59	Average or typical	Handles life's bumps and challenges in emotionally appropriate ways; good self-confidence; predisposed to positive attributions.
≤ 39	Low to very low	Enjoy life, confident, poised, cheerful and infectious mood; perhaps overly optimistic but also quite resilient.

In this latter circumstance we sometimes utilize a different name for the scale in order to communicate the results more accurately to parents, teachers, and other consumers. We sometimes refer to the scale as a measure of "happiness" rather than "depression," a more foreboding term that does not describe the mild nature of the symptoms.

Even extremely high scores on this scale should be explored further via questions regarding vegetative symptoms of the disorder, such as weight gain or loss, fatigue, etc. Vegetative symptoms are not typically included on rating scales (see Kamphaus & Frick, 1996, for a review), the BASC included. Specifically, our scale is an effective measure of the clinical dimension of "depression"; it is not a symptom checklist, like that in the DSM-IV. Table 2.6 summarizes interpretations of the Depression scale.

ATYPICALITY

The rationale and design of the Atypicality scale requires elucidation to ensure proper interpretation. This scale was initially designed to be a psychoticism scale with prototypical item content. A perusal of the items assessing auditory and visual hallucinations and disorganized, delusional, and bizarre mentation supports this contention. As is the case with other psychoticism scales, the reliability coefficients for this scale are also good (Reynolds & Kamphaus, 1992). Nevertheless, this scale has proved challenging because many items can be interpreted as indicators of hyperactivity or other dimensions. For example, a rumination item (e.g., repeats one thought or activity) may be interpreted as a symptom of hyperactivity. Schwean, Burt, and Saklofske (1999) note this problem and conclude the following:

> Items on the Atypicality scale of the BASC are relevant to several different interpretations, with many describing behaviors that parallel those seen in a hyperactive–impulsive disorder (e.g., daydreams, complains about being unable to block out unwanted thoughts, stares blankly, babbles to self, sings or hums to self, rocks back and forth). Several examples will help illustrate this point. Although we typically think of inattentive children as "daydreamy," research has noted that one of the most common observations made by elementary school teachers about hyperactive children is that they appear to be daydreaming (Goldstein & Goldstein, 1992). Hyperactive–impulsive children are also often known to talk excessively and to hum or make odd noises (American Psychiatric Association, 1994; Barkley, 1990). Moreover, irrelevant and purposeless gross bodily movements (i.e., hyperactivity) can easily be confused with more stereotypic motor behaviors. (p. 59)

In our experience, findings on the Atypicality scale are another indicator of a child's hyperactivity in a general referral population. This interpretation is appropriate in many of the cases seen by child clinicians. It is also possible to interpret the Atypicality scale as a measure of psychoticism. However, given the low prevalence of psychotic disorders in childhood, this interpretation is far less likely, unless, of course, one assesses children in inpatient or other settings where the referral base has a higher prevalency rate.

We became alerted to the possibility that the Atypicality scale is prone to multiple interpretations prior to publication. In fact, we feared that the results of this scale, if interpreted in isolation, might lead to overdiagnosis of psychoticism problems. It is for this reason that we labeled the scale "Atypicality," a term that communicates little to anyone, it seems, given the questions we receive about it!

This scale, more than most others, requires clinicians to clarify item responses with informants. Clinicians using the SRP have reported that children or adolescents often affirm that they are "hearing things that are not there." In most cases, however, they will give an explanation for this experience that is not indicative of psychopathology. The use of the computer-scoring option that lists items by scale and their associated responses is recommended as an extremely useful adjunct to interpretation of this scale. Table 2.7 summarizes interpretations of the Atypicality scale emphasizing its psychotic dimensions. Clinicians should not overlook the hyperactivity component.

TABLE 2.7. Atypicality Scale Interpretation Guide

T-score range	Qualitative descriptor	Potential interpretation
≥ 80	Extreme	Severe psychotic symptoms often accompanied by delusions and frequent paranoid patterns; bizarre thoughts are commonplace.
70–79	Clinically significant	Unusual perceptions and sensations, hallucinations, magical thinking, confusion, difficulties with maintaining logic or focus, delusional beliefs; occasionally will elevate due to activity level.
60–69	Mildly to moderately elevated or at risk	Tendencies toward eccentric thought and mild paranoia or questioning of others' motives; may be viewed as somewhat odd or peculiar by others, but daily living skills are intact; agitated.
40–59	Average or typical	Clear, logical thought patterns, without odd or bizarre behavior.
≤ 39	Low to very low	Overcontrolled, high levels of superegoism, nonconfrontational, persuadable, typically very conservative.

WITHDRAWAL

In most cases, the Withdrawal scale is an indicator of withdrawal associated with the presence of psychopathology, *not shyness or timidity*. For example, a score in the at-risk range eventually led us to the diagnosis of separation anxiety disorder in the case of a seemingly well-adjusted child (see discussion of the Anxiety scale). Furthermore, the Withdrawal scale reflects difficulties with emotional bonding and attachment, and is part of the high-point pair, with the Atypicality scale, for children diagnosed with mild mental retardation or autism (see Chapter 5). Table 2.8 summarizes interpretations of the Withdrawal scale.

ATTITUDE TO SCHOOL AND ATTITUDE TO TEACHERS

To some, the behavior reflected in the Attitude to School scale and the Attitude to Teacher scale may be so obvious as to not require quantification. It is now clear, however, that these two scales can produce unexpected findings. For example, clinical experience has shown that some children dislike school or teacher, but not both simultaneously. This finding is reasonable, given that the correlation between these scales is modest (i.e., in the .50–.70 range; see Table 14.8 in Reynolds & Kamphaus, 1992).

TABLE 2.8. Withdrawal Scale Interpretation Guide

T-score range	Qualitative descriptor	Potential interpretation
≥ 80	Extreme	Severely withdrawn, poor emotional bonding, with autistic features common.
70–79	Clinically significant	Withdrawn, actively avoidant, poor eye contact, fear of strangers common, seldom initiates interactions.
60–69	Mildly to moderately elevated or at risk	Withdrawn to point of interfering with major life activities; shuns close friendships or has only one or two friends, trouble making new friends; clingy at younger ages.
40–59	Average or typical	Appropriate in appraising level of interaction and initiating contact; competes on occasion; little fear of strangers.
≤ 39	Low to very low	Outgoing, frequently initiates contact; lacks caution in relationships; too little fear of strangers may be evident.

INTERVIEW 2.2

Mary M. Hartley, PhD
Psychologist
Training Coordinator
Access Behavioral Care
Denver, Colorado

The Behavior Assessment System for Children (BASC) is widely used as a diagnostic tool in the Cherry Creek School District (CCSD). At Campus Middle School (CMS) it is used for three primary purposes. First, the BASC is often used as a global screening device of behaviors prior to an evaluation for possible Special Education services. Grade-level prereferral intervention teams meet weekly to discuss students who are struggling in the school setting. Teachers commonly describe a variety of internalizing and externalizing behaviors believed to be interfering with a student's academic performance. If the team determines that more specific information is needed regarding behavioral concerns, the BASC is one method used to gather further information. Second, the BASC is also used as part of the multidisciplinary team evaluation to determine eligibility for special education services. It is used both by the psychologist and the school social worker who has received training specific to the instrument. This second use of the BASC is widespread across the entire school district. Third, I not only interpret the scores produced by the BASC, but also use the individual BASC items as a springboard for clinical interview questions with teachers, parents, and students. Although the authors may lament that the Atypicality Scale is a miserable failure, I have found that further questioning responses to some of these items have identified some symptoms of psychosis. This contributed to development of a successful course of treatment. Had the child/student not had an opportunity to answer such items about "hearing voices" and "seeing things," the door to further query about these symptoms may not have been opened in the interview process.

In my doctoral dissertation examining the relationship among externalizing behaviors and academic achievement, the BASC proved to be a worthy instrument. Results from my study suggested that problems of attention, rather than problems of externalizing behaviors such as hyperactivity and aggression, are more closely related to learning problems and lower standardized academic achievement scores. These results have many implications for determining which behaviors should be the primary focus of interventions for children and adolescents with ADHD and academic problems. This finding may not be a startling, but when you consider that many other behavior rating scales combine at-

(continued)

tention problems and hyperactivity on the same scale, the finding becomes more interesting. In other words, previous studies using instruments that do not successfully identify and separate problems of attention and hyperactivity, produced results suggesting that academic difficulties were related to hyperactivity when, in fact, they may have been more closely related to attention problems. Using the BASC may prevent clinicians from drawing similar problematic conclusions in practice.

The value of the BASC as a strong diagnostic tool that differentiates among attention problems, hyperactivity, learning problems, or a combination of the three has been supported in my everyday practice as a school psychologist. Along with behavioral observations, anecdotal data from teachers, and family history data, the standardized data from the BASC help make a compelling case for when students and their families need to seek medical intervention for attention problems. Furthermore, I use the BASC because it represents a global picture of child and adolescent behavior. The BASC not only measures problems associated with ADHD, but also successfully identifies other types of externalizing and internalizing behaviors. On more than one occasion, I have received a referral for attention problems that upon further evaluation, reveals problems of learning, anxiety, and depression. This has been particularly true when the SRP is administered. I needed only one experience of this crucial differentiation to convince me that measures focused on only one or two behaviors are most often too narrow in focus, and miss data important for sound diagnoses.

I find the Adaptive Skills Scales of the BASC to be a welcome addition to traditional behavior scales that only measure child/adolescent pathology. These scales help to identify areas of mental "healthiness" that constitute strengths for the student being evaluated. Once identified, these areas of strength can then be used to tailor interventions in a manner the utilizes them to the child's benefit. Identifying and building on those strengths certainly captures the spirit of the direction where educational programming for children/adolescents with learning challenges is headed.

Rather than specific problems using the BASC as an instrument in practice, I have struggled with more systemic issues with its use; specifically understanding the ethical use of such an instrument by other professionals in the educational setting. The BASC is widely used at our school and in some cases, among staff BASC scores have become synonymous with a diagnosis for a disorder, rather than an important piece of information contributing to a diagnosis. In the educational setting it is the responsibility of the mental health staff trained in diagnostics to use the BASC in conjunction with other measures of behavior and mood, such as observations and interviews, to make the best decisions for students. This is an ongoing professional challenge.

Although these scales are not directly related to diagnostic criteria, they can contribute considerable assistance in treatment planning, particularly when attempting to improve adaptation to schooling. It is hard to imagine a child having problems in both of these areas being well adapted to school. School-based personnel will likely need to include these dimensions in treatment or an Individual Educational Plan (IEP) with some frequency. It has always been surprising to us how often these areas are overlooked or minimized, yet schools and teachers have enormous impact on a child's feelings and behavior as well as emotional development. Except for sleeping, a child spends more time at school, with teachers and peers, than in any other single setting. Tables 2.9 and 2.10 summarize interpretations of these two scales.

LOCUS OF CONTROL

This Locus of Control scale is primarily a measure of external locus of control. We have found that elevated scores indicate children or adolescents who perceive others, particularly authority figures, as excessively controlling his or her actions. This interpretation is often valid for children and adolescents who have disruptive behavior problems and are involved in coercive relationships with teachers or parents. In effect, the child's perceptions are correct; authority figures *are* struggling to control the child's behavior, although often with little efficacy.

TABLE 2.9. Attitude to School Interpretation Guide

T-score range	Qualitative descriptor	Potential interpretation
≥ 70	Clinically significant	Dislikes school intensely, wishes to be elsewhere, easily bored, poor motivation to do well.
60–69	Mildly to moderately elevated or at risk	Generally fails to see utility of school, dislikes attending, dislikes being graded.
40–59	Average	Sees school appropriately; tends to like attending but not necessarily enthusiastic.
≤ 39	Low to very low	Likes school more than most at same age; finds being at school a positive experience.

TABLE 2.10. Attitude to Teachers Interpretation Guide

T-score range	Qualitative descriptor	Potential interpretation
≥ 70	Clinically significant	Hostile toward one or more teachers; feels they are unfair, uncaring, and overly demanding.
60–69	Mildly to moderately elevated or at risk	Suspicious of teachers; harbors beliefs that teachers are uncaring, on power trips, and not really concerned about students.
40–59	Average	No strong like or dislike of teachers; gets along well with teachers; sees them as concerned about well-being of students.
≤ 39	Low to very low	Tends to like teachers and believes they are fair, caring individuals; any problems with teachers tend to be situational.

Do low scores indicate an internal locus of control? We are not sure. We have hypothesized such (Reynolds & Kamphaus, 1992), but we need more confirmation from either research or practice to establish a correlation. At this time, low scores are not as easy to interpret as high scores. This obscurity could mean that the Locus of Control scale functions like other BASC clinical scales where a low score simply indicates a relative lack of problems within a dimension. Table 2.11 summarizes interpretations of the Locus of Control scale.

TABLE 2.11. Locus of Control Interpretation Guide

T-score range	Qualitative descriptor	Potential interpretation
≥ 70	Clinically significant	Very high external locus of control; harbors beliefs of having no control over life or events that befall him or her; feels oppressed by others.
60–69	Mildly to moderately elevated or at risk	Feels that others have too much control over life; believes in fate; poor coping skills when faced with adversity.
40–59	Average or typical	Normal attributions of outcomes; some to actions of self, some to fate, some to others; feels at least a modicum of control over life.
≤ 39	Low to very low	Most likely good internal locus of control; believes has influence over outcome of life and common situations; does not experience parents, teachers, or others as overcontrolling.

SENSATION SEEKING

The Sensation-Seeking scale portends great clinical utility; it has been the subject of an insightful newsletter article and we receive numerous anecdotes about interpretations of it. In the sample case later in this chapter, the Sensation-Seeking scale was the only BASC indicator of emerging problems of sexual aggression on the part of a middle-school male.

There is also at least one intuitive interpretation of this scale that may or may not be valid: Although we do not possess any scientific or clinical evidence, to date, that demonstrates a strong relationship between scores on this scale and risk of substance abuse, our clinical experience is suggestive of such a relationship. The Sensation-Seeking scale may indicate the presence of conduct problems in much the same way as the McAndrew Scale of the MMPI-A (Archer, 1991). In fact, clinicians tell us that this scale is often elevated for cases of disruptive behavior problems. In addition, joint elevations on the Attitude to Teachers, Attitude to School, and the Sensation-Seeking scales imply especially poor school adjustment.

Interestingly, a study by Rowe (Rowe et al., 1998) reveals that teachers are often unaware of adolescent sensation-seeking tendencies. If such is the case, the SRP may be clinicians' only access to this domain. Rowe conducted a cluster analysis of the SRP-A, using the national normative sample data set. She produced one cluster of children with substantial problems indicated on the Sensation-Seeking scale, along with other scale elevations. She then examined the TRS-A ratings for the same children. Remarkably, most teacher ratings suggested average behavioral adjustment at school. This provocative finding has implications beyond supporting the potential utility of the Sensation-Seeking scale for identifying problems and propensities toward misbehavior. Specifically, these results suggest that teachers often may be unaware of significant adolescent maladjustment—an oversight due to no malfeasance on their part. To state the obvious, they simply do not have the same access to the adolescent's thoughts and feelings as the student him- or herself has. As noted previously, multiple informants are necessary to gain as much information as possible regarding adolescent functioning. Table 2.12 summarizes interpretations of the Sensation-Seeking scale.

SENSE OF INADEQUACY

The item content of the Sense of Inadequacy scale is designed to have special relevance to school-age children: The majority of items deal with topics such as test taking, grades, completion of schoolwork, and satisfaction with school-

TABLE 2.12. Sensation-Seeking Interpretation Guide

T-score range	Qualitative descriptor	Potential interpretation
≥ 80	Extreme	Extreme needs for novel and varied experiences and unusually willing to take risks to obtain them; high probability of alcohol or drug use and delinquency.
70–79	Clinically significant	Risk taker who needs lots of varied experiences, craves excitement, impulsive, tends to be argumentative; alcohol, drug use, and delinquency more common than with low scorers.
60–69	Mildly to moderately elevated or at risk	Typically not as risk taking as higher scorers; some impulsivity seen; more easily influenced by others to take risks.
40–59	Average or typical	Typical adolescent level of experimentation, limit testing, rule breaking, and related risk-taking behaviors designed to provide novel and varied experiences.
≤ 39	Low to very low	Cautious and reflective; at very low scores, likely anxious and overcontrolled or inhibited.

work. Interestingly, our experience reveals that elevated results on this scale are frequently matched by elevated scores on the Depression scale, which has more diverse item content. This finding makes clinical sense, given that these scales correlate in the .69–.80 range (Reynolds & Kamphaus, 1992). Often, children with elevations on both these scales have simply given up on achievement and have lowered their level of aspiration.

The item content of the Sense of Inadequacy scale may reflect perceptions specifically related to schooling. This possibility suggests that clinicians in nonschool settings should follow-up on scores in the at-risk range with assessments of school functioning. Potential "rule outs" include academic failure, underachievement, cognitive deficit secondary to neurological impairment, mental retardation, and learning disability. Table 2.13 summarizes interpretations of the Sense of Inadequacy scale.

SOCIAL STRESS

Feelings of loneliness, isolation, and stress in social situations figure prominently in interpretations of the Social Stress scale. Most of the items refer to "people"; some refer specifically to "other children" and "friends." It has been our experience that most respondents interpret these items as referring to

TABLE 2.13. Potential Interpretations of BASC Sense of Inadequacy Scale *T* Scores

T score range	Qualitative descriptor	Potential interpretation
≥ 70	Clinically significant	Significant lack of confidence in one's ability to succeed in most tasks of life, especially school, gives up easily, feelings of inadequacy, lacks persistence, may have rejected common achievement goals.
60–69	Mildly to moderately elevated or at risk	Mildly to moderately depressed sense of confidence in ability to master most life tasks, possibly socially alienated, leans toward underachieving peers.
40–59	Average or typical	Makes realistic appraisals of ability to succeed on varied tasks; tries to improve some doubts but common ones we all feel, adequate persistence.
≤ 39	Low to very low	Academically confident individual, believes in self and ability to succeed with hard work and persistence in most areas of life.

peers. As such, this scale may function as the clinical counterpart to the Interpersonal Relations scale (inverse correlation of about .60; Reynolds & Kamphaus, 1992). Consequently, Social Stress scale elevations are likely to indicate peer relationship problems. To this end, at-risk scores should trigger further qualitative or quantitative assessment of peer relationship status and associated treatment needs. Table 2.14 summarizes interpretations of the Social Stress scale.

ADAPTABILITY

Children with severe disruptive behavior problems and those with pervasive problems in both the externalizing and internalizing dimensions have very low scores on the Adaptability scale, often as much as two standard deviations below the normative mean. Research by Huberty, DiStefano, and Kamphaus (1997) and Kamphaus, Huberty, DiStefano, and Petoskey (1997) and Kamphaus et al. (1999) have shown this dimension of adaptability to be very important for optimal adaptation to school and home environments. Findings of this nature demonstrate that improvement in the ability to adapt to changes in routine is important for improving general adaptation.

TABLE 2.14. Potential Interpretations of BASC Social Stress Scale
T Scores

T score range	Qualitative descriptor	Potential interpretation
≥ 70	Clinically significant	Severe levels of stress present, usually associated with peer interactions; some vague paranoia about others' motives evident; few friends, poor social support network; poor levels of resiliency especially if relations with parents also poor.
60–69	Mildly to moderately elevated or at risk	High stress levels associated with feeling like an outcast, occasionally ostracized by others, fearful of making mistakes in front of peers, worries about interactions obsessively.
40–59	Average or typical	Appropriate levels of stress, likely labile in adolescence but high stress episodes resolve appropriately, has friends, generally interacts appropriately with others.
≤ 39	Low to very low	Very low stress levels evident; confident, often socially facile child with good peer support; often a leader in peer group.

A school intervention for children low in adaptability may involve systematically preparing them for transitions by giving prior cues (e.g., teacher raising his or her hand five minutes prior to recess). In addition, coping strategies may be included in the treatment plan. For example, a child can be taught to utilize cognitive self-control strategies when facing abrupt changes in routine (such as a family emergency causes a change in plans).

Of course, the Adaptability scale of the TRS and PRS is only relevant to children between the ages of 2½ and 11. We could not obtain adequate reliabilities at the adolescent age range, which suggests that this dimension is altered with development (Reynolds & Kamphaus, 1992).

A study by Thorpe, Kamphaus, Rowe, and Fleckenstein (2000) suggests that the Adaptability scale may also serve as a proxy for the temperament variable of negative emotionality. Nelson et al. (1999) also found that temperament-associated measures of negative emotionality were related to the BASC adaptability scores. These findings, while in need of cross-validation, provide further evidence of the prognostic significance of the Adaptability scale. Specifically, low scores may be cause for concern about poor prognosis—which, in turn, suggests a need for more aggressive and enduring intervention. Table 2.15 summarizes interpretations of the Adaptability scale.

41

TABLE 2.15. Adaptability Scale Interpretation Guide

T-score range	Qualitative descriptor	Potential interpretation
≥ 80	Extremely flexible	Highly adaptable, resilient, a "good sport," rarely upset by changes in routine, easily soothed.
70–79	Very highly flexible	Very adaptable, adjusts well to changes in routine, seldom complains, likes to try new things.
60–69	Highly flexible	Easily adapts to change if not intrusive, seldom complains, adjusts well overall.
40–59	Average	About as flexible as most kids at this age; occasional upsets and complaints.
≤ 39	Inflexible	Somewhat rigid, easily upset when routines are changed, may be seen as a "poor sport" or may be seen as stubborn.

LEADERSHIP

The Leadership scale has not been systematically studied, nor has it produced noteworthy findings, such as serving as a marker of pathology, health, or resistance in clinical samples. Thus we are left with our original interpretations of the items reflecting good social skills and cognitive abilities associated with good decision making. We may be lacking significant findings for this scale because, to date, high-achieving children have not been systematically studied, and they are seldom referred for special education placement or to clinical practitioners. Table 2.16 summarizes interpretations of the Leadership scale.

SOCIAL SKILLS

Low scores on the Social Skills scale signify an interpersonal skills deficit that adversely affects adaptation to home, school, and/or peer social environments. In addition, indicators of social skills deficits may be of value in making differential diagnoses of conditions such as mental retardation or autism, where children with autism have poorer skill development (Volkmar et al., 1987).

Once a skills deficit is identified, then an intervention package (of which there are numerous kinds) can be applied, typically in a group-based format. It would also be wise to begin the intervention process with a broad assessment of social skills knowledge and use it in order to target specific skills for

TABLE 2.16. Leadership Scale Interpretation Guide

T-score range	Qualitative descriptor	Potential interpretation
≥ 70	Very high	Involved in multiple extracurricular activities; strong self-starter, energetic, good decision-making skills, seen by others as a leader.
60–69	High	Generally speaks up, has initiative, helps problem solve with others, works well with others, and under pressure.
40–59	Average or typical	Generally cooperative, occasionally initiates, adequate group skills, average involvement in extra activities.
≤ 39	Low to very low	Generally lacks initiative, keeps ideas to self, shuns decision making, less involved than peers in activities, seldom chosen as a leader by peers.

intervention. Most intervention packages also include an assessment component that evaluates numerous skills beyond those assessed by this scale.

Alfonso et al. (1997) found that the BASC Social Skills scale and the Social Skills Rating System (SSRS; Gresham & Elliott, 1990) overlap, to a limited extent. The SSRS would be one choice for follow-up assessment, once a social skills deficit has been identified with the BASC. This assessment could lead to further delineation of treatment objectives, beyond those already identified by the BASC. Table 2.17 summarizes interpretations of the Social Skills scale.

TABLE 2.17. Social Skills Scale Interpretation Guide

T-score range	Qualitative descriptor	Potential interpretation
≥ 70	Very high	Socially adept, facile, exceptional manners, helps and encourages others, tends to initiate conversation, good sense of humor, appropriately self-confident and at ease with others.
60–69	High	Overall good social skills; adept at most social interactions; shows interest in others.
40–59	Average or typical	Adequate social skills; occasional discomfort in some social interactions but none that are debilitating or abnormal; social problems tend to be transient.
≤ 39	Low to very low	Poorly developed social skills; problems getting along with others; trouble initiating and maintaining appropriate conversation; socially awkward.

STUDY SKILLS (TRS)

The Study Skills scale, like the Social Skills scale, leads readily to the identification of target behaviors for intervention (skill development). Although this dimension is not included on many teacher rating scales, we think that it is among the most important for treatment planning in schools. Teachers and others are very knowledgeable about the behaviors included in this scale, such as homework completion, reading assignments, and organizational skills. A well-developed body of research literature on such topics has yielded a diverse array of intervention strategies and packages. It is highly likely that a child's teacher already possesses knowledge of interventions for the problematic behaviors. The importance of identifying these skills deficits for school adaptation can sometimes be overshadowed by the stress of dealing with frank symptomatology of aggression, depression, or other more intrusive problems.

Low scores on the Study Skills scale can be used to remind school personnel that study skills deficits may also be contributing to behavioral difficulties. The psychologist can emphasize the importance of such deficits by listing target behaviors for intervention based on item responses—a process that is done automatically by the BASC Plus software package.

We have some scientific evidence to support the view that study skills deficits are obstacles to school adaptation. Huberty et al. (1997) revealed that the dimension of externalizing problems was most important, followed by adaptive skills, with internalizing problems coming in a distant third. We advise that adaptive skills development be an important part of every child's treatment plan. Table 2.18 summarizes interpretations of the Study Skills scale.

SELF-ESTEEM

In our experience, the Self-Esteem scale has indicated problems when a child or adolescent has a negative view of self. Furthermore, this scale, although brief, reflects problems that are typically confirmed by interview or other information. When problems are identified by this scale, it is important to follow-up with a clinical interview or other tool that is aimed at identifying the full extent of the self-esteem problems by assessing the various domains, such as interpersonal effectiveness, appearance, and academic subject areas. These areas can then become the focus of psychotherapeutic intervention. Table 2.19 summarizes interpretations of the Self-Esteem scale.

TABLE 2.18. Study Skills Scale Interpretation Guide

T-score range	Qualitative descriptor	Potential interpretation
≥ 70	Very high	Excellent organizational and study skills overall, completes assigned work on a timely basis, and often goes beyond limits of assignment.
60–69	High	Very good organizational and study skills, typically completes work, reads assignments, knows how to access study resources.
40–59	Average or typical	Adequate study skills; somewhat erratic in studying and handling assignments but most often gets them done, although some are last-minute; may need to cram episodically.
≤ 39	Low to very low	Poor study skills and habits, often late with work, does not read assignments, neglects studies; frequent cramming before tests if studies at all.

TABLE 2.19. Self-Esteem Scale Interpretation Guide

T-score range	Qualitative descriptor	Potential interpretation
≥70	Very high	Exceptionally high levels of self-esteem and self-satisfaction; possible ego inflation.
60–69	High	Strong sense of self and good self-satisfaction; feels comfortable with physical appearance.
40–59	Average or typical	Appropriate perceptions of strengths and weaknesses of self; some insecurity but overall well adjusted to self.
≤39	Low to very low	Poor view of self, poor ego strength, self-critical, very dissatisfied with physical appearance.

SELF-RELIANCE

Low scores on the Self-Reliance scale suggest feelings of irresponsibility, or even guilt, typically related to academics. The theme of irresponsibility is reflected in the scale items, as are themes of academic problems and failure. Such content makes this scale particularly useful for school-age children. Difficulties identified with self-reliance are often reflected in schoolwork. Furthermore, thoughts and associated feelings of irresponsibility may also need to be targeted in psychotherapeutic intervention, as they are likely to diminish a child's motivation to achieve. Table 2.20 summarizes interpretations of the Self-Reliance scale.

MULTIPLE INFORMANTS

The importance of utilizing numerous data sources is highlighted in a study by Rowe, Abelkop, and Kamphaus (1999). They conducted a cluster analysis of the SRP-A, using the national standardization sample of 4,839 cases. Of the eight clusters of adjustment items identified, three were found to have problems requiring intervention, representing 13% of the sample. Of greater interest is the fact that most of these children were not receiving treatment.

TABLE 2.20. Self-Reliance Scale Interpretation Guide

T-score range	Qualitative descriptor	Potential interpretation
≥ 70	Very high	Strong sense of confidence in ability to accomplish tasks of everyday life, both at school and home; feels others can depend upon him or her.
60–69	High	Good sense of confidence in ability to accomplish hard tasks; sees self as good at most things when puts forth effort; likes to tackle problems and believes will be successful.
40–59	Average or typical	Evaluates self realistically, feels confidence in some areas but not others; some anxiety when called on but not debilitating.
≤ 39	Low to very low	Very little confidence in abilities; prefers not to be asked to help for fear of failure; does not like to be called on in class.

One of the groups was labeled moderate distress–internalizing and represented 8.2% of the sample. Of these adolescents, 56% were female and had a mean age of 14.6 years. All racial/ethnic groups were affected in proportion to U.S. Census estimates from 1990. Their mean T scores were: 67 for Depression and 64 for Sense of Inadequacy, Social Stress, Atypicality, and Locus of Control scales. They had T scores of 60, or above, on the Somatization and Anxiety scales, 40 on Interpersonal Relations, and 38 on Self-Esteem. Remarkably, this group was rarely diagnosed (6%) and probably not treated. Of greater concern, as noted, was the finding that teachers are typically unaware of their problems. A subgroup of 70 subjects (who had teacher ratings available) had TRS mean T scores well within the normal range. This finding clearly makes the case for multi-informant data collection.

To restate a cautionary note: We are in no way implying that teachers should necessarily be aware of internalizing problems of their adolescent students. Such problems are often characterized by cognitive symptomatology that is not readily expressed in the classroom and the overt behavior of these children at school may in many cases be compliant. In our view, teachers, parents, and child/adolescent raters have varying access to different types of information and valid differences in perceptions.

CHAPTER 3

Interpretation

This chapter provides a review of interpretive strategies for the BASC that we find helpful. A "top down" approach is used that is consistent with the original BASC manual (Reynolds & Kamphaus, 1992), but individual subscale interpretations are emphasized, followed by a discussion of applying and interpreting the BASC to assess change. As we noted in the manual, the individual subscales of the TRS, PRS, and SRP are the most powerful and useful clinical components of the BASC's formal, standardized assessment. First, a preliminary review of scaling is presented in relation to its meaning for BASC interpretation, the validity of the scales, and their impact on interpretation.

UNDERSTANDING AND USING LINEAR *T* SCORES

Raw scores on a test, rating scale, or other psychometric device are difficult to interpret without consulting multiple tables and calculating a host of sometimes complex transformations—tedious and cumbersome tasks. The use of raw scores is complicated further when the scale items reflect phenomena that may be associated with, or affected by, age or developmental level of the examinee. In addition to the demographic, contextual, and related information needed to interpret scores on psychological and behavioral tests, knowledge of the scale and unit of measurement employed is also a necessity. Raw-score distributions on a multiscore instrument such as the BASC, for example, will change from one subscale to another. For this and other reasons (related

48

to ease of interpretability and applications of scores outside of research environments), raw scores are commonly transformed into a standardized or scaled score. Common transformations for IQ and achievement tests include normalized, age-corrected, and deviation-scaled scores of the Wechsler genre, where composite scores (e.g., Verbal IQ, Full Scale IQ) are set to a predetermined mean of 100 and a standard deviation of 15. Although there is a rational reason why these metrics were chosen decades ago, the metrics themselves are largely arbitrary. Raw-data scores from subtests of intelligence scales and related batteries (e.g., Test of Memory and Learning [TOMAL]; Reynolds & Bigler, 1994) are commonly transformed into scaled scores with a mean of 10 and a standard deviation of 3. These choices, again, are largely by convention.

In the assessment of personality and behavior, it has become conventional to use *T* scores, which denote standardized or scaled scores, set to a predetermined mean of 50 and a standard deviation of 10, and expressed on an interval scale of measurement. Interval scales of measurement are ranked above nominal and ordinal scales (e.g., age equivalents and grade equivalents) for their utility because they convey more detailed information that can be manipulated by basic mathematical operations.

The BASC standard scores for all scales are expressed as linear *T* scores that are on an equal interval scale with corresponding percentiles. Linear *T* scores have particular characteristics that are necessary to understand in order to interpret these scores correctly across subscales. Linear transformations preserve the shape of the latent or underlying distribution of raw scores. In contrast, normalization of score distributions, through what are popularly called area transformations (fitting the area under the bell curve), is often applied when there is a strong theoretical reason to assume that the true population distribution is normal or "Gaussian" in shape. Under this assumption, any deviation from normality is viewed as error variance created by sampling error. Butcher, Dahlstrom, Graham, Tellegen, and Kaemmer (1989) have argued that it is undesirable to use scaled or standardized scores that have not been normalized. However, if the true distribution of scores, as reflected in the raw score distribution, is non-normal, then there is little justification, beyond convenience, for setting the distribution artificially so that it replicates a normal curve. Linear *T* scores have not been transformed to fit the Gaussian or normal curve.

Research on more than 33,000 children examined with the tryout and standardization versions of the BASC, and prior research with other scales, clearly show that behavioral variables such as aggression, hyperactivity, attention, and sensation seeking have distributions that are decidedly non-normal (e.g., see Reynolds & Kamphaus, 1992). As we have discussed elsewhere (Reynolds, 2001a; Reynolds & Kamphaus, 1992), measures of psychopathology frequently show a grouping of individuals in the normal range with a long (skewed) tail stretching to the right side of the distribution. In order to accurately assess the targeted behavior, it is often necessary to design content so that discrimination is most acute in the tail of the distribution. In many domains (e.g., aggression), the majority of people tested produce scores that lump into a normal position on the curve; there are strong theoretical reasons to believe this is how it should be. Since non-normal distributions reflect the true state of behavior in the population, linear T scores were chosen to preserve these relationships.

Each scaling method has its strengths and limitations. The advantage to normalizing the raw score distribution is the resulting consistency in the percentile ranks associated with specific T scores across scales. If scores have been normalized, any given T score (e.g., 60, 70, 80, etc.) has the same percentile rank, regardless of the subscale. In relation to the BASC, this procedure means that all the scales (Aggression, Anxiety, Depression, Sensation Seeking, and so on) have precisely the same number of people who score 2 standard deviations (SD's) above or below the mean. This is not true of linear-transformed T scores, where each scale has a different distribution, and the percentile rank changes across scales for a common T score. For example, for boys ages 8–11 years, a T score of 63 on the Aggression scale has a percentile rank of 87, but the same T score on the Atypicality scale has a percentile rank of 91, and a percentile rank of 89 on the Leadership and Study Skills scales. Because we see these variations as representing true differences in the percentages of individuals showing these behaviors at a common distance from the mean (the linear T score reflects the distance of a raw score from the norm group's mean raw score expressed in SD units), preserving these differences is advantageous.

EVALUATING AND INTERPRETING THE BASC VALIDITY SCALES

The first consideration when interpreting the standardized BASC scales (all levels of the TRS, PRS, and SRP) is to assess the various validity scales. The different BASC forms have different types of validity scales that correspond with the most concerns or problems of potential dissimulation by an examinee. On the hand-scored versions of the BASC, three indexes of dissimulation are available, although not all are provided on all forms: (1) the F, or Infrequency,

index; the *L*, or Lie versus social desirability, index; and (3) *V*, the Validity index. On the computer-scored version, a *C*, or Consistency, index is available
that examines internal discrepancies in responding to similar items. Though
each index is designed for a different purpose, all are intended to detect response biases or (in the case of the *C* index) unreliable responding. Before
beginning an interpretation of the BASC composite or subscale scores, the examiner should review the *V* index to determine whether an interpretable profile has been obtained, and/or whether follow-up with the informant or the
examinee is necessary to clarify the meaning of any elevations (or their absence) in the profile of the referred child.

The *L* index appears only on the SRP-A, reflecting adolescents' tendencies
to deny or minimize emotional or behavioral problems to adults. *L*-index
items, when answered in the keyed direction, reflect denial of common problems or flaws that pervade adolescence: For example, "I have some bad habits," "My parents are always right," and "I always think before I act." While adolescents may actually possess some of 14 unusually virtuous characteristics
represented on the *L* index, one who responds in the keyed direction to eight
or more of the items is likely not being truthful. Raw scores of 10 or more
raise serious concerns about the validity of the profile. Scores as low as 5 represent at least a moderate degree of defensive idealization although the protocol remains valid overall, and the clinician should look for the presence of
more severe problems than those reported in the peak areas of the profile.
We suggest the following guidelines for interpreting SRP-A raw scores on *L*.

Raw score on *L*	Potential interpretation
5–7	*Defensive* response set: Peak scores likely represent more serious problems than revealed.
8–9	*Caution* in the interpretation of profile: Problems are likely deflated, and follow-up interview is warranted.
10–14	*Extreme caution* is necessary: The profile is likely invalid; such scores may reflect a lack of cooperation, frank denial, "faking good," or emotional immaturity and psychological naiveté.

In deciding upon the most appropriate interpretation it is useful to review specific item content. Sometimes a repeat administration after such a review, and the interview with the adolescent, will clarify matters.

The *F* index appears on all standardized BASC scales and at all levels of
the TRS-P, C, and A; PRS-P, C, and A; and the SRP-C and A. Classically con-

structed, the BASC F indexes are composed of items that are infrequently endorsed in the normal population and that have relatively lower correlations with one another than to other items on the various scales. Thus, not only are items on the F index infrequently endorsed, they are items that are least likely to form a coherent or unified construct or syndrome of psychopathology. In a valid profile, elevated F scores are associated with the presence of multiple severe disorders or a frank, psychotic disturbance; however, sometimes they represent a "plea for help" due to acute, psychological distress on the part of the examinee (in the case of the SRP) or distress or exasperation with the behavior of the examinee (in the case of the TRS or PRS). As clinicians, we have all encountered teachers who are so frustrated with a student that an exorbitant number of problems are rated severely to try and get the child removed from the class. Such rating styles will typically cause an elevated F score. The most common interpretation of an elevated F score is an attempt to create an excessively negative impression. However, beyond those noted above, other reasons can result in an elevated F, including reading difficulty, failure to follow instruction, random responding, or a failure to take the task seriously. We suggest the following guidelines for interpreting raw scores on F.

Raw scores on F	Potential interpretation
SRP 2–3 TRS 2 PRS 1	Mildly exaggerated but clearly valid profile; some distress evident; negative evaluation by self or others apparent.
SRP 4–5 TRS 3–4 PRS 2–3	Probably significant problems evident; distress and some exaggeration present; caution necessary to avoid overinterpretation of profile.
SRP 6–7 TRS 5–8 PRS 4–6	Severe, acute distress; invalid responding; frank psychosis, malingering, or failure to follow instructions.

Once again, we must emphasize the need for a follow-up interview with the respondent to clarify the meaning of an elevated F score, since it may range from a true plea for help to psychosis to frank malingering or a purposive attempt to portray the individual in an unduly negative manner.

The V index appears only on the SRP in its two versions. It consists of 5 and 6 nonsensical items for the SRP-C and SRP-A, respectively. The V-index items, listed in Table 3.1, are clearly implausible or nonsensical. They are occasionally misinterpreted by children, however, and we find it useful to question them about their keyed responses to these items.

High scores—defined as equal to or greater than 2 on the V index—

TABLE 3.1. SRP: *V*-Index Items

Child level	Adolescent Level
I drink 50 glasses of milk every day.	I have just returned from a nine-month trip on an ocean liner.
I have never been in a car.	
I have never been to sleep.	I have not seen a car in at least six months.
I have no teeth.	I take a plane trip from New York to Chicago at least twice a week.
Superman is a real person.	
	Superman is a real person.
	Television does not really exist.
	The local newspaper has a story about me almost every day.

indicate misinterpretation of the items, bizarre mentation, lack of cooperation, inability to read, random responding, or a floridly psychotic state that should be evident in conversation.

The *C* index is available only via computer scoring and is listed on the first page of any PRS, TRS, or SRP printout. This index compares responses to thematically similar items, calculates the difference between each possible pair of common items, and compares those deviations to the extent to which individuals were consistent within the standardization sample. This score provides an indication of the relative reliability of an individual respondent. Cautionary statements are generated by the computer-scoring algorithm and guidance for interpretation is given on page 1 of the BASC Plus or BASC Enhanced Assist computer printout.

Once the examiner has determined that a valid or useful profile has been obtained, the next step is to decide whether to follow a top-down interpretive approach, first examining the composite scores and working down to the individual subscales (as detailed in Reynolds & Kamphaus, 1992, Ch. 9), or to move more directly to the subscales.

INTERPRETING COMPOSITE SCORES

Originally, we conceptualized a top-down approach to BASC interpretation that began with the various composite scores—for example, Behavioral Symptom Index, Emotional Symptom Index, Clinical Maladjustment, and the like. Ten years of applying the BASC in our own clinics, interacting with literally thousands of BASC users, and seeing how the BASC is used in the research literature has caused us to rethink this approach. We now view the composite scores as more limited, offering specific types of information but not the greatest benefits. Aside from the BASC multimethod, multidimensional approach and its strong psychometrics, its greatest benefits are contained in the profiles produced on each of the components.

The various composite scores are useful as indexes of the overall level of behavioral pathology present for a specific child, or of the level of more positive or adaptive behaviors seen. In public schools or other arenas where classification rules for special education eligibility are applied, the BASC composite scales are eminently useful as global indexes of behavior, indicating whether the overall pattern of behavior and emotion is deviant to the extent that a child or adolescent would qualify for special education placement. Classification as emotionally disturbed is warranted, more likely than not, whenever the Clinical Maladjustment scale of the SRP, the Externalizing or Internalizing composite scores, the Behavioral Symptoms Index (BSI), or the Emotional Symptoms Index (ESI) is elevated at a $T \geq 70$. An exception is when the elevation is due to Conduct Problems on the TRS or PRS, in which case, the possibility of social maladjustment must be given serious consideration.

The composite scores can be elevated when none of the individual component scores is elevated. For example, a child could have a T of 72 on the SRP Clinical Maladjustment composite but score below 70 on all of its component scales (Atypicality, Locus of Control, Somatization, Social Stress, Anxiety), if a majority of these scales are above the mean T of 50. While at first blush, this may seem to be an inaccurate finding, it happens for the same reason a child with Verbal IQ of 129 and Performance IQ of 129 on the WISC-III has a composite or Full Scale IQ that is higher than either of its component parts, 131. It is more unusual, and hence further from the mean, for a person to be above the mean on multiple scores by more than one or a few. What this means clinically is that a child who has multiple subsyndromal problems and/ or multiple scales in the at-risk range, may be severely troubled and require placement and intervention, even though a specific DSM-IV diagnosis may not be applicable. This is the arena of most utility for the composite scores.

INTERPRETING INDIVIDUAL SCALE SCORES

The individual scales are perhaps the most powerful interpretive force available for the rating scales and the SRP. These scales are highly interpretable because of the manner in which they were developed, with a particular emphasis on the content validity of the individual scales. The highly recognizable content of most of the scales helps render their interpretation intuitive. However, it is still useful to review the congruence between the individual scale and its composite to assess the breadth of the problems seen.

It may be necessary to evaluate the item content of a scale to understand the reasons for a high or low score, particularly a score that is inconsistent with the composite score. An example would be a child referred for attention problems who obtains a high Atypicality score on the TRS, in addition to high Attention Problems and Hyperactivity scores. The Atypicality items should be evaluated carefully to determine the reasons for the elevation. Items describing inattentive or hyperactive behaviors might be responsible, such as "Eats things that are not food" (the child may chew on erasers in class) or "Sings or hums to self" (this is not an unusual behavior for a child with motor hyperactivity). In this case, the high T score would not be indicative of psychotic thought processes but of motor hyperactivity, consistent with a diagnosis of ADHD. On the other hand, if items describing behaviors such as "Tries to hurt self" or "Sees things that are not there" have been marked as occurring frequently, the examiner would need to evaluate other sources (such as other BASC components) to determine whether there is evidence of a psychotic disorder.

The normative analysis of the scales and the inspection of the critical items provide a strong basis for interpretation. However, normative analysis does not capture all of the useful information in a child's profile. For example, a child whose clinical-scale T scores are all above 60 and whose adaptive-scale T scores are all below 40 is clearly having extraordinary difficulties, but some of the problems may be considerably worse than others.

Next we present methods for more in-depth interpretation of the individual subscales, using a three-level model. Throughout this discussion on interpretation, it is important to keep in mind the need for a simultaneous consideration of the context in which the behaviors occur and the information gleaned from the SDH and the clinical interview with the child.

Three Levels of Scale Interpretation

In general, we formulate three interpretations at the scale level: (1) clinically significant problems requiring diagnosis and/or treatment (and/or the child's strengths), (2) subsyndromal problems requiring monitoring and/or preventive intervention, and (3) problems or adaptive skills requiring no specific action. We will demonstrate how we use these interpretations via hypothetical examples of one child with different scores on the Depression scale of the SRP.

1. "Jasper's" Depression scale T score of 70 and his symptoms of depression—which include expressions of hopelessness and suicidal ideation (without a specific plan), frequent tearfulness, decreased appetite, weight loss, inability to enjoy previously pleasurable activities, and decreased energy—are severe enough to warrant a diagnosis of major depressive episode, moderate. Symptomatology of this severity requires immediate treatment. Individual psychotherapy is recommended along with a referral to a psychiatrist to determine whether psychopharmacotherapy is appropriate and medically safe for the young man.

2. Jasper is unhappy most of the time, as indicated by multiple sources of information, including a Depression scale T score of 62 on the SRP. He complains of tearfulness, decreased appetite, and some feelings of hopelessness. Although he does not experience sufficient symptomatology to warrant a diagnosis, his symptoms are beginning to impact his relations with parents and teachers, primarily in the form of increased irritability. It is recommended that he be monitored periodically by the school psychologist, his parents, and his pediatrician to ensure that these problems do not worsen. Simultaneously, preventive intervention, in the form of cognitive–behavioral therapy and supportive counseling, is recommended at school and in the community, if his parents deem it necessary as well.

3. Jasper does not display significant depressive symptomatology (Depression scale T score of 55) as noted by teachers, parents, and himself. He does admit to experiencing some occasional unhappiness with a depth and frequency that is within normal limits at this time.

Of course, most youth possess more than one problem area, and some of these scales do not lead directly to diagnosis or classification decisions although they contribute to case formulation. Withdrawal, Study Skills, Social Skills, Leadership, Learning Problems, Interpersonal Relations, Self-Reliance, Social Stress, Attitude toward Parents, Teachers, and School, Sense of Inadequacy, and Aggression are examples of scales of this type. Three interpretations are offered for the Aggression scale, again using "Jasper.".

1. Jasper displays significant problems with aggression, including verbal cursing, threatening, and bullying (T score = 70). In addition, the school history indicates that he has been cited for pushing and punching others and has been suspended twice this year twice for fighting. He requires treatment for these problems in both school and community.

2. Jasper has some problems with verbal aggression, including cursing at peers and anger outbursts (in which he throws objects) primarily noted at

home and in the community (*T* score = 61, BASC PRS-C). These problems should be monitored to see if they respond to the new parenting strategies being adopted by his parents. If they do not, additional interventions should be implemented to reduce aggression. No significant aggression problems are reported in the more structured environment of school at this time (*T* = 51, BASC TRS-C).

3. Jasper does not display significant problems with aggression, as rated by teachers and his parents (*T* = 51 on both TRS and PRS).

As noted, BASC interpretation is described in detail in Reynolds and Kamphaus (1992). However, we develop additional interpretive guidance as new research findings become available. The following proposals for additional interpretive steps are offered to supplement those found in the BASC manual.

Three Interpretive Steps

In an effort to simplify interpretation and yet ensure a thorough approach we advise the following steps as a starting point.

• **Step 1.** *Write down (or highlight, circle, or in some way mark) all scales with* T *scores at or above 60 for the clinical scales and at or below 40 for the adaptive scales.* Scores in this range are identified as either "at-risk" or "clinically significant" on BASC printouts. By utilizing scores in this range for screening, diagnostic, and treatment purposes, we are likely to reduce "false negatives" and errors in the direction of "false positives." In addition, utilization of scores in this range allows for the identification of subsyndromal problems that may require treatment because they are associated with functional impairment (Cantwell, 1996).

We generally do not list the composite scores at this stage unless we are trying to answer a question that is associated with a composite score (see Reynolds & Kamphaus, 1992). Types of these questions include, for example, "Is Victor's behavior generally worse than that of other boys his age?" (BSI), or "Does Victor have more internalizing problems than other boys his age?" (Internalizing composite). Another instance is a composite score exceeding *T* of 69, with lower scores on the subscales—a noteworthy combination suggesting that the sum of this child's problems clearly exceeds it parts. For the clinical purposes of diagnosis, classification, or treatment planning, the individual scales provide the specificity necessary to answer these questions; the composite scores do not.

The TRS and the PRS subscales show good levels of test specificity (defined as unique and reliable variance associated with scores on a particular scale), although parent ratings (the PRS) have been found to have greater specificity across scales than teacher ratings (TRS; Daniel, 1993). This finding means that parents' ratings will produce profiles with greater variability than teachers' and will denote less influence by the higher order factors (e.g., internalizing and externalizing). Daniel (1993) contends that these findings indicate that parents may be more sensitive to specific aspects of their child's behavior. This is a reasonable view; given parents' greater exposure to their children, they can likely make finer distinctions regarding behavior and may be influenced less by any positive or negative halo. These interpretations are consistent with TRS and PRS profiles for various diagnostic groups reported in the BASC manual as well.

In the sample tables that follow, all potentially important T scores are identified in **boldface** type for the case of "Victor," discussed in Chapter 4.

	Teacher	Mother	Father
Hyperactivity	**83**	58	52
Aggression	57	39	39
Externalizing Problems composite	57	48	45
Anxiety	50	47	42
Depression	45	39	39
Somatization	43	49	37
Internalizing Problems composite	45	43	36
Atypicality	**74**	37	41
Withdrawal	41	29	33
Attention Problems	**78**	**73**	**73**
Behavioral Symptoms Index	**69**	48	47

On the Adaptive scales, scores below 30 are considered clinically low, but scores from 31 to 70 are also representative of high-risk areas.

	Teacher	Mother	Father
Adaptability	44	**61**	**61**
Social Skills	42	**66**	57
Adaptive Skills composite	42	**65**	**60**

• **Step 2.** *For each scale listed, identify supportive and nonsupportive evidence of a significant problem or competency.*

Scale	Supportive evidence	Nonsupportive evidence
Hyperactivity	• Parents and teacher report an inability to learn basic academic concepts, such as numbers and letters, a high level of activity, and an inability to focus on academic tasks. • Father reports his own lifelong problem of sitting still. • Teacher reports that he cannot focus on task at hand and, as a result, his problem is worsening. • Current teacher reports that he is always on the run, talks excessively, is unable to stay seated for any period of time, and frequently interrupts class activities.	• Parents report some difficulty with fine and gross motor skills. He is not yet able to catch a ball or tie his shoes, although he is able to ride a bike. His teacher also reports that he has a difficult time writing his letters, coloring, or drawing (could be a case of general developmental delay or mental retardation). • Teacher reports that he is unable to retain information over even short periods of time (further evidence of developmental delay).
Atypicality		• Parents report some difficulty with fine and gross motor skills. He is not yet able to catch a ball or tie his shoes, although he is able to ride a bike. His teacher also reports that he has a difficult time writing his letters, coloring, or drawing (could be a case of general developmental delay or mental retardation).

(continued)

Scale	Supportive evidence	Nonsupportive evidence
Atypicality (continued)		• Teacher reports that he is unable to retain information over even short periods of time (further evidence of developmental delay).
Attention Problems	• Parents and teacher report an inability to learn basic academic concepts, such as numbers and letters, a high level of activity, and an inability to focus on academic tasks. • Teacher reports that he cannot focus on task at hand and, as a result, his problem is worsening. • During testing, his inability to focus on task at hand or sustain attention for even small lengths of time caused him to miss many items he would otherwise have gotten correct.	• Parents report some difficulty with fine and gross motor skills. He is not yet able to catch a ball or tie his shoes, although he is able to ride a bike. His teacher also reports that he has a difficult time writing his letters, coloring, or drawing (could be a case of general developmental delay or mental retardation). • Teacher reports that he is unable to retain information over even short periods of time (further evidence of developmental delay).
Adaptability	• Parents report that he is responsible for keeping his room clean, is very polite, well-mannered, and able to dress and bathe himself.	
Social Skills	• Parents report that he is responsible for keeping his room clean, is very polite, well-mannered, and able to dress and bathe himself.	

• **Step 3.** *For each scale remaining, draw conclusions regarding diagnosis, subsyndromal problems, and competencies.* Victor has significant problems with inattention and hyperactivity, as indicated by BASC *T* scores and other measures (see test results in Chapter 4). Although his PRS Hyperactivity scale *T* scores are not significant, these results reflect underestimations of his activity level at home when compared to the parents' verbal descriptions of their management of his activity level at home (see Chapter 4). There is overwhelming evidence for the diagnosis of ADHD, combined type. Moreover, the potential alternative cause of developmental delay or mental retardation is effectively ruled out by the various cognitive test results, which were consistently average to low-average. He tended to score lower on tests requiring spatial and visual motor skills, which could be attributed to a mild developmental delay.

Although his parents report adaptive strengths at home and they clearly have a very favorable opinion of his behavior, noting that he has many friends, this is not the case at school. Qualitative information and behavior ratings from his teacher do not support this conclusion. Hence, it is probably premature to conclude that he has above-average adaptive competencies in comparison to other children his age (see full report in Chapter 4).

In this case, the Atypicality scale functions as another indicator of hyperactivity, as demonstrated in Chapter 2. Therefore, this result can be subsumed under the Hyperactivity scale results.

No noteworthy subsyndromal problems (*T* = 60–69) were identified for Victor. This conclusion suggests that his ADHD symptomatology is not accompanied by any current evidence of emerging comorbidities, with the possible exception of a learning disability, for which he will be observed (see Chapter 4).

While we recognize that these three steps represent a simplified version of the complex set of heuristics typically used by clinicians, they do provide a structure for initiating BASC scale interpretation. The report for Victor, presented in Chapter 4, includes more of the nuance that characterizes clinical case formulation. To facilitate understanding and interpretation of various score levels on all standardized subscales of the BASC, we have provided rapid summary tables, one for each BASC subscales previously mentioned in Chapter 2. Now we turn to explore additional interpretive steps that may enhance the BASC's utility.

Critical Items

Individual test items provide narrow views of behavior, and item reliabilities pale in comparison to the reliability of a composite of items (a subscale). However, reviewing item content and following up with questions can prove extremely useful to gaining a deeper understanding of a pattern's etiology. Some items cry out for follow-up by virtue of their content (e.g., "Sometimes I want to hurt myself"). Such items are tagged as Critical Items on all levels of the BASC TRS, PRS, and SRP, on both the hand-scored and computer-scored options. Examples of Critical Items from the SRP-A are:

I can't seem to control what
  happens to me.
I don't seem to do anything right.
Someone wants to hurt me.
No one understands me.
I hear voices in my head.
I have fainting spells.
I just don't care anymore.
Sometimes I want to hurt myself.

Nothing goes my way.
Nothing about me is right.
Nobody ever listens to me.
I cannot control my thoughts.
Other kids hate to be with me.
Sometimes voices tell me to do bad
  things.
I get into fights at school.
I cannot stop myself from doing
  bad things.

As is apparent, these items deal principally with issues of self-harm, loss of control, bizarre symptoms, and dejection/rejection—all critical issues for adolescents that may denote more severe problems than have otherwise been detected or revealed. Follow-up questioning and sometimes confrontation may be necessary although many times a clear, rational explanation for the behavior or feeling is given by the child.

Examples of Critical Items from the rating scales are also instructive. The following are designated as Critical Items on the PRS-A:

Tries to hurt self.
Sleeps with parents.
Uses medication.
Uses illegal drugs.
Says, "I want to die," or "I wish I
  were dead."
Has muscle spasms.
Has a hearing problem.
Says, "I'm afraid I'll hurt someone."

Has seizures.
Has eye problems.
Is in trouble with the police.
Says, "I want to kill myself."
Stutters.
Plays with fire.
Drinks alcoholic beverages.
Says, "I hate myself."
Threatens to hurt others.

Common themes of violence, poor sense of control, and odd behaviors, in conjunction with well-established developmental flags (e.g., "Plays with fire") and somatic complaints (e.g., muscle spasms, hearing or eye problems, seizures) should prompt a medical referral if the child has not been seen lately by his or her primary care physician. Critical items on these and all other BASC standardized scales are clearly identified when endorsed, regardless of whether the clinician uses the hand score BASC forms or any of the BASC computer scoring programs.

According to Butcher (1990), and reiterated by Graham (2000), the primary and most appropriate use of Critical Items is to detect highly specific problems or behaviors that are important but might not be reflected in clinical profile elevations. Highly salient themes in the child's life may be illuminated. However, as single items, Critical Items have limited reliability, and the types of problems depicted are restricted in range. They are thus a supplement to subscale interpretation, not a substitute or an independent interpretive process. Endorsement of Critical Items should lead the examiner to inquire further into areas designated by the items.

INTERVENTION PLANNING AND EVALUATION

The interpretive steps described are primarily useful for case formulation, classification, and diagnostic purposes. The following discussion offers principles intended to enhance the utility of BASC results for treatment of behavioral and emotional difficulties in children and adolescents.

Specifying Treatment Objectives and Target Behaviors

Results from the BASC may form the basis for establishing treatment objectives. Examiners are cautioned to avoid establishing unrealistic objectives—and therefore expectations—for change. Indeed, it may be inappropriate to offer treatment objectives for all BASC constructs. It may not be warranted, for example, to expect change on the Withdrawal or Anxiety scale if somatic therapy for Hyperactivity and Attention Problems is the only treatment being used. Similarly, pharmacological treatments for ADHD (e.g., amphetamines) have not been shown to affect internalizing problems in predictable ways (discussed more later). Therefore, it seems unwise to communicate the expectation that these scales will change when, in fact, there is no treatment aimed at changing the behavior designated by the construct. On the other hand, if comorbid depression is being treated through medication and cognitive–behavior therapy, then change in the Depression scale may be an appropriate treatment objective. Treatment objectives should always be linked to actual treatments delivered in order to ensure that parents, teachers, and others have realistic expectations regarding change.

Any of the four BASC components (PRS, TRS, SRP, SOS) can then be used to identify target behaviors for intervention. Erhardt and Conners (1996) support their suggestion that deviant scales and items be used to set target behaviors by observing that "it is reasonable in drug studies to use the most elevated scales on rating measures as predictors of drug treatment outcome, as well as primary target behaviors for medication effects" (p. 130).

The BASC Plus computer scoring program offered by American Guidance Service provides recommended target behaviors that are useful for prioritizing interventions. The selection of these behaviors was heavily influenced by surveys of teachers and more than 500 school-age children during the development of the BASC. These teachers and students listed, in prioritized order, behaviors they most disliked in others. Frequency and saliency were determined from these ratings; those most likely to result in a child being ostracized were retained on the BASC. The BASC Plus identifies these behaviors when marked by a teacher or a parent. These are often behaviors associated with aggressive tendencies, which typically cause children to be excluded from activities with normally behaving, nonaggressive children. By targeting these behaviors for intervention—unless self-harm is noted, which would take priority—children are less likely to experience exclusion and ostracization. Children who display inappropriate behavior benefit from being with normal and well-behaving peers who model appropriate behavior. Due to the level of saliency among peers and teachers and the resultant social validity and potential for positive impact, these target behaviors should receive careful, due consideration as a starting point whenever they are detected.

Recording Treatment Data

The major interpretive inference made by the BASC user is a link between treatment and outcomes. Careful treatment records are necessary in order to draw such inferences. The reverse side of the Parent and Teacher Monitor forms that are part of the BASC ADHD Monitor, for example, provides space for documenting the types of various treatments, including their onset, cessation, and adherence. Although adherence is probably the most difficult to document, attempts should be made to do so. It may be necessary to use telephone interviews with parents, teachers, and/or clinicians, or conduct reviews of clinical records in order to assess adherence to treatment regimens. The collection of treatment information allows clinicians to be confident in their assessments of change.

Collecting at Least Three Data Points

The BASC forms and software are designed to facilitate the collection of three or more data points so as to encourage frequent follow-up and a more accurate assessment of a child's underlying change trajectory. Francis, Fletcher, Stuebing, Davidson, and Thompson (1991) observed that individual growth is difficult to measure accurately with only two data points, such as a pretest and posttest.

Assessing Change: Clinical Significance

The assessment of change is characterized by numerous methodological confounders and issues. Jacobson and Truax (1991) criticize the use of meta-analyses for assessing change by observing that statistical significance may be unrelated to the clinical significance of change. They cite the example of weight loss where a loss of 2 or 3 pounds may be deemed statistically significant yet hardly satisfying to many of those undergoing treatment. In relationship to change subsequent to psychotherapy, they note that there are three potential indicators of clinical significance. We believe these indicators apply to all types of psychological interventions and have rephrased them here to reflect their more general applicability:

1. The level of functioning subsequent to behavioral intervention should fall outside the range of the dysfunctional population, where the range is defined as extending 2 *SD*'s beyond (in the direction of functionality) the mean of the population.
2. The level of functioning subsequent to behavioral intervention should fall within the range of the functional or normal population, where the range is defined as within 2 *SD*'s of the mean of that population.
3. The level of functioning subsequent to behavioral intervention places the client closer to the mean of the functional population than it does to the mean of the dysfunctional population.

To these we would add an important fourth:

4. The response to treatment makes a positive difference in the day-to-day life of the patient.

Consider, for example, a child who has a severe case of ADHD and responds to psychopharmacotherapy to a degree that reduces his score on the Hyperactivity scale from 90 to 75. This child is still more overactive than 99% of children at his age. Nevertheless, if he can now attend a regular classroom with peers who have good social skills, as opposed to attending a segregated classroom with children who have behavioral problems and less developed social skills, then the treatment would be successful.

Whether or not such goals are realistic for ADHD and other developmental disorders, however, remains in question. If ADHD is conceptualized as a developmental disorder, there may be cause for modest expectations for change, whereas we would not expect children with mental retardation to ever test within the normal range. However, in accordance with criterion (4), an intervention allowing a person with mental retardation to handle activities of daily living independently would make a huge difference in quality of life and be judged successful. Similarly, expectations for change due to treatment of children with syndromes of reading disabilities or autism might not include a return to the normal range of functioning for many. For a child with autism to be able to engage in interactive play, or for a child with dyslexia to develop positive self-esteem, a high level of self-acceptance, and compensatory skills are all big successes that do not attain "normalcy" but should be recognized and encouraged. Other potential indicators of acceptable change could include change that is recognizable by peers, teachers, parents, or others, and/or reduced risk for various health problems (Jacobson & Truax, 1991). Certainly the limitations of statistical indicators of change should not be overlooked.

For the above reasons, it is essential that clinical significance be considered when assessing change. In part, clinical significance will eventually become evident through research on the outcomes of children with various disorders. Until then, the clinical assessor of change must decide on a measure of clinical significance that is appropriate for each child. Perhaps the best way to proceed is to define clinical significance by setting objectives that are commensurate with the treatment objectives for the child, parents, and/or caregivers. In fact, setting appropriate goals for change may be an important topic to discuss with parents and others prior to the implementation of treatment. If treatment objectives are not specified and/or realistic for a given child, the effectiveness of treatment will remain ambiguous. Therefore, the establishment of treatment goals is a key step in BASC interpretation. Detailed information on development of treatment plans and objectives can be found in Hersen and Bellak (1998), Hughes (1999), Martens, Witt, Daly, and Vollmer (1999), and Leahy and Holland (2000).

Assessing Change: Other Methodological Issues

Francis et al. (1991) have offered statistical procedures and formulae for individual growth models of change. These authors also discuss some of the measurement prerequisites that are necessary for the accurate assessment of change. Francis et al. (1991) concluded that measures of change, such as the BASC, should (1) have interval scales of measurement, (2) be relatively free of ceiling or floor effects, (3) encourage collection of three or more observations in order to assess an individual growth trajectory, and (4) not use age-based standard scores for measuring change. Each of these criteria will be discussed as they apply to the BASC.

The BASC strives to produce an interval scale of measurement through the use of *T* scores. An interval scale is necessary for assessing change because a scale with unequal units would not allow for the precise computation of change indices. The methods of scaling the BASC (Reynolds & Kamphaus, 1992) ensure the existence of an equal-interval scale of *T* scores.

Because ceiling and floor effects would detract from the usefulness of a scale for assessing change, the BASC *T*-score range is not artificially restricted to a prespecified range. The *T* scores were scaled based on the distributional properties of the construct, as sampled from the population (see Reynolds & Kamphaus, 1992). Ceiling and floor effects are rarely encountered with the BASC, and when they do occur, are almost exclusively present on the SRP.

The BASC does use age-based standard scores (*T* scores) as the featured score for measuring change. For many children, however, the effects of age standard scores on the interpretation of change are nonexistent, because raw scores are not significantly different across age groups, as is indicated by the use of the same norm tables for large age groups of children. In the case of the PRS, the raw scores did not differ significantly for ages 8–11, allowing for the use of one norm table for this age range. For example, if a child is diagnosed initially at age 8, the same raw score to *T*-score conversion table is used until the child reaches age 11. In the case of a 7-year-old child, however, different norm tables will be used for the computation of *T* scores at age 8, which could result in an inaccurate assessment of change. When norm tables change for children, it may be wise for clinicians to consider raw scores, in addition to *T* scores, when assessing change over this time period. Raw scores can be used to assess change for a child or a group of children in a common age range but should not be used for classification or diagnostic purposes.

Another methodological issue to consider is the reliability of different (pretest–posttest) scores. Since an inverse relationship exists between the reliability of a difference score and the correlation between the pretest and posttest, unreliable difference scores may reflect the possibility that the trait being measured changes little over time or in response to treatment (Francis et al., 1991). The long-term stability of the BASC scales is currently established only for a 7-month period (see Reynolds & Kamphaus, 1992), but additional information, when it becomes available through future research, may shed light on the malleability that may be detected by the scales. However, when groups of children are considered, regression effects and unreliability of change scores are easily accommodated.

Informing Treatment Providers and Caregivers

Due to the complexity of symptoms commonly associated with children's disorders, children often receive multimodal therapies, including somatic, behavioral, and educational interventions. The involvement of multiple treatment providers makes communication critical. BASC output is designed to foster communication among parents, physicians, teachers, psychologists, and other clinicians by offering straightforward graphics. *T* scores and percentile ranks are also provided to enhance quantitative interpretation.

We recommend that BASC results be shared generously among all individuals involved with a case. Results, however, should always be accompanied by competent interpretation in order to ensure that they are used appropriately.

ADDITIONAL INTERPRETIVE ISSUES

Child–Adult Agreement

We expect disagreement between adult and child raters, even when common items and scales are utilized. Handwerk, Larzelere, Soper, and Friman (1999) compared parent Child Behavior Checklist (CBCL) and adolescent Youth Self Report (YSR) ratings and found that the adolescent raters significantly underreported their problem behaviors whether they were being treated in acute-care psychiatric shelter, psychiatric inpatient, or residential placement settings. In addition, the adolescents were able to describe their internalizing symptoms with only a minimal level of accuracy. Specifically, parent reports exceeded clinical cut scores 58% of the time, whereas children exceeded cut scores with 22% frequency for the Internalizing scale; the corresponding values for the Externalizing scale were 78% and 30%. In light of these and other data, the authors concluded that, in this specialized treatment setting, parents tended to overrate the prevalency of externaling symptoms compared to external criteria, such as incident reports. Hence, both child and parent raters showed evidence of bias regarding the reporting of externalizing problems. It should be noted, however, that these samples were clinical in nature, with the residential sample including adolescents who had a minimum of two and a half psychiatric diagnoses per case.

In another study, Kamphaus et al. (2000) found that the mean scores for children in normative samples were similar for parent and teacher ratings. We compared the parent and teacher ratings of four groups of children: U.S. Anglo, U.S. African American, U.S. Hispanic, and metropolitan Medellin, Colombia. We found that parents tended to rate their children as having more adaptive skills and significantly more problem behaviors than teachers did.

The Kamphaus et al. (2000) study is also the largest comparison study of mean gender and ethnic group differences. Generally speaking, the results can be summarized as follows (although there were a few exceptions):

• Child gender produced the most consistent trends for the total U.S. and Colombian samples. In the Colombian sample teachers rated boys as having more aggression, atypicality, conduct problems, and hyperactivity, whereas parents rated boys as having more problems in all those areas as well as attention. Girls were not rated by teachers as having more problems than boys; however, parents viewed girls as having more problems with anxiety (ages 6–18), withdrawal (ages 4–11), depression (ages 12–18), and somatization (ages 12–18). (These results also support Handwerk et al.'s conclusion that parents were more severe raters than teachers.) Finally, both parents and teachers generally agreed that girls have better adaptive skills than boys (indicated for most age levels on all of the BASC Adaptive scales). This finding is consistent with the BASC standardization data.

• Few of the differences between the four ethnic groups were as consistent as the gender differences. For example, the four groups did not differ on ratings of aggression by teachers. Parents of Colombian and U.S. Anglo children rated their children as more aggressive than did parents of U.S. African American and U.S. Hispanic children. There were, however, some differences at individual age levels. For example, parents of U.S. Hispanic children, ages 4–5, rated their children as being as aggressive as parents of Colombian and U.S. Anglo children rated theirs. These data reveal that the ethnic and linguistic differences are much less interpretable than the clear cut gender differences, which are much more consistent across rater and ethnic group.

• Some of the ethnic group differences were more consistent within rater categories. For example, although teachers did not observe significant differences in somatization, parents consistently identified their U.S. African American and Colombian children as having more somatization problems than did parents of U.S. Hispanic and Anglo children (see Kamphaus et al., 2000, for a full report of these findings).

• Analyses of socioeconomic status (SES) for the Colombian sample revealed that teachers rated fewer differences, with the exception of low-SES children having more problems with somatization and conduct. Many differences were noted among parents by SES groups, as groups in the lower SES strata rated their children as having more aggression, atypicality, depression, hyperactivity, and conduct problems. Other differences were quite variable by age group.

Our interpretation of these findings are that (1) child gender is the most important determinant of both teacher and parent ratings, and (2) child ethnicity and SES are more likely to affect parent than teacher ratings. Of course, the significance of these findings is tempered by the fact that these were nonclinical samples. Nevertheless, results may have implications for research and theory development regarding the interplay of child gender, family SES, and ethnic and language group influences on child behaviors and adult perceptions of these behaviors.

Teacher and parent ratings of young children have been found to be good predictors of behavioral maladjustment over a 6-year period (Verhulst, Koot, Van der Ende, 1994). Verhulst and colleagues used parent and teacher ratings on the CBCL to predict behavioral maladjustment, based on interviews with parents, six years later. Interestingly, although both teacher and parent ratings were predictive, teacher ratings were significantly better predictors, despite the fact that the criteria data were collected from parents. This finding underscores our belief that both parent and teacher reports are necessary in each case we evaluate.

Kamphaus and Frick (2002) emphasize an interpretive approach that considers all information, regardless of the source, to be of potential value. Take the case of Victor, for example. If he were old enough to take the SRP, his results would also be submitted to the same three steps of interpretation. We agree with this approach and advise our trainees similarly—to consider all sources of information as potentially valuable. Case studies in the next chapter demonstrate the value of child/adolescent ratings as well. In addition, we wish to point out that we developed the SOS and SDH for one reason: observations and interview findings are of considerable importance for case conceptualization.

ADHD Comorbid with Mental Retardation

The most recent diagnostic manual of the American Association on Mental Retardation (1992) suggests that all individuals with mental retardation should receive a full social/emotional evaluation because they are at greater risk of depression, ADHD, schizophrenia, and a long list of other psychiatric disorders. The prevalence of ADHD is, indeed, higher in this group than in the remainder of the population. Unfortunately, due to inclusion of a codicil to this effect in the DSM-IV, clinicians may consider ADHD symptomatology to reflect a developmental delay that is associated with the child's mental age. Well, it is conceivable that the DSM-IV is simply incorrect on this point. Pearson and Annan (1994) conclude that this is the case:

> Findings suggest that chronological age should be taken into consideration when behavior ratings are used to assess cognitively delayed children for ADHD. However, the results do not support guidelines stating that mental age must be used to determine which norms should be applied when such children are evaluated clinically. (p. 395)

The use of mental age as a consideration in making the ADHD diagnosis for children with mental retardation may result in the denial of somatic and behavioral treatments that are known to have demonstrated efficacy.

CHAPTER 4

Case Studies

We include several case studies (well disguised but real) in this chapter, written by various colleagues and students. The psychological reports are presented in a format similar to their original formulation to provide models of report writing. General advice regarding the written communication of BASC results is necessary first.

First, we suggest that clinicians begin their reporting of BASC findings by utilizing the descriptions of scale results offered in the BASC software and the suggested interpretations offered in Chapter 3 of this book. The software descriptions of BASC scales and results are the product of considerable effort and the fine editing of many; they are the most accurate and literate available. Those in Chapter 3 offer somewhat finer discriminations across various score ranges. Usage of these two sources of descriptions makes report writing based on BASC user results much easier.

Second, change the names of scales if the situation so dictates to mitigate against misinterpretation. As noted, we have already done this in the case of the Atypicality scale. When it became obvious that our "Psychoticism" scale was prone to other interpretations (i.e., hyperactivity), we changed the name to the innocuous "Atypicality." Such name changing may also be necessary in other circumstances. For example, a child with some symptoms of depression who is clearly not syndromal for depression may not be served by describing the problem as one of *depression*. In some subsyndromal cases, it may be more accurate to label Depression scale results as indicators of "unhappiness" or even "negative affectivity." Likewise, a child with minor anxiety problems may be best described as suffering from "worry" at the present time. Because we could not possibly anticipate all such circumstances, we do not want to limit clinicians' inventiveness with regard to score reporting. However, before making such changes in name or interpretation of a specific scale, the pattern of item responses should be reviewed. The BASC Enhanced Assist and the BASC Plus computer scoring programs provide the option of listing every BASC item, grouped by scale, and the response given by the parent, child, or teacher.

Third, written reports can either emphasize or downplay the obtained T scores, depending on the case. For example, we have seen cases of clinical depression where the Depression scale T score did not fully communicate the seriousness of the condition. In one case (SRP Depression T score = 64; no PRS or TRS Depression scores greater than 60), the adolescent experienced both homicidal and suicidal ideation. Here it was most important to emphasize the specific symptomatology and its seriousness more than the T-score finding. Above all, we wish to encourage clinicians to exercise their clinical acumen in their reports of BASC findings. Clinical interviews of children and adolescents will always have a place in diagnosis and in making sense of any objective test results.

Finally, the *BASCforum.com* web site is described at the end of this chapter. The various discussions, sample reports, and "FAQs" available at this site are a valuable resource for those charged with interpreting and reporting BASC results.

PSYCHOLOGY CLINIC
PSYCHOLOGICAL EVALUATION REPORT

Name: David R. Becker
DOB: 09/26/89
Age: 10 years 0 months
Parents: Jodie and Travis Becker
Address: 4433 Snowy Trail
   Anchorage, AK 99286
School: Elm Street Elementary
Grade: Fourth
Teachers: Mrs. Hart and Ms. Wright

Dates of evaluation: 09/16-09/17/99;
   10/7/99; 10/10/99
Psychologists: Tom Goldstein, PhD
   Inga Howard, PhD

Assessment Procedures

Wechsler Intelligence Scale for Children—Third Edition
Woodcock–Johnson Psycho-Educational Battery—Revised Tests of
   Achievement
Wide Range Achievement Test–3
Oral and Written Language Scales
Beery–Buktenica Developmental Test of Visual–Motor Integration
Structured Interview for the Diagnostic Assessment of Children
Achenbach Child Behavior Checklist—Parent Form
Parenting Stress Index
Behavior Assessment System for Children—Parent Rating Scales
Behavior Assessment System for Children—Self Report of Personality
Child Depression Inventory
Child Interview
Parent Interview

School visit and interview with classroom teachers
Behavior Assessment System for Children—Student Observation
   System

Differential Abilities Scale

Other
Phone Conversations: Dr. K. Albertson, Dr. M. Jones, Dr. G. Short

Referral Question

David is a fourth-grade student who was referred for an evaluation by his parents, Travis and Jodie Becker, to determine the formal psychiatric diagnosis that best describes David's current emotional and behavioral profile. They are seeking a formal diagnosis to better guide his medication protocol and to direct therapeutic intervention. Historically, his primary difficulties have revolved around "angry rages," "depression," and defiance.

David is currently under the care of a psychiatrist, Dr. Kathleen Albertson, who is prescribing 20 mg of Adderall three times/day (at 7, 11, and 3) and 30 mg of Prozac in the morning daily. Under Dr. Albertson's orders, Depakote (1,000 mg daily) was discontinued one month ago, and the Adderall was discontinued for the first 2 days of the evaluation (10/26–10/27). On the second

2 days of the assessment (11/3 and 11/5), David was taking his regular doses of both Adderall and Prozac. A secondary goal of this evaluation was to assess the impact of Adderall on David's performance.

Background Information

David is a 10-year-old boy who lives with his mother, father, 12-year-old brother, Justin, and 5-year-old sister, Rachel, in Anchorage, Alaska. Mrs. Becker completed high school and is currently a homemaker. Mr. Becker obtained a college degree and is currently employed in marketing.

Relevant History

Developmental and Psychological History

The Beckers report that Mrs. Becker's pregnancy with David was planned and uncomplicated, although she had "ulcers and reflux" during the first 6 months of the pregnancy and was prescribed "stomach tranquilizers." During the pregnancy, Mrs. Becker fell down and experienced some bleeding; bed rest was ordered for several days. The prenatal history is also significant for cigarette use (i.e., 3–5 per day). Mrs. Becker went into labor at 40 weeks, and the delivery was apparently lengthy, at 52 hours. Mr. Becker was present during the delivery. David weighed 6 pounds, 7 ounces at birth and was reportedly in good condition overall, with Apgar scores at "7 or 8." However, immediately upon delivery, David reportedly experienced breathing difficulties due to fluid in his lungs, although supplemental oxygen was not required. David also received phototherapy for jaundice.

David was breast-fed for 6 weeks, then switched to a bottle until 18 months. Mrs. Becker reported that he was an "eager" eater and did not experience significant symptoms due to reflux. Later, David reportedly developed "picky" eating habits and would not eat fruits and vegetables. As a baby, the Beckers describe David as "difficult," "intense," and "serious." He was reportedly somewhat difficult to soothe, and his mood changed more frequently than average. Response to novel situations and rhythmicity was reportedly average, whereas activity level and extroversion were slightly above average. Overall, David's health as a baby was insignificant, except for recurrent ear infections. At 9 months, "tubes" were put into his ears, and David was reportedly a "different child," crying significantly less. Motor and language developmental milestones were met within normal limits.

David was a "strong-willed," "defiant," and "difficult" toddler. For example, the Beckers reported that they had to use locks on the windows and doors to keep him in his room. David also threw his dinner across the kitchen on occasion, because he didn't like what was served to him. Throughout the toddler and preschool periods, David resisted taking naps, even when clearly tired. David was defiant and would lay and scream at his bedroom door until falling asleep on the floor. In general, he was defiant whenever his parents tried to direct his behavior across a range of situations. Sometimes David's behavior placed him in danger, such as the time that he drank a bottle of his sister's perfume. He also swallowed "stomach tranquilizers" and had to have his stomach pumped when he was 4 years old.

David exhibited difficulties during this period primarily with his parents. For example, as a preschooler, he attended a half-day program 3 days a week for 2 years. The teacher–student ratio was low (i.e., six student teachers to 12 children), and David performed "like an angel" in this setting. He responded appropriately to demands and enjoyed his time at preschool. David's performance at school has been, and continues to be, significantly better with one-on-one attention.

Although David was reportedly difficult "from birth," his problems apparently escalated around the time his sister was born and when he started formal schooling (the timeline of events is unclear). Around age 5, the Beckers took David to Somerset Hospital for evaluation. They did not receive a formal report or diagnosis at this time; they report being told that they were "just not strict enough" with David. At some point in this general time frame, a psychiatrist (unknown) put David on Paxil for "depression," even though he did not formally proffer a diagnosis. They did not continue seeing this psychiatrist, and David did not take Paxil long enough for the Beckers to notice any change in behavior. Again around this time, David's pediatrician, Dr. Perez, prescribed Ritalin, which seemed to stabilize his behavior. However, the Beckers reported that whenever the Ritalin wore off, David would experience "rebound" effects, with severe "mood swings" and even more severe tantrums. Therefore, the pediatrician changed his medication to Adderall, which they believe was helpful. He was able to focus better, his emotional state was much more stable, and he did not experience rebound effects. David reported that the Adderall "keeps me awake" and that he feels tired when not taking it.

In kindergarten, David was referred to the Student Support Team due to being "a little below grade level in reading and writing," according to the referral sheet. The teacher also noted that he had difficulty concentrating, lacked confidence, was easily frustrated in front of others, had difficulty completing his work, and was overly anxious to please. Some interventions were already in place at this time, including visits with the school counselor for "anger," and sitting close to the teacher so that she could "motivate and encourage" him.

In first grade, the Student Support Team Intervention Documentation sheet stated that David's behavior was "beginning to be unusual," although this statement was not explained. The teacher also noted that he "appears to be frustrated" and makes "frequent comments about not liking himself." She added that he "appears sad." It was noted that he was seeing the school counselor regularly.

Although David's behavior apparently stabilized for a time, it soon escalated when he entered the second grade. David experienced several major life events around this time, including moving to a new home nearly 2 miles from their old neighborhood after the school year had started. David was reportedly upset (i.e., crying, sad, and angry) about having to leave his friends, make new friends, and attend a new school. Further, his uncle had recently died, and his neighbor, a good family friend and someone with whom David enjoyed spending time, was suffering from a serious illness. In general, the timeline of these psychosocial stressors in relation to the exacerbation of David's symptoms is unclear. However, around this time (approximately age 6½ years), David reportedly was obsessed with the color black, drew a number of pictures of skulls and blood, and talked about "dying and killing people." In addition, when he did not get his way with his parents, he would have "huge outbursts," wherein he screamed, punched, and destroyed property. The Beckers noted that when David did not get his way, they knew there would be a "price to pay," such as when David threw an expensive clock out of the window. During this time, the Beckers took David to Dr. Jones, a psychologist, who reportedly told the Beckers that David was "clinically depressed." In a phone conversation, Dr. Jones reported that his major concern was the amount of negative feedback David was receiving at home and at school due to his behavior. David was also reportedly "emotionally labile," "depressed," and disruptive in the classroom. Problems noted in the second-grade classroom, as reported by Mrs. Becker, included chronically defiant behavior toward teachers, taking other's papers, tripping students as they walked past his desk, acting the class clown, and appearing very sad. His behavior was so disruptive that he was not allowed to participate in the class musical.

Dr. Jones reported asking for a reevaluation of David's medication status in January of 1998, due to concerns about David's depressed presentation. David was taken to see Dr. Short, a psychiatrist, who added Prozac to his medication protocol. Mrs. Becker believes that the Prozac beneficially affected David's levels of aggression, anger, and sadness, whereas Mr. Becker disagrees;

he could see no benefits beyond those of Adderall. David reported that he "has no clue" what the Prozac does.

David was seen in individual therapy with Dr. Jones for six months, and according to the Beckers, he seemed to like the psychologist. In addition, Dr. Jones reportedly worked with the classroom teacher on behavior management issues. Dr. Jones noted that, after he had worked with the family and teacher (and apparently after David began taking Prozac), David's behavior looked more typically like ADHD and he became "harder to manage." The Beckers were unable to continue working with Drs. Short and Jones due to an insurance change.

At the beginning of David's third-grade year, he again experienced significant psychosocial stressors. His beloved dog, Ginger, died. Ginger had been with the family since David was 1 year old, and he was reportedly "devastated" by the dog's death. In addition, David's paternal grandmother, with whom he shared a special relationship, died after an extended illness.

During David's third-grade year, his behavior problems again escalated both at home and at school. According to the Beckers, his teacher reported significant difficulties, and he was sent to the principal's office frequently. David was reportedly "calling out," and he exhibited a few simple motor tics, such as head rolling. Mrs. Hart, his resource teacher for the past and current years, reported that he made odd noises to his classmates. She believes that these noises were more like a vocal tic than a voluntary behavior (i.e., "he did not have any expression on his face" and he was not acting the class clown at the time). David reported that he does not believe that he ever made such noises in class. Other problem behaviors included punching holes in his papers, drawing on himself, repetitively reorganizing his book bag, failing to complete work, bringing forbidden objects to school (such as his skateboard), and acting like the class clown. In response, David was referred to the Student Support Team at school, and an IEP meeting was scheduled for January of that year. On a special education referral form (dated 2/05/99), David's teacher noted that the reasons for referral included below-average academic performance (reading, math, and writing), "severe mood swings," and his inability to work in a group situation. Other problem behaviors noted on this sheet included "compulsive behaviors, such as continually erasing marks on his paper, arranging items in his desk over and over, and clenching his hands and fists continually . . . focusing on tasks, and often never gets started with what he is supposed to do before time is out." Based on Dr. Short's evaluation of David, he was deemed eligible for special education in the category of "other health impaired" and began to receive services. According to David's permanent school record, Dr. Short had diagnosed David with attention-deficit/hyperactivity disorder (subtype unknown), obsessive–compulsive disorder, and oppositional defiant disorder.

Reportedly, the third-grade classroom teacher (Mrs. Foster) told Mrs. Becker that at one point she considered him a conduct problem, but changed her mind when she began to believe that he could not control his own behavior. Following the development of an IEP, he began to see the school counselor regularly and attend a self-esteem group. He also was placed in a resource room for the last 9-week grading period, where his grades changed from C's and D's to A's and B's. Again, David demonstrated that he responds well to individualized attention and instruction.

At the end of his third-grade year, the Beckers took David to a new psychiatrist, Dr. Danbury, who added Depakote to his medication protocol (i.e., Adderall, Prozac, and Depakote). Again, Mrs. Becker felt that the addition was helpful, especially with the tics and repetitive behavior and for the "leveling effects" on his mood, whereas Mr. Becker did not believe that it was helpful.

Following David's third grade year, David also began to see a new psychologist, Dr. Davidson, and a new psychiatrist, Dr. Kathleen Albertson. He currently sees Dr. Davidson once a month. In a phone conversation, Dr. Davidson reported that the primary issues in David's treatment concern temper tantrums, defiant behavior (e.g., refusing to get dressed), anger outbursts, stealing (e.g., money from his mother's purse and father's wallet), lying (Mrs. Becker says he lies "always to get out of trouble"), and the destruction of property (e.g., his sister's new CD). Dr. Davidson reports that he is taking a crisis management approach at this time by helping the Beckers find ways to contain and manage their son. Dr. Davidson added that, when asking David questions, he takes a long time to respond ("you think he's forgotten") but eventually produces a clear answer. David denies feeling depressed but appears to be "slowed and depressed." Dr. Albertson is responsible for David's current medication protocol.

Academic History

In kindergarten at Valley Elementary School, David's academic progress appears unremarkable for learning or behavior problems. His overall conduct was evaluated as satisfactory in each grading period. In regard to social and emotional development, David was rated as consistently demonstrating such skills as following directions, accepting rules and authority, completing tasks, and demonstrating a positive self-concept. He was rated as "sometimes" on *demonstrates self-control*. However, as noted above, the referral process to Student Support Team was initiated in kindergarten.

In the first grade, also at Valley, the teacher noted that David put a great deal of effort into his work. She also noted delays in reading and writing at the end of the school year. His progress was graded as satisfactory in all subjects except language arts, where he was evaluated as "needs to improve." In regard to behavior, David received a "needs to improve" mark in several areas: *shows self-control* (all four grading periods), *controls talking* (last two grading periods), and *listens and follows directions* (last two periods). The teacher noted that David especially enjoyed reading and making artwork.

In the second grade, at Adamsville Elementary, David's grades declined. He received C's and D's in social studies, B's and C's in math, and B's, C's, and D's in language arts. He received all A's in science. The teacher noted that David's behavior, including his ability to focus, "changed drastically" in the third grading period. Although he did not receive any "needs to improve" marks in the first two grading periods, he received many such marks in the third and fourth grading periods, including: *shows self-control, controls talking, shows good manners, respects others, works independently, listens and follows directions*, and *uses materials and time wisely*. Although his overall mark in conduct and work habits was "satisfactory" in the second grading period, he was marked as "needs improvement" in the third and fourth grading periods. She also noted that David is very artistic and that he began to "open up" with other students in the second period, although he needed to find more appropriate ways to do so.

In the third grade, also at Adamsville, David's grades declined; he was mostly making C's and D's in all areas but science, in which he made B's and C's. The teacher noted that when David tries, he succeeds, although by the fourth grading period he was placed in the resource class for language arts and math. His grades did not change dramatically even with the added attention. This year, David received an overall mark of "needs improvement" in conduct and work habits with specific marks in the following areas: *shows self-control, controls talking* (third only), *shows good manners, works and plays well with others* (second only), *respects others* (fourth only), *listens and follows directions, completes assignments on time, completes homework* (fourth only), *accepts responsibility* (first only), and *uses time wisely*.

Overall, David's academic performance and behavioral scores have declined from kindergarten to third grade.

Family History

Both maternal and paternal family histories are significant for psychological problems. Travis Becker's maternal aunt was diagnosed with bipolar disorder, as were three of her four children. Travis's nephew was also diagnosed with bipolar disorder. According to Travis, all of these family members evidenced good premorbid functioning in childhood, and symptom onset did not occur until adulthood.

Jodie Becker's mother was diagnosed with bipolar disorder when Jodie was 12 years old, and Jodie's younger sister was reportedly diagnosed with bipolar disorder as an adult. One maternal aunt has twin grandsons, both of whom have experienced difficulties. One of these children (13 years old) is currently taking lithium, although he has not been formally diagnosed, and the other has been diagnosed with attention-deficit/hyperactivity disorder. According to Jodie, most of her diagnosed family members began to experience difficulties in childhood. Interestingly, Jodie's aunt recently visited the family and reportedly told her that David reminds her very much of Jodie's mother when she was a child. According to this aunt, her mother was "careless," "strong-willed," "defiant," and "artistic like David." Furthermore, the aunt also suggested that David acts like the grandson who is currently taking lithium.

Travis Becker reports that he was "hyperactive" as a child. For example, he was put on a "leash system" in the backyard and was restrained to keep him in bed. He also experienced reading difficulties in the second grade and was retained. Jodie Becker noted that she "struggled" in the lower grades and has had continued difficulties with reading. Finally, David's older brother has been diagnosed with a reading disability and attention-deficit/hyperactivity disorder (subtype unknown).

Clinical Presentation

Presenting Problem

The Beckers concerns are reflected in the their scores on the Achenbach Child Behavior Checklist, Behavior Assessment System for Children, and Parenting Stress Index. They are primarily concerned with David's defiant behavior ("defying authority"), his not following directions, his destructive behavior, lack of consequential thinking, response to being disciplined, and his depression and mood problems.

In general, David is defiant when his parents try to direct his behavior across a range of situations, such as after school when he is supposed to be completing homework, in the evening when he is told to take a shower, or when he is "fussed at" for trying to sneak forbidden objects (e.g., trading cards) into his book bag to take to school. His behavioral responses are also unpredictable, except that progression into a more severe response appears to be prompted mostly by discipline. David demonstrates three levels of bad behavior: "acting foolish," "temper tantrums," and "rages." The Beckers agree

on operational definitions for each of these categories of behavior and which
behaviors fit into each.

Response to Discipline

Specifically, when acting crazy and silly, David might create a mess (e.g., getting into Mom's make-up), yell and bang on the walls on the way to the
shower (without creating permanent damage), and stomp his feet. He often
acts foolishly when asked to take a shower. His parents reported that David
sometimes talks excessively to "make people mad" and will not stop; they
once pulled over the car, telling him they would go no farther unless he
stopped talking—to no avail. One time when he was supposed to take a
shower, they heard him tell his brother to stop beating him up, and his dog to
stop biting him. However, when his father went into David's room, neither
the dog nor his brother was present. David's parents describe his behavior at
the clinic (i.e., throwing Legos up in the air and making noises) as "crazy/silly"
behavior. When disciplined or asked to stop his crazy behavior, David is likely
to escalate into a temper tantrum—which according to the Beckers, consists
of crying, kicking his bedroom door, and sulking. If sent to his room, he might
continue the tantrum or escalate into a "rage" (i.e., "pure anger"), especially if
his parents are angry and agitated themselves. Although rages are more likely
to occur when David is "fussed at," attempts at discipline are not always followed by escalations into a rage. During his rages, David exhibits heavy
breathing, "seeth[es] as if smoke is coming out of his ears," holds his head in
his hands, and screams, curses, or shouts, "I'll kill you" (about which his parents comment, "It looks like he could, but it's just an expression"). David cre-
ates permanent damage during these rages. For example, in his bedroom he
has sliced lampshades, put holes in his walls, and slashed walls with a knife.
Following a rage, he might sleep for a half hour to an hour, after which he
may act "like a new person" or apologize; other times he says that he cannot
remember acting badly.

His rages are not predictable, except that they are more likely to occur if he
is having a bad day and has already had a rage. They do not seem to occur several
days in a row, although Mrs. Becker believes that, at times, he might have two
"up days" (*up* refers to anger) followed by two or so "down days." However, he
might have several bad days in a row, although he is not usually "bad" for the entire day. Mrs. Becker maintains that his rages are more likely to occur before
school and before bedtime; Mr. Becker was unsure. Although most of David's
uncontrollable behavior occurs in the company of his parents, he has also en-
acted severe tantrums in public. During one such time, he had to be physically
carried off a nearby playground, where his siblings were playing.

Destructive Behavior

David's destructive activities do not always occur in the context of a rage. These activities, referred to as "David's projects" by his parents, are not destructive in the traditional sense of rendering something unusable. Instead, they are highly goal-directed and elaborate activities. For example, on one occasion he neatly painted the baseboards of the upstairs rooms with red paint; on another occasion, he painted elaborate designs on the living room floor. The Beckers do not believe that David perceives his "projects" as destructive but rather as "making improvements." He also engages in dangerous activities, such as jumping on the roof of the house. Again, his parents do not believe that he engages in such activities with the intent to destroy property or harm himself or others.

Additional Symptoms

The Beckers report a number of other symptoms as well. David continues to exhibit simple motor tics (head rolling, shoulder shrugging), although they have reduced in frequency, and he demonstrates compulsive behaviors. For example, they maintain that David organizes each part of his room (e.g., top of the desk) in a *very* specific way—"It has to be certain way." For example, they note that he positions the radio, Kleenex box, TV remote, and so on, in a particular configuration on his dresser. After his mother cleans and moves these items, he moves them back to exactly how they were—though he does not appear to be distressed that she moved his things. Further, they note that "he has to redo things until they are perfect." For example, if he does not like the way his homework looks, or if he has accidentally skipped a line on the paper when numbering problems, he will erase the entire sheet and start over. The teacher says that "he is always reorganizing his desk," according to Mrs. Becker. As noted, the Beckers also report that David steals (e.g., money out of Mom's purse), lies ("only to get out of trouble"), and exhibits a number of difficulties related to inattention and impulsivity.

Discipline Strategies

To discipline David, the Beckers typically yell, take away privileges (e.g., prohibiting television watching or bike riding for the day) after three to four warnings, and "ground" him. They spank him approximately one time per month and contend that this is the only discipline that is effective with him. If he destroys property, they may also make him pay for the damage out of his allowance. David often responds to discipline by sneaking out of the house, throwing a temper tantrum, or engaging in rageful behavior. David responds very well to praise, although they have observed that the effects are short-lived. At this point, the Beckers feel that they have to "choose their battles" with David and not respond to some of his bad behavior. Otherwise, "he could be grounded all day and never have any positives" in his life. They are also beginning to "back off more and more" as he gets older.

Social Adjustment and Personal Characteristics

The Beckers describe David as a "serious" child who does not smile very often. They do not believe that he is either sad or happy but "numb most of the time or mad." Nevertheless, the Beckers also described their son as displaying positive attributes as well. They note that he is generous with other children (e.g., giving a friend lunch money because he forgot to bring his own), loves animals and is good with them (Mrs. Becker wrote that she hopes he will become a veterinarian), and is handsome, artistic, athletic, and sometimes lovable. Indeed, David described the animals in his household at length and noted that he often feeds his sister's turtle because she usually forgets.

David does not appear to have had past difficulties with social relations, nor is he experiencing problems in the present. In fact, his brother's friends used to come over and ask David to play, even though they are older. At this point in time, David's friends appear to be his age. The Beckers are able to list several friends and describe, in detail, the activities in which he engages with them in the neighborhood. For example, a "gang" of several boys will go from one house to the next, trading cards, riding bikes, playing soccer, playing computer games, and so forth. According to the school reports, his peers have never rejected him, although he did "hang around some troublemakers" last year.

Family Relations

The Becker family appears to have an extensive social life; the parents play golf in their neighborhood association on the weekends and attend social functions nearly every weekend as a family. David is "great" when at other people's homes. The Beckers attribute this dramatic shift to his being entertained and kept busy. When asked, they did not reject the idea that they are less likely to discipline David when at someone else's home, although they added that he does not behave as badly when he is occupied. "As a rule," they eat dinner together as a family, unless Mr. Becker is out of town on business (i.e., 2 days per week) or one of the children has a sporting event after school.

The family is currently experiencing a great deal of tension and stress. The Beckers note that they expend most of their energy dealing with David. There is "a lot of hollering" in the home, mostly out of "sheer frustration." David's brother and sister also yell at David and even "tattle" on him. In short, sibling relations are not positive, according to the Beckers. Although David can be very sweet and loving with his sister, he also can be very hateful. David reported that Rachel tattles on him for taking forbidden objects to school (e.g., trading cards) and that Justin "beats me up pretty bad" (e.g., punching him in the stomach) when David goes into his room.

The Beckers are extremely frustrated by, and worried about David's current behavior and developmental trajectory. When asked about their greatest fears for their son, Mrs. Becker became very emotional and said that she is worried that David will end up with no positives in his life and possibly endanger his own life, as an adolescent, through his reckless and rageful behavior. She is worried that he may eventually turn to drugs to "self-medicate." Mr. Becker's worst fear is that there is something "really wrong" with David and that he will not have the aptitude to succeed in life. He is also concerned about the effects that medication is having on David's health and development.

Current School Performance

David currently spends 15 hours per week in the resource room for language arts and math. The resource teacher, Mrs. Wright, does not report any disruptive or defiant behavior from David. However, she noted that he will "fiddle with something until it's broken . . . without you knowing." David will not complete his work unless she keeps him on task. However, at the end of the day when Mrs. Wright reads aloud to the class, David pays attention and is able to follow the story (demonstrated by answering follow-up questions). Mrs. Wright believes that the nature of David's problems is primarily "internalizing." She described David as a polite child who wants to help others and who "rarely" smiles. David looks forward to and enjoys going to the resource room, according to his regular classroom teacher, Mrs. Hart.

In his regular classroom, David is unable to complete any of his work independently. However, he responds well to mild intervention to keep him on task: For example, the paraprofessional in the room will come stand by his desk, put her hand on his shoulder, and so on. David regularly uses up an entire package of erasers when completing his work, punches holes in and makes tears in his workbooks, makes noises, mumbles so that the girls on either side of him often ask to be moved, and speaks out in class. Mrs. Hart noted that he is becoming more difficult as the year progresses, "more open in his movements," popping his neck, "fiddling" with the contents of his desk, calling out, and such. She does not believe that he is disrupting the entire class at this time, however. When asked how his behavior compares to a typical ADHD child, Mrs. Hart responded that he is more "nervous-acting" (e.g., wringing his hands) and "jittery" (although not agitated) and that he attempts to work on his assignments, unlike an ADHD child. During the classroom observation, David appeared to be very focused on his writing assignment, but Mrs. Hart noted that his hands were shaking and he appeared anxious and as if he were trying hard to stay on task. It was her impression that David knew we were going to visit that day, because he cleaned out his desk for the first time. She noted that David can "hold it together" when he is being observed; usually he "squirms in his seat more," "falls off his seat," "fiddles in his book bag," and on and on.

Assessment

Observations and Child Interview

David's mood was subdued when he arrived with his mother and father. When the Beckers were asked if this was a typical presentation for him, they answered with the observation that his behavior had been atypical in the last week: He had been "fairly good," not arguing much. Overall, David appeared to be significantly depressed throughout this first day of the evaluation (09/16). During the interview, which was the first activity of the day, David did not smile (though he did he exhibit polite behaviors, such as pushing in his chair when he stood up to leave the room) and he demonstrated significant lethargy, psychomotor retardation, and flat affect. Even though he did not report depressed feelings, he scored above the clinical cutoff on the Sense of Inadequacy scale, and his scores were elevated in the areas of depression and locus of control on his SRP. When asked questions, he took a very long time to answer. However, he did not appear to be defiant and oppositional but seemed to be experiencing a decelerated rate of processing. With few exceptions, his answers were brief and lacking in emotional content. When asked how he was feeling, for example, he said only that he was tired and suggested that it was due to getting up one hour early to come to the assessment. Finally though, he offered that he was feeling "weird," because this was a new situation for him.

A negative cognitive set appeared to influence most of David's answers. For example, he described not having any friends in his neighborhood and being rebuffed by a child he "tries to hang out with." However, his parents were able to name many friends and list specific activities in which he participates around the neighborhood after school and on weekends. As noted, his parents report no concerns about his social relationships. The only time that David spontaneously elaborated on a topic was when he was talking about the death of his dog, Ginger, and how much he cried when she died.

During testing on the first day, David appeared sluggish and tired, as he had during the interview. For the stimulus items that required a deeper level of thinking and concentration, he typically took the maximum time allotted in order to respond. During this time, he appeared to be studying the item and thinking about his answer. When prompted to respond, to the harder questions, he usually said that he did not have an answer. He often rested his head in his hands, covering his face, and frequently pulled his hat down over his face.

When the family arrived on the second day of the assessment (09/17), David appeared more energetic though agitated, and the Beckers appeared tense. David spent his time in the waiting room throwing crayons in the air while shouting nonsense words. Later, Mr. Becker reported that David had smacked him on the back of the head repeatedly during the drive from their home to our clinic. David was again polite in the presence of the examiners, but on several occasions, he was observed to behave in a more agitated manner when the examiner left the room. For example, he made obscene gestures at the camera, acted as if he were going to punch the chair (but would pull back at the last moment), and shoved the table repeatedly. Despite appearing more energetic before testing, once testing began, he behaved in a fatigued manner and was again slow to respond to stimulus items; he often yawned and closed his eyes. One noticeable difference was his restlessness. He often readjusted his position in the chair to the point where he had turned the chair completely around, with the back toward the table. Later in the session, he knelt on his chair and used the chair next to him as a table on which to write his responses. He did not lose focus during testing, however.

Cognitive Ability Measures

David was administered the Wechsler Intelligence Scale for Children—Third Edition (WISC-III) in order to assess his level of cognitive functioning. Sixty-eight percent of the general population receives scores of 85–115. David received a Full Scale score of 90, which is in the average range. There is a 90% chance that David's true score falls between 86 and 95. The WISC-III Full Scale score is an average of the Verbal and Performance composite scores.

David received a Verbal score of 85, which is in the lower end of the average range. Some subtests loading on the Verbal score include Vocabulary, for which the child is asked to define words, and Similarities, for which the child is asked to find a common link between two items or concepts. David received a Performance score of 98, which is solidly in the average range. Some subtests loading on the Performance score include Picture Arrangement, for which the child arranges picture cards in a sequential order, and Block Design, for which the child manipulates blocks to copy a two-dimensional pattern.

The WISC-III also yields four additional composite scores. David's scores for Verbal Comprehension and Visual/Perceptual were in the average range. However, there is a 90% chance that David's score on the "Third Factor" would fall between 71 and 86, which is below average. Subtests that contribute to this score include Arithmetic, for which the child is asked to make mental calculations, and Digit Span, for which the child is asked to repeat a number series in sequence. Both of these subtests require focused concentration and the ability to retain information mentally for a short period of time. There is also a 90% chance that David's score for Processing Speed would fall between 61 and 78, which is below average. Subtests that contribute to the Processing Speed score are Coding and Symbol Search. Both of these subtests are timed and require the child to recognize and copy unfamiliar symbols. These two subtests are fairly low-level cognitive tasks. David's low score in this area is consistent with observations that he is slow to respond to stimulus items.

Achievement Measures

David was administered the Woodcock–Johnson Psycho-Educational Battery—Revised Tests of Achievement (WJ-R ACH), a broad band measure of school-related skills. Most of David's scores on this test fell in the average range and were consistent with David's cognitive ability scores. However, David's score for the Calculation subtest was below average. There is a 90% chance that David's true score in this area would fall between 63 and 71.

David was also administered the Arithmetic subtest from the Wide Range Achievement Test–3 (WRAT-3). For this subtest, the child is required to calculate arithmetic problems on paper with a 15-minute time limit. During this test, the examiner instructed David to recheck his answers carefully and to use the opposite side of the paper as scratch paper for calculations. Although he did not take the full 15 minutes to complete the test, he did indeed check his answers, using the scratch paper. David received a standard score of 51 for this subtest, which is significantly below average. By examining David's responses to this test, it became apparent that he does not understand the basic mathematical concepts that are expected of children his age. David's scores on the Arithmetic subtest of the WISC-III, Calculation subtest of the WJ-R ACH, and Arithmetic subtest on the WRAT-3 are consistently low relative to age.

David also was administered the Oral and Written Language Scales (OWLS), which contain subtests in the areas of Listening Comprehension, Oral Expression, and Written Expression. David's standard score on each of these areas fell in the average range and was consistent with his other achievement and cognitive ability scores.

Visual–Motor Abilities

David was administered the Beery–Buktenica Developmental Test of Visual–Motor Integration (VMI). This test, in which children are required to copy line images using a pencil without an eraser, is designed to identify children who have difficulty integrating and coordinating their visual and motor abilities. David received a standard score of 95 on it, which is in the average range and is consistent with his achievement and cognitive ability scores.

Observations

The week following the initial assessment (10/10/99), David was administered the Differential Ability Scale (DAS). David was taking his prescription of Adderall again and appeared to have more energy compared to the previous week. When asked how he felt, David stated that he "felt fine" and that he was "not tired." Additionally, he responded to the stimulus questions more quickly than he had during testing the previous week.

Cognitive Abilities Measure

The DAS yields a General Conceptual Ability (GCA) score as an estimate of overall intelligence. David's GCA score of 89 falls in the average range; there is a 90% chance that David's true GCA score would fall between 84 and 95. The DAS also yields a Verbal Cluster score, a Nonverbal Cluster score, and a Spatial Cluster score. David's scores for all three clusters fell in the average range and were consistent with the scores he received on the WISC-III. Subtests that comprise the Verbal Cluster score include Word Definitions, for which the child gives definitions to vocabulary words, and Similarities, for which the child looks for a common link among three objects or concepts. Subtests that comprise the Nonverbal Cluster score include Matrices, for which the child chooses an answer to complete a logical puzzle, and Sequential and Quantitative Reasoning, for which the child chooses an answer to complete a logical sequence. Subtests comprising the Spatial Cluster Score include Recall of Designs, for which the child memorizes and recreates a figure, and Pattern Construction, for which the child is required to manipulate blocks to match a two-dimensional figure.

The DAS also contains several diagnostic subtests that yield T scores with a mean of 50 and an SD of 10. The Recall of Objects subtest, designed to measure verbal memory, requires the child to memorize and name objects from a stimulus card immediately and after a 15-minute interval. David's scores for both immediate and delayed recall fell in the average range. The Speed of Processing subtest, designed to measure the speed at which a child is able to process simple information, times the child while he or she marks the largest number in a row of numbers. David's score on this subtest was in the average range, and it was significantly higher than the score he received on the Processing Speed subtest in the WISC-III. Lastly, the Recall of Digits, a subtest designed to assess short-term memory, requires the child to repeat a series of digits in order. David's T score on this subtest was below average, in the fifth percentile, which means that 95% of children David's age received a higher score on this subtest. The WISC-III contains a nearly identical subtest, Digit Span, on which David's score also fell in the low-average range.

Clinical Impressions and Diagnosis

David is an attractive child who presents with a complex symptomatic profile. He has been previously diagnosed with attention-deficit/hyperactivity disorder (ADHD), oppositional defiant disorder (ODD), and obsessive–compulsive disorder (OCD). However, David's current difficulties are not easily captured by these diagnoses.

First, David was rated by his parents and described by his teachers as having difficulties attending to and completing school-related tasks. However, the scope of David's difficulties do not appear to be accounted for by ADHD. During our observations of him across three different days, David did not present as inattentive, distractible, hyperactive, or impulsive. Even off of Adderall, he was able to sustain attention and respond to task demands for his entire time in the clinic. Even though he was observed to exhibit a very decelerated rate of information processing, and took a considerable time to respond to questions, he did not lose focus. Even with the unusual testing situation in the clinic, given the one-on-one attention and minimized distractions, it would be unlikely that an ADHD child could sustain attention, resist distractions, and respond appropriately to task demands across an entire day of testing, especially on difficult tasks. Although David clearly has difficulties concentrating in the classroom and sustaining attention to tasks, he does have the *capacity* to concentrate, attend, and sustain focus. Furthermore, he did not exhibit an impulsive style when responding to task demands. He was observed to check his answers, and he was not penalized on WISC—III subtests, such as Coding and Symbol Search, for careless errors. His scores were low on these subtests because he was slow.

Second, David's parents described a number of conduct-related difficulties. However, David does not meet criteria for conduct disorder. He does not meet any criteria under the subcategories "aggression to people and animals" and "serious violations of rules," and he meets only two criteria for the remaining two categories; "destruction of property," and "deceitfulness or theft." David has deliberately destroyed someone else's property (e.g., his sister's CD), but although he has started fires, he does not appear to have engaged in fire-setting behavior with the intent of causing serious damage; and he has stolen items of value. However, in regard to lying, he reportedly lies only as a way to escape punishment, not for the explicit purpose of obtaining goods or favors. David's conduct-related difficulties do meet criteria for oppositional defiant disorder (ODD), however: He often loses his temper, argues with adults, defies adults' requests, and is angry. However, even though he meets criteria for ODD, this alone does not explain the overall pattern of David's behavioral difficulties.

Third, David exhibits a number of compulsive behaviors, such as continually reorganizing his desk and maintaining the objects on his dresser in a particular configuration. However, he does not appear to meet criteria for obsessive–compulsive disorder at this time. He does not perform behaviors to reduce distress or prevent some feared event from happening. Furthermore, his compulsive behaviors do not appear to cause him "marked distress" and do not significantly interfere with his normal routine or daily functioning. David's compulsive behaviors appear to fit better under the category of obsessive–compulsive personality disorder, which is characterized by a preoccupation with orderliness, perfectionism, and control. However, diagnosing a child David's age with a personality disorder is not appropriate.

The etiology of David's simple motor tics (and possible vocal tics) is unclear. His tics appear to have emerged after he started taking stimulant medications and may have resulted from this class of medication. David does not appear to be distressed by them, and they do not appear to be causing him marked impairment. However, if David's calling out behavior is determined to be a vocal tic, and it continues to increase in its disruptiveness to the classroom, then a diagnosis of Tourette's disorder may be appropriate.

The primary difficulties that David displays are mood disturbance and emotional dysregulation. His range of symptoms may be accounted for best by the possibility of an emerging bipolar disorder. Bipolar disorder (I or II) is characterized by manic or hypomanic episodes, which are typically followed by major depressive episodes. Even though David's symptom presentation is atypical and he may not meet formal criteria for bipolar I or II disorder, according to DSM-IV, he appears to meet research criteria. Recent research suggests that mania in children presents differently than in adults (e.g., AACAP Work Group on Quality Issues, 1997; Biederman et al., 1996; Fristad, Weller, & Weller, 1995; Geller & Luby, 1997; Weller, Weller, & Fristad, 1995), and DSM-IV criteria for a manic episode were developed for use with adults. For example, mania in children is more likely to appear as irritability and emotional lability than the typical euphoria, elation, and grandiose delusions. Furthermore, it is difficult to identify discrete episodes in manic children, and they may cycle more rapidly than adults. Weller et al. (1995) describe the clinical presentation of mania in childhood as including a "worsening of behavior, moodiness . . . impulsivity . . . inability to concentrate . . . episodic short attention span, low frustration tolerance, and explosive anger followed by guilt, sulkiness, depression, and poor school performance." David's "rages" may be analogous to the "explosive anger" that these researchers describe. David has exhibited periods of distractibility, increased focus on goal-directed activities (e.g., "projects"), and psychomotor agitation. He may have experienced periods of pressured speech and episodes of involvement in pleasurable activities that have a high potential for painful consequences (e.g., fire setting).

It also appears that David has experienced a number of major depressive episodes in the past, as well as currently. Within a 2-week period, he has appeared depressed and irritable to others (and reported depressed mood before starting antidepressants), reported fatigue (i.e., in the interview), experienced feelings of worthlessness (e.g., Sense of Inadequacy scale on the PRS), and exhibited significant psychomotor retardation and a diminished ability to concentrate. In addition, he has experienced recurrent thoughts of death. In the assessment, as noted, David displayed a decelerated processing speed and poor memory, both of which are associated with depression.

Because David does not yet meet criteria for either bipolar I or bipolar II disorder, he is being diagnosed with the more conservative bipolar disorder not otherwise specified. His symptom presentation and significant family history strongly suggest that he is experiencing a developmental progression toward bipolar I or II disorder.

DSM-IV Diagnoses

Axis I: 296.80 Bipolar disorder not otherwise specified
            313.81 Oppositional defiant disorder
Axis II: V71.09 No diagnosis on Axis II
Axis III: (Rule out medical condition)
Axis IV: Psychosocial stressors: significant discord with parents and siblings, academic problems
Axis V: Current GAF = 35

Recommendations

- A medication consult with David's psychiatrist is recommended. His current medication protocol may not be the most appropriate for him at this time.
- A neurological consult and thorough physical evaluation is recommended. As recommended by the American Academy of Child and Adolescent Psychiatry, a mood disorder due to a medical condition should be ruled out. Several neurological conditions (e.g., brain tumor, CNS infection, multiple sclerosis, temporal lobe seizures, Klein–Levin syndrome) and systemic conditions (e.g., hyperthyroidism, uremia, Wilson's disease, and porphyria) can produce symptoms of mania (AACAP Workgroup, 1997). His rages are consistent clinically with temporal lobe seizure disorder (a.k.a. complex partial seizure disorder), and specific evaluation of this possibility is warranted.
- David should continue individual therapy. Parent management training is also strongly encouraged. The Beckers have reported that David's rages are more likely if either one of them responds to him in anger. Therefore, treatment should focus, in part, on ways to manage David's defiant behavior to reduce the likelihood that it will progress to a rageful level.

- Reevaluations every 2 to 3 years (or sooner, if needed) should be completed, either by staff at the School Psychology Clinic or another facility. David should be seen and evaluated by a consistent source over the course of his development.
- David's current educational situation appears to be optimal. Mrs. Wright and Mrs. Hart appear to have developed highly appropriate and sensitive interventions that are currently meeting David's educational needs.

Tom Goldstein, PhD   Inga Howard, PhD

Recommended References

AACAP Workgroup on Quality Issues. (1997). Practice parameters for the assessment and treatment of children and adolescents with Bipolar Disorder. *Journal of the American Academy of Child and Adolescent Psychiatry, 36,* 157S–176S.

Biederman, J., et al. (1996). Attention-Deficit Hyperactivity Disorder and juvenile mania: An overlooked comorbidity? *Journal of the American Academy of Child and Adolescent Psychiatry, 35,* 997–1008.

Fristad, M. A., Weller, R. A., & Weller, E. B. (1995). The Mania Rating Scale (MRS): Further reliability and validity studies with children. *Annals of Clinical Psychiatry, 7,* 127–132.

Geller, B., & Luby, J. (1997). Child and adolescent Bipolar Disorder: A review of the past 10 years. *Journal of the American Academy of Child and Adolescent Psychiatry, 36,* 1168–1175.

Weller, E. B., Weller, R. A., & Fristad, M. A. (1995). Bipolar Disorder in children: Misdiagnosis, under diagnosis, and future directions. *Journal of the American Academy of Child and Adolescent Psychiatry, 34,* 709–714.

Psychometric Summary

Wechsler Intelligence Scale For Children—Third Edition (WISC-III)

The WISC-III is an individually administered clinical instrument for assessing the intellectual ability of children ages 6–16 years, 11 months. The child's performance on 12 subtests is summarized in an overall intelligence score called the Full Scale standard score. The WISC-III also yields Verbal and Performance scale scores. Verbal activities include defining words, answering factual as well as commonsense questions, and doing arithmetic problems without pencil and paper. Performance activities include putting together puzzles and picture sequences, making designs with blocks, and pointing out missing parts of a picture.

The following subtest scaled scores have a mean of 10 with an *SD* of 3; scores of 7–13 are considered average.

Verbal	Scaled scores	Performance	Scaled scores
Information	9	Picture Completion	11
Similarities	7	Coding	4
Arithmetic	4	Picture Arrangement	9
Vocabulary	8	Block Design	13
Comprehension	9	Object Assembly	11
(Digit Span)	7	(Symbol Search)	2

The following composite scores have a mean of 100 with an *SD* of 15. Scores of 85–115 are considered to be within the average range and reflect 68% of the general population.

Composite score	Standard scores	90% Confidence interval
Verbal	85	81–91
Performance	98	91–105
Full scale score	**90**	**86–95**
Verbal Comprehension	91	86–97
Visual/Perceptual	107	99–113
Freedom from Distractibility (Third Factor)	75	71–86
Processing Speed	64	61–78

Differential Ability Scales (DAS)

The DAS is an individually administered intelligence test consisting of 6 "core subtests" as well as achievement and diagnostic subtests. Only the core subtests are used in the calculation of the General Conceptual Ability (GCA) score, an estimate of overall intelligence. The DAS core subtests are also used to calculate cluster scores for verbal abilities, nonverbal reasoning, and spatial abilities.

The following composite standard scores have a mean of 100 and an *SD* of 15. Scores of 85–115 are considered to be within the average range and reflect 68% of the general population.

Domain	Standard scores	90% Confidence Interval
Verbal Cluster	87	79–96
Nonverbal Cluster	90	83–98
Spatial Cluster	95	88–102
General Conceptual Ability	**89**	**84–95**

The following subtest *T* scores have a mean of 50 and an *SD* of 10. Scores of 40–60 are in the average range.

Domain	*T* scores
Core subtests	
Word Definitions	46
Similarities	39
Matrices	48
Sequential and Quantitative Reasoning	41
Recall of Designs	40
Pattern Construction	55
Diagnostic subtests	
Recall of Digits	34
Recall of Objects, Immediate	49
Recall of Objects, Delayed	50
Speed of Information Processing	46

Woodcock–Johnson Psycho-Educational Battery—Revised Tests of Achievement (WJ-R ACH)

The WJ-R ACH is an individually administered achievement test containing various subtests whose scores are combined into composites: Broad Reading, Basic Reading Skills, Broad Mathematics, Broad Written Language, and Broad Knowledge.

The WJ-R ACH yields standard scores with a mean of 100 and an *SD* of 15. Standard scores of 85–115 are considered to be within the average range and reflect 68% of the general population.

	Standard scores	90% Confidence interval
Letter–Word Identification	90	86–94
Passage Comprehension	92	87–97
Broad Reading	**91**	**88–94**
Basic Reading Skills	**90**	**87–93**
Calculation	67	63–71
Applied Problems	96	91–101
Broad Mathematics	**81**	**77–85**
Dictation	91	86–96

Oral and Written Language Scales (OWLS)

The OWLS, an individually administered test of oral and written language for children and young adults, consists of three scales: Listening Comprehension, Oral Expression, and Written Expression. Results may be used to determine broad levels of language skills as well as specific performance in the areas of listening, speaking, and writing.

The OWLS yields standard scores with a mean of 100 and an *SD* of 15. Standard scores of 85–115 are considered to be within the average range and reflect 68% of the general population.

	Standard scores	90% Confidence interval
Listening Comprehension	89	79–99
Oral Expression	95	85–105
Written Expression	91	
Oral Composite	**91**	**84–99**
Language Composite	**89**	**83–96**

Wide Range Achievement Test–3 (WRAT-3)

The WRAT-3 is an individually or group administered test of achievement. Specific areas tested include Reading/Word Decoding, Spelling/Written Encoding, and Arithmetic. Standard scores of 85–115 are considered to be within the average range.

	Standard score
Arithmetic	51

Developmental Test of Visual–Motor Integration (VMI)

The VMI is a developmental sequence of geometric figures that requires the child to copy each design exactly as it appears. The VMI measures how effectively the child can integrate and reproduce what he or she sees, using fine motor skills. The VMI yields a standard score with a mean of 100 and an *SD* of 15. Scores of 85–115 are considered to be within the average range and reflect 68% of the general population.

Standard score	95
Percentile	37

Achenbach Child Behavior Checklist—Parent Form (CBCL)

The Achenbach CBCL is a questionnaire that is completed by parents regarding the behavioral and emotional problems of their children. The CBCL yields *T* scores with a mean of 50 and an *SD* 10. Scores of 67–70 are considered borderline significant. A score above 70 is indicative of significant problems.

	T scores	
Domain	Mother	Father
Withdrawn	70	58
Somatic Complaints	64	50
Anxious/Depressed	74	64
Social Problems	52	50
Thought Problems	64	50
Attention Problems	69	63

Delinquent Behavior	81	73
Aggressive Behavior	90	64
Internalizing Composite	**73**	**60**
Externalizing Composite	**84**	**68**
Total Composite Score	**75**	**63**

Behavior Assessment System For Children—Parent Rating Scale (BASC PRS)

The BASC-PRS is a questionnaire completed by parents in order to assess the behavioral problems, emotional difficulties, and social competence of their children. The BASC-PRS yields T scores with a mean of 50 and an SD of 10. Scores above 70 are considered to be indicative of significant problems.

	T scores	
Composites and scales	Mother	Father
Hyperactivity	76	60
Aggression	89	71
Conduct Problems	94	83
Externalizing Problems composite	**92**	**75**
Anxiety	53	48
Depression	77	62
Somatization	44	39
Internalizing Problems composite	**60**	**50**
Atypicality	76	59
Withdrawal	54	44
Attention Problems	81	73
Behavioral Symptoms Index	**86**	**67**

On the Adaptive scales, scores below 30 are considered significantly low.

Adaptability	22	33
Social Skills	31	38
Leadership	32	30
Adaptive Skills composite	**25**	**31**

Behavior Assessment System for Children—Teacher Rating Scale (BASC-TRS)

The BASC-TRS is a questionnaire completed by teachers rating adaptive skills and behavior and emotional problems of students; it yields T scores with a mean of 50 and an SD of 10. Scores above 70 are considered to be indicative of significant problems.

Composites and scales	T scores
Hyperactivity	49
Aggression	66
Conduct Problems	55
Externalizing ProblemsComposite	**57**
Anxiety	49
Depression	51
Somatization	51
Internalizing Problems composite	**50**
Attention Problems	67
Learning Problems	65
School Problems composite	**67**
Atypicality	61
Withdrawal	45
Behavioral Symptoms Index	**59**

On the Adaptive scales, scores below 30 are considered significantly low.

Adaptability	38
Social Skills	30
Leadership	35
Study Skills	31
Adaptive Skills composite	**31**

Behavior Assessment System for Children—Self-Report of Personality (BASC-SRP)

The BASC-SRP is a self-report measure designed to evaluate the personality and self-perceptions of children. Components of two composites comprise

100

the Emotional Symptoms Index; Clinical Maladjustment and Personal Maladjustment. In addition, three scales—Attitude to School, Attitude to Teachers,
and Sensation Seeking—comprise the School Maladjustment composite. The
BASC-SRP yields T scores with a mean of 50 and an SD of 10. Scores above 70
are considered to be indicative of significant problems.

Clinical scales	T scores
Atypicality	60
Locus of Control	64
Social Stress	57
Anxiety	49
Depression	63
Sense of Inadequacy	71
Clinical Maladjustment composite	**59**
Attitude to School	61
Attitude to Teachers	62
School Maladjustment composite	**63**
Emotional Symptoms Index	**59**

Scores below 30 on the Personal Adjustment scales are considered significantly low.

Personal Maladjustment Scales	T scores
Relations with Parents	45
Interpersonal Relations	49
Self-Esteem	46
Self-Reliance	43
Personal Adjustment composite	**44**

BASC Scale and Composite Score Classification

Adaptive scales	T score range	Clinical scales
Very high	70 and above	Clinically significant
High	60–69	At risk
Average	41–59	Average
At risk	31–40	Low
Clinically significant	30 and below	Very low

Parenting Stress Index (PSI)

The PSI was designed as an overall measure of stress in the parent's life. Two domains are sampled: stress associated with parenting this particular child, and stress in other parts of the parent's life. The composite scores (Total Stress, Child Domain, and Parent Domain) are the most reliable scores for interpretation. Percentile scores above 90 are considered to be indicative of problems.

	Percentiles	
Scale	Mother	Father
Adaptability	99+	40
Acceptability	99+	16
Demandingness	99+	20
Mood	99+	98
Distractibility/Hyperactivity	93	89
Reinforces Parent	98	87
Child Domain score	**99+**	**78**
Depression	60	20
Attachment	99+	15
Restriction of Role	65	10
Sense of Competence	80	20
Social Isolation	10	15
Relationship with Spouse	93	15
Parent Health	50	10
Parent Domain score	**80**	**9**
Total Stress score	**97**	**33**

Child Depression Inventory (CDI)

The CDI is a self-report rating scale of depression for children. *T* scores between 40–60 are considered average.

CDI *T* score   43

Structured Interview for the Diagnostic Assessment of Children (SIDAC)

The SIDAC is a list of questions to which parents and teachers answer yes or no to indicate the presence of symptoms relating to DSM-IV diagnosis. In this case, only the questions relating to ADHD were administered. The DSM-IV criteria require the endorsement of six symptoms in the category of inattention and/or six symptoms in the combined categories of impulsivity/hyperactivity.

DSM-IV items endorsed:
Inattention	8/9
Impulsivity	2/6
Hyperactivity	3/3

PSYCHOLOGICAL EVALUATION (CONFIDENTIAL)

Subject: Julianne
DOB: 10/19/84
Exam Date: 11/24/99
Chronological Age: 15 years 1 month
Date of Report: 11/30/99
Examiner: M. Markus, PhD

Tests and Procedures

Clinical Interview
Mental Status Exam
1. Substance Abuse Subtle Screening Inventory
2. Revised Children's Manifest Anxiety Scale
3. Human Figure Drawing
4. Kinetic Family Drawing
5. Incomplete Sentences Blank
6. Bender Visual–Motor Gestalt Test
7. Trauma Symptom Checklist for Children
8. BASC: Structured Developmental History (mother)
9. BASC: Parent Rating Scale—Adolescent (mother)
10. BASC: Self-Report of Personality—Adolescent
11. Collateral Interview with Mother

Background Information and Reason for Referral

Julianne was referred for psychological evaluation by the victim coordinator at the County sheriff's office. Julianne was sexually assaulted by an 18-year-old acquaintance on 10/23/99. Both Julianne and the alleged perpetrator are reported to have been using alcohol at the time of the alleged assault. She was referred due to concerns about her current emotional state and potential effects of the assault. She did not initially report the assault. According to the mother, Julianne cried at school throughout the week after the assault and was finally persuaded by friends to tell a school counselor. Since that time, the mother notes that she has had sleep problems and seems very depressed and to have shut down emotionally. The mother, a mental health professional, complains that Julianne seems angry, has anxiety problems, a decreased appetite, and that her grades at school have become a problem for the first time . She further notes that her daughter seems hyperirritable and has engaged in a regressive use of language since the day after the assault. Julianne is currently seeing Dr. Susan Kraft, a local psychologist, for psychotherapy.

History and Development

The mother was available to provide a developmental and psychosocial history. She completed a Structured Developmental History and a follow-up collateral interview.

By the mother's report, Julianne has resided with her parents her entire life. The mother is the executive director of a local mental health center and the father is a political liaison in the statehouse. Whenever a parent is not available, the maternal grandmother provides child care as needed. There have never been any divorces, separations, or deaths in the immediate family. The mother believes that Julianne is somewhat closer to her than to the father. She has two older brothers, ages 19 and 30, who reside outside the home, and a 12-year-old sister living in the home. The sisters are reported not to be getting along well at this time.

Julianne is reported to participate in routine family activities such as meals, movies, conversations, trips with relatives, and the like, and she sees her grandparents frequently. The mother enjoys what she describes as Julianne's calm and caring spirit but finds it difficult when Julianne becomes quiet, internalizes her feelings, and does not communicate with others. The parents have appropriate aspirations for her. The mother is primarily in charge of discipline in the home and tends to use grounding and writing assignments as intervention techniques.

By the mother's report, she was under a doctor's care throughout her pregnancy with Julianne, during which there were no complications. She was 35 years old when Julianne was born, via C-section, 44 weeks of gestation and 3 days of labor. A 7-ounce ovarian cyst was located at the age of 3 days, and an ovary was removed. Subsequent to her surgery, Julianne remained in the hospital for nearly a month.

Developmental milestones were achieved within normal limits, according to the mother's recall. No special problems were noted in the early years. Julianne has had measles, chickenpox, and a tonsillectomy. She is not known to have any respiratory, cardiovascular, gastrointestinal, genitourinary, musculoskeletal, dermatological, or neurological problems. She has never taken any long-term medication or tranquilizing medication. She has allergies to airborne allergens, such as ragweed and cedar. She has no hearing or vision problems. She is followed medically by Dr. Earl Young of Ellis. Prior to the therapy following the current episode, she had never had psychological counseling or therapy. She has never undergone neurological, psychological, or psychiatric exams.

The family health history is positive for cancer, multiple forms of cardiovascular disease, and migraine headaches; an uncle has an unspecified mental illness and a history of alcohol and drug abuse. Neither parent has any history of significant health problems, and no one in the family has ever attended special education classes.

By the mother's report, Julianne has no problems relating to or socializing with others her age. She tends to act as a leader in her peer group and enjoys a variety of sports and hobbies, including art. The mother states that, over the last month, Julianne's interest in her favorite activities has declined as she has become more depressed. At present, she is reported to seem unhappy most of the time. She becomes angry at perceived invasions of privacy, particularly her sister's unauthorized entry into her room.

Adaptive behavior is developing appropriately for her age. She attended both preschool and kindergarten and has not experienced any academic problems until the last month. The mother reports that Julianne has begun to dislike school, whereas she previously enjoyed it a great deal and was an honor student. She has never had any disciplinary problems associated with her schooling.

Observations, Behaviors, and Interview

Julianne was brought to the evaluation session by her mother. Her height and weight are within normal limits for a teenage girl of her age. She has dark hair, brown eyes, and was dressed appropriately for her age (in jeans, a sweat shirt, and tennis shoes). She was oriented appropriately to person, place, time, and circumstances. Speech was within normal limits for rate, volume, and articulation. She showed no dyspraxic or dysarthric speech, dysfluencies, or disorganized thought. Her mood was notably subdued, and her affect was restricted. Language use was quite good, and attention and concentration were within normal limits. Memory was appropriate, and insight and judgment both appeared to be particularly good, relative to her age. Intellectual function was estimated to be high average or better, based upon her language usage and results of the mental status exam. These observations are consistent with her educational and family histories.

Julianne described her living circumstances accurately and appropriately. She was able to give a history of her life that is generally consistent with that provided by the mother. She stated that she gets along "pretty well" with her mother and noted that her mother enjoys talking a lot and that sometimes she (Julianne) prefers to go to her room and be alone. She believes her mother is open and listens well to her. She reported having a particularly strong relationship with her father until approximately 2 years ago, when she had a brief episode of declining grades and some disagreements with a teacher. At that time she distanced herself from others and had difficulty getting along with her dad, as well as her sister. She grew apart from her dad during this episode and never worked to reestablish her prior relationship with him. She and her sister get along better than they have in the past, when they fought a lot. She sees her brothers only episodically but gets along with them quite well.

Julianne enjoys going out with her friends to nearby Montgomery (a larger town) or to their home with them. She used to enjoy more athletic activities but now she is too busy with social aspects of her life. She performs in the school band, where she plays percussion. She reported finding high school to be quite different from what she had expected. She had not anticipated all of the rules and had expected to have more freedom than in the earlier grades.

Julianne gave no history of any physical abuse but said that she did feel emotionally abused by a teacher in kindergarten, who called her names. She denied any history of sexual abuse other than the incident that brought her to my office and one earlier incident of assault by the same young man. She has never been arrested. She has not been hospitalized since her surgery as an infant. She was struck on the head several years ago but had no loss of consciousness and has no known sequelae. She reported that she takes no medication currently, other than episodic antihistamines. She experimented once with marijuana several years ago but has not used any form of illicit substance since. She stated that the episode of intoxication at her friend's home, during which she was allegedly assaulted, was her only episode of intoxication. She denied having used tobacco products of any form. She has a 17-year-old boyfriend (Martin) whom she has been dating since the beginning of the current school year.

With regard to the episode of alleged assault, Julianne indicated that she was spending the night with a close friend, Anna. On the way to Anna's house, Anna's mother stopped and purchased a bottle of fortified wine for Julianne, at Anna's request. Julianne stated that Larry, Anna's brother and the alleged perpetrator, and Anna already had bottles. They then stopped and rented movies to watch. Once there, they began drinking, and each of the teens drank a full bottle of the wine. Anna and Julianne then drank one and possibly more wine coolers. During the drinking and the movie watching, Larry approached Julianne and whispered lewd requests into her ear. She told him to stop on each occasion. During the second movie and after consuming the wine, Julianne reported that she either fell asleep or passed out and was awakened by the sensation of Larry fondling her. She told him to stop and went back to sleep. She awoke later to find her shorts pulled down, Larry's pants pulled down, and him on top of her, penetrating her, and then performing intercourse. She told him to stop, and after a few seconds of continuing intercourse, he stopped, pulled out, and got off of her. She stated that her vision was somewhat blurry at the time; she believes that she then rolled over and passed out again. The next morning, she woke early, went home, and went out shopping with her mother, where the mother noted the regressive behavior. Julianne reported that during the next week at school (the experience occurred on a Friday night and/or early Saturday morning), several of her friends were concerned about her crying, and she related to them what had happened. Over the course of the week, they eventually persuaded her to tell a school counselor, who then reported it to local law enforcement.

Julianne reported that she has been interviewed six times about the assault, the first five interviews occurring on the day she reported it to the school counselor. No videotape or other recording of any interview was made.

According to Julianne, she has experienced a number of difficulties since the assault. She stated that she has had significant sleep initiation problems since that time along with problems with unusual dreams that she does not know how to characterize. The first several weeks following the incident, she woke up in the middle of the night repeatedly, but this has now resolved. Still, she continues to experience morning fatigue, with episodes of increased fatigue in the afternoons. According to Julianne, she sees Larry at school but does not talk to him, and her relationship with Anna, Larry's sister, is quite different now: They do not spend time together or even talk. She reported a loss of interest in school, described not doing her work on time, and expressed fear that her grades are slipping. Her friendships with everyone seem different, and she believes people talk to her differently. She worries about every little thing that happens at school and what might happen the next day—

which contributes to her inability to fall asleep at night. She complained of episodic thought intrusions and said that she has to work very hard to force herself not to think about what happened. Episodic flashbacks also occur. Following the flashbacks, she begins to feel "really lousy" and then weak and tired. She feels very insecure now and is experiencing some paranoia: She feels like someone is in her room at home or outside, watching her get dressed. She is much more careful about where she dresses in her room and stays out of window range. She wears pants more often, feeling uncomfortable and exposed whenever she wears shorts. Approximately one week ago, she began having crying episodes at night and does not know why. She feels that she needs to be a lot more careful in her life now, particularly about trusting others.

Julianne was open and forthright in discussing the episode that brought her to the office and the problems she was experiencing. As noted, her affect was clearly restricted and her mood subdued. It was difficult at times for her to talk about the assault, but she persisted. She then related an additional episode of assault, also by Larry, that occurred last year. She stated that he came into Anna's bedroom, where Julianne and Anna were both lying on the bed. She thought that he was drunk; he jumped onto the bed between the two of them, shoved his hands down Julianne's pants, and penetrated her digitally. She ordered him to stop and he did. He got up, left the room, and then left the house with a friend. Julianne did not report this incident at that time, but subsequent to it her mother noted a number of changes over several months that she believes resolved over time. Julianne has a significant desire to be seen in a positive light and does not want to experience, or have others know that she is experiencing, any problems as a result of these attacks. She thus attempts to minimize any particular problems that she experiences.

Test Results and Interpretation

Due to the involvement of alcohol in the incident described by Julianne, she was asked to complete the Substance Abuse Subtle Screening Inventory. On this scale, her alcohol and drug dependency ratings were both below the mean, relative to other females her age. She has few obvious attributes of teenage alcoholics and even fewer subtle attributes of teenagers who are dependent upon alcohol or drugs. She was less defensive in responding to these items than the typical girl at her age, and there are no indications of any problems with alcohol or related chemical dependencies. These results, coupled with her history, support the view of the recent episode of intoxication as a singular incident of alcohol abuse.

Results of the formal personality assessment indicate a young woman who is responding particularly well to the episodes of trauma she has experienced. She has begun to experience some school maladjustment problems and has a number of somatic complaints that are in the at-risk range at this time. She has more somatic complaints than 91% of girls her age. She has a mildly increased anxiety level overall; however, her physiological symptoms of anxiety exceed those of 92% of girls her age. Her adaptive skills, including her relations with parents and peers and her continued ability to rely upon herself and see herself in a positive light, remain within normal limits.

This overview is generally consistent with the projective responses seen. Although she was mildly avoidant during the projective assessment, indicating a preference for avoiding emotional conflict, her anxieties nevertheless penetrated. Her self-portrait is of a subdued and emotionless young woman. She has a number of concerns about her family and an increased need for nurturance and emotional support, which she sees as lacking for a significant period of time, particularly from her father. She feels somewhat adrift emotionally and recognizes she has closed herself off from some of the support that might otherwise be available to her. Her scores on the Trauma Symptom Checklist for Children indicate that she is adapting well to the assault and suggests a positive prognosis. Nevertheless, Julianne continues to experience significant sleep problems and increased somatic complaints that appear to be related to the episode of sexual assault. She reports alterations in her social relationships; these alterations may have a negative impact on her coping skills. She has become hypervigilant and experiences episodes of thought intrusion as well as flashbacks. Vague paranoid ideation has developed and has not yet resolved. She has had a recent onset of crying episodes, particularly at night. She does not display overt behavioral problems and has a number of strengths that likely will enable her to experience an above-average level of recovery from the trauma. She has particularly good social skills and the capacity to be a leader among her peers. At the present time, however, she is withdrawing and turning inward. Historically a competitor, Julianne is attempting to avoid and deny the problems she is experiencing as a result of the assault.

Her pattern of symptoms is consistent with the presence of a posttraumatic stress disorder, and she meets the diagnostic criteria specifically for this diagnosis at this time. She is strongly encouraged to continue in individual psychotherapy, which will likely be necessary for a period of at least 6 months and possibly as long as 2 years. Given that her sleep disturbance has persisted more than 30 days since the incident, a consultation with her family physician would be appropriate to determine the advisability of short-term psychopharmacotherapy with an antidepressant (an antidepressant in the tricyclic class might be most helpful in assisting her with sleep regulation). It is anticipated that such psychopharmacotherapeutic intervention, should it be determined to be appropriate by her physician, would be of a short term nature. In addition to her continuing individual psychotherapy, which is targeted at her current symptom pattern, separate family therapy sessions would also appear to be appropriate. Julianne recognizes the need for greater nurturance and emotional support within the context of her family but is unable to reach out, particularly to her father, at this time. Brief family therapy, directed at the reestablishment of the close family relationships that existed in the past, would facilitate Julianne's emotional development not only on an acute basis but long term as well. Children and teenage victims of sexual assault are at high risk for a variety of future problems. Continued treatment, as has been initiated, along with family therapy, are appropriate interventions for circumventing the known risk patterns for victims of sexual assault.

M. Markus, PhD
Psychologist

Supplementary Psychometric Summary

Substance Abuse Subtle Screening Inventory

All T scores $\leq$ 49.

Revised Children's Manifest Anxiety Scale T Scores

Total Anxiety	$T = 55$
Physiological Anxiety	$T = 63$
Worry/Oversensitivity	$T = 50$
Social Concerns/Concentration	$T = 53$
Lie	$T = 60$

Trauma Symptom Checklist for Children

All T scores below 50, except:

Anxiety	$T = 60$
Posttraumatic Stress	$T = 65$
Dissociation	$T = 67$

110

BASC: Self-Report of Personality T Scores, General Norms

CLINICAL SCALES

1. Attitude to School	$T = 60$
2. Attitude to Teachers	$T = 62$
3. Sensation Seeking	$T = 48$
4. Atypicality	$T = 49$
5. Locus of Control	$T = 44$
6. Somatization	$T = 65$
7. Social Stress	$T = 46$
8. Anxiety	$T = 58$
9. Depression	$T = 43$
10. Sense of Inadequacy	$T = 44$

ADAPTIVE SCALES

1. Relations with Parents	$T = 53$
2. Interpersonal Relations	$T = 57$
3. Self-Esteem	$T = 58$
4. Self-Reliance	$T = 52$

BASC: Parent Rating Scale T Scores, General Norms

CLINICAL SCALES

1. Hyperactivity	$T = 37$
2. Aggression	$T = 50$
3. Conduct Problems	$T = 49$
4. Anxiety	$T = 46$
5. Depression	$T = 40$
6. Somatization	$T = 37$
7. Atypicality	$T = 39$
8. Withdrawal	$T = 47$
9. Attention Problems	$T = 35$

ADAPTIVE SCALES

1. Social Skills	$T = 62$
2. Leadership	$T = 66$

SCHOOL PSYCHOLOGY SERVICES
PSYCHOEDUCATIONAL EVALUATION
(CONFIDENTIAL)

Name: Anne Windsor
Age: 17 years
Educational Attainment: High School Graduate

Assessment Procedures

Parent Interview

> Behavior Assessment System for Children (BASC)—Structured
> Developmental History
> Behavior Assessment System for Children (BASC)—Parent Rating Scales
> Achenbach Child Behavior Checklist—Parent Form (CBCL)
> Parent–Child Relationship Inventory (PCRI)
> Parenting Stress Index (PSI)
> Parent Interview

Child Assessment

> Wechsler Intelligence Scale for Children—Third Edition (WISC-III)
> Wechsler Individual Achievement Test (WIAT)
> Woodcock Reading Mastery Tests—Revised (WRMT-R)
> Oral and Written Language Scales (OWLS)—Written Expression Scale
> Developmental Test of Visual–Motor Integration (VMI)
> Children's Memory Scale (CMS)
> Torrance Tests of Creativity (TTCT)—Thinking Creatively with Pictures
> Behavioral Assessment System for Children (BASC)—Self-Report of
> Personality
> Achenbach Youth Self-Report for Ages 11–18 (YRS)
> Piers–Harris Children's Self-Concept Scale (PHCSCS)
> Reynolds Adolescent Depression Scale (RADS)
> Revised Children's Manifest Anxiety Scale (RCMAS)
> Beck Depression Inventory (BDI)
> Child Interview

School Information

Behavioral Assessment System for Children (BASC)—Teacher Rating Scale
Achenbach Teacher Report Form (TRF)

Reason for Referral

Anne was referred to evaluate her educational and personal goals. Anne graduated from high school this year and has been accepted to Northern College for the fall semester 2000. She recently decided to delay pursuing her college education, but she still plans to move away from home. Anne's mother is concerned that the reason for this sudden change of plans is Anne's relationship with her boyfriend, with whom she plans to live this summer.

Background Information

Anne is a 17-year-old female who lives with her mother and her 10-year-old sister. The father died when Anne was 3 years old.

Family History

The Windsor family has experienced many stressful events. Following the death of her sister 5 years ago, Mrs. Windsor became depressed; she felt isolated without close friends and family in the community, but she did not seek treatment then. At the same time, Mrs. Windsor's employment was terminated following a theft, for which she was sentenced to 2 years probation. After completing her probation, Mrs. Windsor had difficulty finding a job in the community, and her financial situation worsened. Currently, she is working as a secretary. Three years ago, she underwent individual counseling and has been on antidepressant medication periodically since that time.

Two years ago, when Anne was 15, she was raped by four acquaintances. On Anne's request, the rape was not reported to police. Mrs. Windsor sought professional help for Anne, but Anne refused to participate and the relationship between her and her mother grew increasingly difficult. Then her older half brother was arrested for possession of drugs, for which he was sentenced to probation. Recently, Anne's younger sister was expelled permanently from the private school she was attending because of threats she had made against another child. The most recent stresses in the family relate to Anne's abrupt change of plans to delay college enrollment and to move to Augusta to live with her 28-year-old boyfriend, whom she has been dating for just over a month.

Developmental and Medical History

Mrs. Windsor reported that Anne was a healthy child who met developmental milestones without delays. Anne's medical history is not remarkable, except for suffering from migraines for the last 3 years, for which she takes medication when needed.

Social and Emotional Development

Mrs. Windsor described Anne as a talented, smart, happy, vivacious, and outgoing child who was involved in many activities throughout her childhood, including acting, cheerleading, playing piano, and horseback riding. She loves animals. Although she got along well with others, she was always a headstrong child. She showed early signs of separation anxiety, refusing to stay in the day-care center while Mrs. Windsor was at work. Although Anne was attached to her father, no significant changes were noticed following his death. She was close to her maternal grandfather, who died 6 months after her father. Mrs. Windsor feels that she and Anne were close when Anne was a young child.

Mrs. Windsor first noticed defiant behavior toward herself in Anne's teenage years. After the rape, her defiance intensified and communication within the family deteriorated, including Anne's relationship with her sister and older brother. According to Mrs. Windsor, Anne continues to balk at authority and is defiant and verbally aggressive toward her. After the rape, Anne experienced anger outbursts, cried, and argued with her mother, began suffering from migraines, and evidenced significant weight loss. Anne and Mrs. Windsor did not seek medical or psychological help immediately after the rape. Anne still feels irritable, sad, and angry. She also feels tired, often sleeps long hours, naps during the day, and does not have a good appetite.

Following the multiple rape, which was unfortunately her first sexual contact with another, Anne became involved in a year-long relationship with a boyfriend, her first, who had problems with alcoholism and drugs and was both verbally and physically abusive.

Educational History

Anne has a history of successful academic and extracurricular performances. She began her education in public school but moved to a private school in fifth grade after being "picked on." She stayed there through ninth grade, then transferred to a new school 3 years ago. The move was motivated by the gossip that spread among the students following the rape, not to mention her discomfort seeing and interacting with the alleged perpetrators in school. She was particularly disturbed by talk that portrayed the trauma as her responsibility. Mrs. Windsor placed Anne in a residential psychiatric facility for an evaluation, but Anne was expelled allegedly because of hostility.

Anne successfully adapted to her new school, where she completed the high school program in 3 years. She felt comfortable in this school and enjoyed the freedom to pace herself and work independently. She got along well with her teachers and peers but did not develop close friendships with peers.

The evaluation of Anne's school records from grades 5–8 shows performance at above 80% mastery, with the exception of algebra, in which she achieved around 70% mastery. Her scores declined after the rape; Anne completed ninth grade with scores ranging from 66% mastery in algebra to 81% mastery in English. Anne's grades recovered in high school, and she completed 12th grade with all A's, except for one B in applied math. Her Iowa Tests of Basic Skills (ITBS) scores in grades 5–8 closely reflect her grades, ranging from average to high above-average, with the lowest scores achieved in reading. Anne took the SAT but did not reveal those results to her mother.

Anne was accepted at Northern College for the fall semester, where she planned to study art photography. However, she has recently decided to enroll at a larger regional university instead. First, however she wants to take a few months off from school; she feels that she needs to move away from home, find a part-time job, and take time to think about her educational and personal goals. She is currently working part-time at a restaurant.

Interview Information

The interview with Mrs. Windsor revealed feelings of frustration and helplessness regarding her relationship with her daughter. The communication between mother and daughter became especially difficult in the last 6 months, during which conflicts intensified. The most recent conflicts relate to financial difficulties and Anne's decision to postpone her college education and move away from home with her boyfriend. Mrs. Windsor describes Anne as inconsiderate about financial limitations; for instance, she demands money for car maintenance but does not contribute any money to the household. She feels that Anne is withdrawing emotionally from her and behaving in a manipulative manner. When denied her way, Anne complains that her mother does not love her.

According to Mrs. Windsor, Anne sleeps long hours and spends a lot of time with a group of friends or with her boyfriend. Mrs. Windsor worries about this most recent relationship with her 28-year-old boyfriend and is particularly concerned about Anne's decision to live with him. She feels that Anne will not enroll in college and that the relationship will not last. Her attempts to talk to Anne end up in conflicts, and good times between them are rare. Anne is overly sensitive, especially to criticism, which Mrs. Windsor attributes to a lack of self-confidence that has been evident since Anne was a young child. Mrs. Windsor describes herself as an inconsistent parent who has never been dominant in her role. She is aware that she was not available for Anne during the last 3 years, because of her own emotional difficulties following her criminal conviction and Anne's rape. Mrs. Windsor felt unable to cope and blamed herself for being unable to protect Anne. She feels that Anne's anger at the whole event is directed toward her, and she (Mrs. Windsor) does not know how to deal with it.

Behavior during Testing:

Anne unwillingly accompanied Mrs. Windsor to the clinic and did not communicate with her mother or brother while sitting in the waiting room. Her responses to the examiner's questions were polite but short. During the introductory session, with Mrs. Windsor and Anne both present in the room, Anne looked angry, though her eyes were teary and her voice quiet as she answered questions directed to her. She avoided eye contact with both the examiner and her mother. During the first day of testing, Anne's attention was adequate, and she followed directions without difficulty. She completed tasks required of her without complaints. However, she showed a lack of enthusiasm and motivation for the testing portion of the evaluation, and after the first day of evaluation, she said that she had not tried hard enough. Anne became more willing to divulge personal information during the clinical interview. During the second day, Anne was more spontaneous and relaxed. She smiled and showed positive emotions toward the examiner. Although signs of fatigue were noticed, Anne showed interest in completing all assignments.

Assessment Results and Interpretation

Cognitive Development

On the Wechsler Intelligence Scale for Children—Third Edition (WISC-III), Anne achieved a Full Scale score of 122, in the above-average range. Taking measurement error into account, Anne's true Full Scale score is between 118 and 125. Her strengths are in verbal areas, where she performed in the above-average range, achieving a Verbal score of 128. She showed well above-average performance on tasks requiring knowledge of vocabulary, information, comprehension, and comparison of similar words. She had more difficulty with tasks requiring arithmetic skills, which is consistent with her school reports and the ITBS scores that both indicate a relative weakness in math. There was more variability among Performance subtest scores, ranging from average to above average. Her Performance score was 110, in the high average range. Anne showed strengths in abstract thinking and discrimination skills on nonverbal material, but she had more difficulty on tasks requiring spatial skills.

Achievement

On the Wechsler Individual Achievement Test (WIAT), Anne's scores were within the average range (total composite of 108, Reading composite of 110, Language composite of 101, and Mathematics composite of 100). Her Writing composite of 118 was in the above-average range. Anne's overall performance on the WIAT was lower than would be expected based on her cognitive ability scores.

Her Woodcock–Johnson—Revised Tests of Achievement (WJ-R ACH) scores were consistent with those on the WIAT, ranging from average to high average. On the WJ-R ACH, Anne's strength was shown in the area of reading (Broad Reading of 115). Broad Math and Broad Knowledge were within average limits, and Broad Written Language was in the low-average range. The inconsistency in Written Language performances on the two achievement tests could be attributed to fatigue. The results of the WJ-R ACH and the WIAT are consistent. The more than 20-point difference between Anne's average standard scores in achievement and her above-average scores in intelligence suggest that she is underachieving academically, even given her high grades. The gap is even bigger when achievement scores are compared with her verbal intelligence, which is well above average. Her achievement scores may indicate that her high school did not provide an adequate academic challenge for her.

Social and Emotional Development—Parent Report

Information provided by Mrs. Windsor on several rating scales is consistent with that provided during the parent interview. On the Behavior Assessment System for Children—Parent Rating Scales (BASC-PRS-A), she endorsed conduct problems and withdrawal at clinically significant levels. Conduct problems relate to Anne's defiant behavior toward Mrs. Windsor, her choice of friends, use of tobacco and alcohol, and lying. Withdrawal behaviors relate to Anne's need to be left alone and her refusal to talk to her mother. The at-risk social skills and the lack of leadership skills endorsed by Mrs. Windsor reflect Anne's private nature and her need to be alone, as well as her lack of energy and enthusiasm for group activities and leadership roles.

Similar behaviors were confirmed on the Achenbach Child Behavior Checklist (CBCL), where Mrs. Windsor endorsed aggressive and delinquent behaviors at clinically significant levels, as well as elevated ratings on the withdrawal score. She also endorsed a number of symptoms related to depression, such as sadness, feelings of worthlessness, worries, underactivity, loneliness, and feelings of being unloved. On the Parenting Stress Index (PSI), Mrs. Windsor revealed very high levels of stress associated with parenting Anne. Problems include demands Anne places on her, Anne's moods, and negative feedback she is receiving from Anne. Mrs. Windsor's stress is also related to perceptions of her own low competence in parenting and to feelings of isolation, lack of attachment, and depression.

Social and Emotional Development—Teacher Report

There is great consistency between home and school reports regarding Anne's behavior. On the Behavior Assessment System for Children—Teacher rating Scales (BASC TRS-A) and the Achenbach Teacher Report Form (TRF), Mr. Smith, Anne's English and social studies teacher, endorsed the same conduct and delinquent behavior problems as Mrs. Windsor. He also identified a number of symptoms related to depression and anxiety, such as worrying, feeling worthless, insecurity, nervousness, anxiety, sensitivity, fatigue, and inattention in class. However, unlike Mrs. Windsor, he endorsed great leadership potential and good social skills. He did not endorse any behaviors related to withdrawal, which may suggest that withdrawal problems are specific to the mother–daughter relationship.

Social and Emotional Development—Self Report

The interview with Anne revealed a number of issues related to family relationships, dating, future plans, and past traumatic events. However, the Behavior Assessment System for Children—Self-Report of Personality (BASC-SRP-A), the Achenbach Youth Self-Report (YSR), and the Beck Depression Inventory (BDI) did not confirm any of these issues. Anne admitted to being less than forthcoming with her answers because of a lack of motivation to participate in this evaluation and a desire to protect her privacy. Thus, this portion of the report is based only on information during the assessment interview.

Anne described herself as an open-minded and outgoing person who is not afraid to take chances. That is also how she thinks her friends perceive her. However, she feels that her mother perceives her as stubborn, argumentative, and rebellious. When around her mother, Anne feels irritable and short-tempered. Their relationship deteriorated in the course of the last 3 years to the point that they do not have anything in common. Anne's trust was violated, she reported, when Mrs. Windsor revealed private information to other people. In response, Anne refuses to tell her mother anything of consequence. According to Anne, Mrs. Windsor was unavailable to her children during much of their upbringing, but the problems inherent in this unavailability escalated after Anne was raped. Anne felt violated not only by the rapist, who blamed *her*, but by her mother who also held her responsible, according to Anne. These events and their related feelings were not openly discussed between Anne and Mrs. Windsor. Anne's trust further deteriorated when her mother reportedly arranged residential treatment for her daughter without talking to her first. Further, according to Anne, Mrs. Windsor did not inform her about the nature of this present evaluation. This compounded miscommunication drove Anne to spend more time with friends away from home and to stay in her room when at home. Anne spends her time at home sleeping long hours or just lying in bed. Although she still likes to read, she is no longer passionate about any of the activities she used to enjoy as a child. As noted, she suffers from migraines and has recurring nightmares about her former boyfriend.

The aftermath of the rape, the physically and emotionally abusive relationship with her first boyfriend, and the tragic deaths of three of her close friends in recent years has left Anne mistrustful and feeling betrayed. She has withdrawn emotionally from her mother and other family members. According to Anne, she had never had a good relationship with her older brother, of whose life-style she does not approve, and her younger sister annoys her. She feels tired from what she describes as an intense high-school program and does not feel ready to pursue a college education. She is also unsure about what she wants to study, though she has interests in journalism and art. She describes her boyfriend as "nice, fun, and pretty." Anne gave very vague answers about the nature of their relationship and is not sure what kind of expectations he may have of her.

Summary and Conclusions

Anne was referred for assistance in assessing her future educational and personal goals. Mrs. Windsor is concerned about Anne's decision to move away from home and postpone her college education. She feels that the real reason for the sudden change of plans is Anne's relationship with her 28-year-old boyfriend. Mrs. Windsor is concerned about the breakdown in communication between her and Anne, which began three years ago, but has worsened in the last 6 months. She describes Anne as smart and talented but defiant and rebellious.

The results of this evaluation confirmed that Anne's cognitive abilities and achievement levels would potentially allow her to continue with any college program of her choice. Her general cognitive skills are well above average limits, with strengths in the verbal area. However, successfully completing a college education depends on more than ability level; motivation, persistence, and commitment are also needed. Anne's achievement scores are average, pointing to a significant discrepancy between her abilities and performance. Although she graduated from high school with top grades, results indicate that she is not performing at a level commensurate with her abilities. Her educational history shows a variability in grades that seems to reflect fluctuations in degree of commitment as well as emotional difficulties. The discrepancy between Anne's high academic performance and average achievement scores may also indicate the lack of challenge presented by her most recent curriculum.

From the age of 14, when Anne was raped, she has shown signs of depression and irritability that have not ceased and for which she has not received professional help. A number of traumatic events that followed the rape, including an abusive relationship and tragic deaths of three of her friends, most likely intensified Anne's emotional difficulties and diminished her coping abilities.

She withdrew emotionally from her mother and other family members and formed stronger attachments to a group of friends. Symptoms including sadness, nervousness, hypersomnia, nightmares, fatigue, migraines, poor appetite, low self-esteem, diminished interest and pleasure in activities, and feelings of hopelessness all provide evidence of a mood related disorder. These symptoms have caused significant distress in Anne's relationship with her mother, who also suffers from depression. It is likely that these symptoms also diminished Anne's ability to perform academically at the level expected for her cognitive skills. The early onset of symptoms and the course of Anne's depression during the last three years suggest a chronic course of illness with less likelihood of spontaneous recovery.

Diagnosis

Anne meets the diagnostic criteria for dysthymic disorder, early onset (300.4), as delineated in the DSM-IV. The following symptoms were identified: depressed and irritable mood for the last 3 years, markedly diminished interest or pleasure in most activities, feelings of worthlessness and hopelessness, poor appetite, hypersomnia, fatigue, and low self-esteem. These problems have caused significant distress in relationships and likely diminished Anne's academic performance.

Recommendations

The following recommendations address areas related to individual and family therapy, parent–child relationship, peer relationships, and career counseling.

1. Anne would benefit from individual therapy that focused on her cognitions, feelings about herself, and issues related to isolation from peers, social interactions, and communication and coping skills.

2. It would be beneficial for Mrs. Windsor to seek individual therapy for her own emotional problems as well as family therapy focused on the relationship between her and Anne. It seems that Mrs. Windsor's parenting style, in conjunction with Anne's irritability and temper, causes problems in communication and render the mother's well-intentioned actions ineffective and even detrimental.

3. To reclaim positive aspects of their relationship, it is important that both Mrs. Windsor and Anne take opportunities to engage in pleasurable and relaxing activities together. Companionable experiences might alleviate the tense emotions and feelings of unhappiness that have long characterized their relationship.

4. Anne needs to take a more active role in financially supporting her education and life-style. Shouldering an increased responsibility for contributing to the household finances could also serve as an opportunity to involve her more actively in family life. However, keep in mind that at the age of 17, she is still dependent and may be limited in finding ways of supporting herself. Terminating all financial support might prevent her from continuing with higher education and further alienate her from her mother and family. Anne needs emotional support and encouragement in developing independence.

5. Even when she does not approve of Anne's friends, Mrs. Windsor should show more acceptance of them. At this point, these friends are a major

source of emotional support for Anne, and attempts to ban such relationships will likely create additional conflicts. However, Mrs. Windsor should also monitor Anne's relationships and activities outside the home.

6. It is important to recognize Anne's many strengths. Mrs. Windsor should demonstrate, as often as possible, how much she appreciates Anne and trusts her coping abilities. Even Anne's smallest efforts should be acknowledged and rewarded. At this point, Anne's anger, disappointments, worries, and low self-esteem are probably overpowering her ability to feel hopeful and positive. Anne needs help to deal with such feelings. Gaining a positive attitude toward oneself is extremely important for making positive changes in other areas.

7. Mrs. Windsor should continue to closely monitor changes in Anne's moods and behaviors, including sadness, irritability, and anger. In order to develop an understanding of what causes Anne's irritability and unhappiness, Mrs. Windsor should initiate communication about Anne's feelings. It would be helpful if Mrs. Windsor could model ways to avoid interpersonal conflicts or resolve them in a more positive and constructive manner. Negative attention is often perceived as better than no attention at all, and arguments with Mrs. Windsor may serve as reinforcement for Anne.

8. Mrs. Windsor should try to share her own feelings about events and traumas in their lives with Anne. Openness is necessary to restore a trusting relationship between them.

9. To prevent anger, arguments, and resentment from taking over their relationship, dominating their communication and time spent together, Mrs. Windsor should remind herself of all those things that make Anne a loving daughter. Mrs. Windsor is Anne's only parent, and it is very important that Anne feel safe, accepted, and supported by her. It is obvious that Mrs. Windsor loves Anne and cares for her, but it is important that she clearly communicates this love to her daughter. Anne needs frequent reassurance about how much she is loved and that the problems in their relationship do not change her mother's feelings toward her.

Natalie Grace, PhD
Licensed Psychologist
Certified School Psychologist

Psychometric Summary

Cognitive Development

WECHSLER ADULT INTELLIGENCE SCALE—THIRD EDITION (WAIS-III)

The WAIS-III is an individually administered clinical instrument for assessing the intellectual ability of adolescents and adults 16–89 years of age. The individual's performance on the subtests is summarized in three composite standard scores—Verbal, Performance, and Full Scale—which provide an estimate of the individual's intellectual abilities. The following subtest scaled scores have a mean of 10 with an *SD* of 3. Scores of 7–13 are considered average.

Verbal subtests	Scaled scores	Performance subtests	Scaled scores
Information	15	Picture Completion	12
Digit Span	9	Picture Arrangement	10
Vocabulary	18	Block Design	9
Arithmetic	10	Digit Symbol-Coding	15
Comprehension	16	Matrix Reasoning	12
Similarities	18	(Object Assembly)	9
		(Symbol Search)	10

The following composite standard scores have a mean of 100 with an *SD* of 15. Scores of 85–115 are considered to be within the average range and reflect 68% of the general population.

Composite scores	IQ index	90% Confidence interval
Verbal	128	123–131
Performance	110	104–115
Full Scale Score	**122**	**118–125**
Verbal Comprehension Index	**142**	**136–145**
Perceptual Organization Index	105	99–111
Processing Speed Index	114	105–120

123

Achievement

WECHSLER INDIVIDUAL ACHIEVEMENT TEST (WIAT)

The WIAT is a comprehensive, individually administered battery for assessing the achievement of children ages 5 years–19 years, 11 months. The WIAT yields standard scores with a mean of 100 and an *SD* of 15. Standard scores of 85–115 are considered to be within the average range and reflect 68% of the general population.

	Standard scores	90% Confidence interval
Basic Reading	105	97–113
Mathematics Reasoning	103	95–111
Spelling	118	109–127
Reading Comprehension	116	105–127
Numerical Operations	95	85–105
Listening Comprehension	89	78–100
Oral Expression	107	99–115
Written Expression	112	102–122
Reading composite	110	102–118
Math composite	100	93–107
Language composite	101	92–110
Writing composite	118	110–126
Total composite	**108**	**103–113**

WOODCOCK–JOHNSON PSYCHO-EDUCATIONAL BATTERY—REVISED TESTS OF ACHIEVEMENT (WJ-R ACH)

The WJ-R ACH is an individually administered achievement test containing various subtests, whose scores are combined into the following composites: Broad Reading, Basic Reading Skills, Broad Mathematics, Broad Written Language, and Broad Knowledge. The WJ-R ACH yields standard scores with a mean of 100 and an *SD* of 15. Standard scores of 85–115 are considered to be within the average range and reflect 68% of the general population.

Subtests	Standard scores	90% Confidence interval	Age equivalent
Letter–Word Identification	110	106–114	21
Passage Comprehension	119	114–124	30
Calculation	100	96–104	17
Applied Problems	99	95–103	16.1
Dictation	99	94–104	16.1
Writing Samples	83	78–88	10.4
Science	104	98–110	19
Social Studies	101	97–105	17.4
Humanities	96	91–101	15

Composite Scores

	Standard scores	90% Confidence interval	Age equivalent
Broad Reading	115	112–118	15
Broad Math	100	97–103	16.6
Broad Written Language	93	88–98	13.7
Broad Knowledge	99	96–102	16.6
Skills	103	100–106	17.8
Math Reasoning	99	95–103	16.1

ORAL AND WRITTEN LANGUAGE SCALES (OWLS)

The OWLS is an individually administered test of oral language for children and young adults. Results may be used to determine broad levels of language skills as well as specific performance in the areas of listening, speaking, and writing. The OWLS yields standard scores with a mean of 100 and an *SD* of 15. Standard scores of 85–115 are considered to be within the average range and reflect 68% of the general population.

Listening Comprehension:
Standard score (age)	115
90% Confidence interval	106–124
Percentile	84
Age equivalent	21

Socioemotional Development—Self-Report

BEHAVIOR ASSESSMENT SYSTEM FOR ADOLESCENTS—SELF-REPORT
OF PERSONALITY (BASC-SRP-A)

The BASC-SRP is a self-report measure designed to evaluate the personality and self-perceptions of children. Two major syndromes comprise the Emotional Symptoms Index: Clinical Maladjustment and Personal Maladjustment. In addition, three scales—Attitude to School, Attitude to Teachers, and Sensation Seeking—comprise a School Maladjustment composite.

The BASC-SRP yields T scores with a mean of 50 and an SD of 10. Scores above 70 are considered significantly high on the Emotional Symptoms Index; scores below 30 on the Personal Adjustment scale are considered significantly low.

Clinical scales	T scores	Range
School Maladjustment composite	41	
Attitude to School	38	
Attitude to Teachers	39	
Clinical Maladjustment composite	40	
Atypicality	47	
Locus of Control	44	
Social Stress	38	
Anxiety	36	
Additional Clinical scales		
Depression	43	
Sense of Inadequacy	37	
Personal Maladjustment composite	54	
Relations with Parents	37	At risk
Interpersonal Relations	57	
Self-Esteem	58	
Self-Reliance	59	
Emotional Symptoms Index		
F Index		Acceptable
V Index		Acceptable
Response Pattern		Acceptable
Consistency		Acceptable

ACHENBACH CHILD BEHAVIOR CHECKLIST—YOUTH SELF-REPORT (CBCL-YSR)

The CBCL-YSR is designed to obtain students' reports of their own competencies and problems in a standardized format that permits comparison with reports by others, such as their parents and teachers. The CBCL-YSR yields T scores with a mean of 50 and an SD of 10. Scores of 67–70 are considered to be borderline significant; a score above 70 is considered to be clinically significant.

	T scores
Withdrawn	55
Somatic Complaints	50
Anxious/Depressed	50
Social Problems	50
Thought Problems	50
Attention Problems	50
Delinquent Behavior	55
Aggressive Behavior	50
Internalizing composite	48
Externalizing composite	49
Total composite score	**45**

BECK DEPRESSION INVENTORY (BDI)

The revised Beck Depression Inventory (BDI) is a 21-item instrument designed to assess the severity of depression in adolescents and adults. The symptoms and attitudes assessed by the BDI include mood, pessimism, sense of failure, self-dissatisfaction, guilt, punishment, self-dislike, self-accusations, suicidal ideas, crying, irritability, social withdrawal, indecisiveness, body-image, change, fatigability, loss of appetite, weight loss, somatic preoccupations, and loss of libido. Each symptom and attitude is rated by adolescent on a 4-point scale in terms of severity. The items are chosen to reflect the severity of depression.

Total score: 8

Socioemotional Development—Parent Report

BEHAVIOR ASSESSMENT SYSTEM FOR CHILDREN—PARENT RATING SCALES
(BASC-PRS-A)

The BASC-PRS is a questionnaire that is filled out by parents in order to assess the behavior problems, emotional difficulties, and social competence of their children. The BASC-PRS yields T scores with a mean of 50 and an SD of 10. Scores above 70 are considered to be indicative of significant problems.

BASC Scale and Composite Score Classification

Adaptive scales	T score range	Range
Very high	70 and above	Clinically significant
High	60–69	At risk
Average	41–59	Average
At risk	31–40	Low
Clinically significant	30 and below	Very low

	T scores	
Clinical scales	Mother	Range
Hyperactivity	49	
Aggression	55	
Conduct Problems	76	Clinically significant
Externalizing Problems Composite	62	
Anxiety	56	
Depression	55	
Somatization	50	
Internalizing Problems Composite	54	
Atypicality	53	
Withdrawal	70	Clinically significant
Attention Problems	51	
Behavioral Symptoms Index	54	

On the Adaptive scales, scores below 30 are considered significantly low.

T scores

Adaptive scales	Mother	Range
Social Skills	35	At risk
Leadership	40	At risk
Adaptive Skills Composite	36	At risk

ACHENBACH CHILD BEHAVIOR CHECKLIST—PARENT FORM (CBCL)

The Achenbach CBCL is a questionnaire that is completed by parents regarding the behavioral and emotional problems of their children. The CBCL yields *T* scores with a mean of 50 and an *SD* of 10. Scores of 67–70 are considered borderline significant; a score above 70 is indicative of significant problems.

T scores

	Mother	
Withdrawn	68	Borderline
Somatic Complaints	51	
Anxious/Depressed	62	
Social Problems	50	
Thought Problems	50	
Attention Problems	51	
Delinquent Behavior	73	Clinically significant
Aggressive Behavior	62	
Internalizing composite	62	At risk
Externalizing composite	67	Clinically significant
Total composite score	**63**	**At risk**

PARENTING STRESS INDEX (PSI)

The PSI was designed as an overall measure of stress in the parent's life. Two domains are sampled: stress associated with parenting this particular child and stress in other parts of the parent's life. The composite scores (Total Stress, Child Domain, and Parent Domain) are the most reliable scores for interpretation. Percentile scores above 90 are considered to be indicative of problems.

Mother		
Scales	Raw score	%
Distractibility/Hyperactivity	27	75
Adaptability	29	83
Reinforces Parent	22	99+
Demandingness	33	99+
Mood	15	97
Acceptability	18	95
Child Domain score	154	99+
Sense of Competence	45	99+
Social Isolation	22	97
Attachment	20	97
Health	16	85
Role Restriction	21	70
Depression	24	80
Relationship with Spouse	17	55
Parent Domain Score	165	93
Total Stress score	**319**	**99**

Teacher Report

ACHENBACH TEACHER REPORT FORM (TRF)

The TRF is a questionnaire to be completed by teachers in order to report behavioral and emotional problems. The TRF yields T scores with a mean of 50 and an SD of 10. Scores of 64–70 are considered to be borderline significant; a score above 70 is clinically significant.

TRF	T-Scores
Withdrawn	50
Somatic Complaints	58
Anxious/Depressed	63
Social Problems	61
Thought Problems	58
Attention Problems	57
Delinquent Behavior	75

Aggressive Behavior	50	
Internalizing composite	59	
Externalizing composite	61	At risk
Total composite score	**60**	**At risk**

BEHAVIOR ASSESSMENT SYSTEM FOR CHILDREN—TEACHER RATING SCALE
(BASC-TRS-A)

The BASC-TRS is a questionnaire completed by teachers to obtain ratings of
adaptive skills and behavioral and emotional problems of students. The BASC-
TRS yields *T* scores with a mean of 50 and an *SD* of 10. Scores above 70 are
considered to be indicative of significant problems.

Clinical scales	*T* scores	
Hyperactivity	46	
Aggression	47	
Conduct Problems	62	At risk
Externalizing Problems composite	52	
Anxiety	45	
Depression	47	
Somatization	56	
Internalizing Problems composite	49	
Attention Problems	46	
Learning Problems	51	
School Problems	48	
Atypicality	42	
Withdrawal	39	
Behavioral Symptoms Index	44	

On the Adaptive scales, scores below 30 are considered to be significantly low.

Adaptive scales	*T* scores
Social Skills	69
Leadership	63
Study Skills	60
Adaptive Skills Composite	65

PSYCHOLOGICAL EVALUATION (CONFIDENTIAL)

Subject: Jeffrey D.
DOB: 12/26/80
Exam Date: 8/18/96
Chronological Age: 15 years 8 months
Date of Report: 8/19/96
Examiner: M. Markus, PhD

Tests and Procedures

Clinical Interview
Mental Status Exam
Wechsler Intelligence Scale for Children—Third Edition (short form)
Kaufman Test of Educational Achievement
Bender Visual–Motor Gestalt Test
Human Figure Drawing
Kinetic Family Drawing
Revised Children's Manifest Anxiety Scale
BASC: Structured Developmental History (father)
BASC: Parent Rating Scale—Adolescent (father)
BASC: Self-Report of Personality—Adolescent
Review of Records

Background Information and Reason for Referral

Jeffrey was referred for psychological evaluation by the Honorable Jack Briscoe in the county court at law of Warrant County, Texas, sitting as a juvenile court. The court, on 8/10/96, requested a psychological evaluation to assist in determining appropriate levels of supervision, treatment, and/or placement with regard to this young man. He has a history of juvenile complaints extending over approximately 3 years and include various acts of destruction of property, burglary of a habitation, and, recently, arson. He has been placed on probation on several occasions. According to his probation officer, neither alcohol nor drug abuse is suspected or implicated in his difficulties.

Jeffrey was seen for psychological evaluation on 8/18/96. He was brought to the examination by his father and his probation officer, Mr. Howard Castle. He was provided with his psychological Miranda warnings in the presence of his father and Mr. Castle. The father explained several of the issues with regard to his rights to him as well. The father then deferred to Jeffrey, who determined that he would participate in the examination and understood that the results would be released to the court. He further indicated clearly his understanding that results of the exam may or may not be seen by him as helpful to his desired outcome in the matters now before the court. The father subsequently signed a consent for release of the results of the examination to the court and to the local probation office.

History and Development

The father, Jake D, completed a Structured Developmental History that provided the following information. Jeffrey currently (and since birth) resides with his parents, Jake and Mandy. They live in Warrenton, Texas, where the mother is employed as a certified nurse assistant with the local hospital, and the father is self-employed in the construction business. There have been no parental separations, deaths, or divorces. Jeffrey is reported to be equally close to both parents. He has a 17-year-old brother and 12-year-old sister also residing in the home. The father left blank questions about the relationship between Jeffrey and his siblings. Jeffrey is reported to participate in some routine family activities, such as meals, conversations, television, and movies. He sees his grandparents a few times each year.

The father states that he enjoys Jeffrey's "brightness" most of all but finds his inability to help his son recognize his total worth to be the most difficult aspect of rearing him. The father would like Jeffrey to attend a technical or vocational school in the future and generally be successful in whatever he chooses to do. The father notes that he is primarily in charge of discipline in the home and that he and his wife do not agree on disciplinary techniques. The father's disciplinary techniques consist of sending him to his room or grounding him from attending certain events.

The father provided a limited history of the pregnancy and delivery. The mother broke her pelvic bone during the pregnancy, but no other complications were noted. She was noted to smoke one pack of cigarettes per day. Jeffrey was subsequently born to a 29-year-old mother (length of gestation was not known). The father noted that both mother and child were healthy at the time of birth but could not provide any further details. He was unable to answer any questions concerning early motor or language development and unable to provide any medical or psychological history. Jeffrey denied any recollection of prior psychological or psychiatric examinations. There is a family health history of cancer, diabetes, cardiovascular disease, and alcohol abuse. Both parents are reported to be in good health, although the mother has adult-onset asthma. The father and Jeffrey both denied that Jeffrey had ever attended a special education program; however, this contention is inconsistent with information provided by the probation office. Special education records had been requested from the school system but were not received in time to meet the report deadlines set by the court. The father did note that Jeffrey had difficulty early in school and was retained in second grade. However, he is not noted to have any difficulties with his studies at this time.

According to the father, Jeffrey has no difficulties relating to, or participating in activities with, other children. He denied reports of frequent fighting and noted that Jeffrey enjoys swimming, walking, hiking, baseball, and football. Jeffrey, in contrast, reported that he enjoys wrestling and does not play baseball at all. The father noted that Jeffrey seems easily overstimulated, overly energetic, and perhaps impulsive in play, has a short attention span, seems unhappy most of the time, hides his feelings, and withholds affection. Adaptive behavior appears to be developing appropriately for age, and no concerns are evident in this domain.

Jeffrey noted that he was expelled from school for the entire second semester last year due to "being written up too many times" for talking out and getting into fights with others. Jeffrey stated that although he has never been in special education, he did go to a school counselor for some time in the past. He could not specify the time period in which this occurred and could not recall the specific reason for his counseling.

The present evaluation was undertaken to assist the court in making a proper determination as to what would be in Jeffrey's best interest at this time.

Observations, Interview, and Behaviors

Jeffrey arrived at the appointed time for his evaluation. His height and weight are within normal limits, and he has jet black hair and hazel eyes. He was dressed appropriately for his age in a pullover shirt with jeans and tennis shoes. He was neat and clean, and there were no indications of personal neglect. He was accompanied by his father and probation officer, as noted. He cooperated fully with the examiner at all times, despite numerous complaints about the length of the examination. He nevertheless answered all questions and participated fully in the exam process.

Jeffrey was oriented appropriately to person, place, time, and circumstances, relative to his age. Speech was within normal limits for rate, volume, and articulation, and there was no pressured speech or flight of ideas, and no evidence of dysarthric or dyspraxic speech. He showed no signs of disorganized speech or any other psychotic symptoms and has no known history of psychotic disorders. His mood was euthymic and affect was full range. He denied any significant history of alcohol, illicit drug, or tobacco use. Attention and concentration were appropriate throughout the nearly four hours of one-on-one examination. He had no specific difficulties staying on task and was not impulsive in his responding. However, he reported having received a diagnosis of "ADD" but added that he had stopped taking Ritalin several years ago—a decision made with his mother's concurrence. According to Jeffrey, the Ritalin had not helped him. During the four hours with the examiner, his observable behavior showed no indications of attention-deficit/hyperactivity disorder. The father did not recall this diagnosis or treatment history.

Jeffrey demonstrated impaired judgment in his responses and demeanor in the current exam and had little insight into his behavior or the behavior and difficulties of others. He had little awareness of his vocational future or plans for employment activities as an adult. Memory function was within normal limits for age, as was language usage. Intellectual function was estimated to be average based upon the interview data, which was confirmed in formal testing.

On examination, Jeffrey was found to be aware of most of the charges in his legal history. He reported three arrests but denied his most recent charges of criminal mischief, arguing adamantly that he was never arrested. He was unable to give any real explanation for his actions other than they "seemed like a good idea at the time." He then quickly proclaimed his innocence on each occasion, then blamed others for drawing him into these illegal actions. He was unable to explain why it is inappropriate to break into a person's home, steal things from it, or even burn it down, except for noting that such activities are wrong and illegal. He is able to state that they are wrong but can give no explanation as to why it is considered wrong to engage in such acts. His limited development of conscience and morality is consistent with his significantly immature psychological and emotional development in general.

Jeffrey reported no difficulties with sleep or other vegetative functions, and he denied symptoms of depression. He had little insight into the seriousness of the matters currently before the court, believing that his probation will probably be extended for a year. Jeffrey's efforts as well as his cooperation and compliance with the examiner indicate that his performance has provided valid indications of his current levels of cognitive and affective function.

Test Results and Interpretation

On testing with a six-subtest short form (three Verbal, three Performance) of the WISC-3, Jeffrey scored a Verbal IQ of 89 and Performance IQ of 111, resulting in a Full Scale IQ of 99. On the WISC-3, this level of performance falls near the midpoint of the average range, exceeding 47% of adolescents at his age. The 22-point discrepancy between the Verbal and Performance IQs, even using a short form, is significant. The discrepency indicates that he performs at a significantly higher level when required to use nonverbal means to demonstrate his intelligence, such as through manipulative materials, than when restricted to the use of verbal modalities. This pattern of intellectual abilities has an extremely high incidence rate within the delinquent population. The short form of the WISC-3 was used due to the length of the examination and scheduling problems with the father's work schedule. Nevertheless, the results were highly consistent across the various components of the short form, with a range of 3 points between highest and lowest scores on each scale, indicating a high degree of probability that the results obtained are stable. These results are consistent with informal estimates made during the mental status examination as well.

Assessment of basic academic skills on the Kaufman Test of Educational Achievement netted standard scores in the application of mathematics (82), mathematics computation (81), word recognition (87), and reading comprehension (88). These scores are all completely consistent with his measured verbal IQ but certainly fall far below his nonverbal level of intellectual functioning. Academic skills are typically correlated more highly with verbal skills. These results are consistent with the presence of a learning disability in the area of mathematics, although lack of educational opportunity cannot be ruled out due to his recent, lengthy, expulsion. However, his difficulties are also consistent with the presence of a language-related learning disability, and a learning disabilities program should be strongly considered by the school and the parents. Indeed, he may have been in such a program, and further consultation with school officials will be necessary to obtain an accurate record of prior placements.

Assessment of personality and behavior, utilizing multiple methods and multiple informants, is consistent with an absence of any significant symptoms of anxiety, depression, or other disorders of an internalizing nature. In fact, Jeffrey reported fewer anxieties than most adolescents at his age—which is particularly significant, given his current legal circumstances. He did report difficulties in adjusting to school and getting along with teachers. In his responses to the multiple self-report personality scales administered, however, he denied any symptomatic pattern of psychopathology. This denial is due, in part, to his general psychological naivete and emotional immaturity, which were observed in interview and demonstrated in his projective responses. His projectives do indicate significant anxieties about himself and what is going to happen to him, although these anxieties appear to be evident more at a subconscious than conscious level. Jeffrey does appear to make chronic use of repression and denial. as defense mechanisms, facilitated by his lack of psychological sophistication and evident intrapersonally and interpersonally.

Results of an objective rating scale completed by the father indicate significant problems with conduct and attention. The highest elevations appear on these two scales with lesser, but noteworthy, indications of depressive symptoms (denied by Jeffrey) and very mild developmental deficits in social skills and related behaviors.

The overall pattern of results seen in the current exam indicates the presence of multiple psychiatric disorders, including, most prominently, the presence of a specific developmental disorder in math and a conduct disorder. Special education programming is strongly encouraged as an intervention for his learning disability in math. There is not sufficient symptomatology at this time to support diagnosis of attention-deficit/hyperactivity disorder, although he has received this diagnosis in the past but discontinued Ritalin because it was not effective. He does not experience anxiety about his behavior and has only a technical understanding of why his actions are wrong, particularly in the context of theft. He does not appreciate the seriousness of his actions or the potentially serious consequences that could result from burglarizing a home or setting fires. He has been unable to control his behavior even while on probation. A period of residential placement that would include group psychotherapy would appear to be appropriate as an intervention.

Jeffrey requires close supervision and a carefully structured environment to enable him to develop appropriate cognitive control systems and an appreciation for the seriousness of his actions. Work in an offenders group would also be appropriate; the power of the group process with peers would be needed to break through his coping mechanisms of denial and repression. As a treatment for conduct disorder, parent training is supported strongly in current research literature; it is recommended that Jeffrey's parents seek out and attend a parenting class led by an individual experienced in providing training for parents with children who have a diagnosis of conduct disorder.

Jeffrey's DSM-IV diagnosis is as follows:

Axis I: 315.1 Mathematics disorder
312.8 Conduct disorder, adolescent onset, severe
314.01 Rule out attention-deficit/hyperactivity disorder, combined type

Axis II: 301.81, Rule out narcissistic personality disorder
Axis III: No diagnosis
Axis IV: Severe problems with education and schooling, legal problems
Axis V: Current GAF: 35
          Highest last year: 55

M. Markus, PhD
Psychologist
Jeffrey D.

Supplementary Psychometric Summary

Revised Children's Manifest Anxiety Scale T scores

Total Anxiety	$T = 35$
Physiological Anxiety	$T = 38$
Worry/Oversensitivity	$T = 32$
Social Concerns/Concentration	$T = 35$
Lie	$T = 62$

BASC: Self-Report of Personality T Scores, General Norms

CLINICAL SCALES

Attitude to School	$T = 60$
Attitude to Teachers	$T = 62$
Sensation Seeking	$T = 59$
Atypicality	$T = 55$
Locus of Control	$T = 41$
Somatization	$T = 45$
Social Stress	$T = 54$
Anxiety	$T = 46$
Depression	$T = 49$
Sense of Inadequacy	$T = 54$

ADAPTIVE SCALES

Relations with Parents	$T = 37$
Interpersonal Relations	$T = 31$
Self-Esteem	$T = 54$
Self-Reliance	$T = 37$

BASC: Parent Rating Scale T Scores, General Norms

CLINICAL SCALES

Hyperactivity	$T = 55$
Aggression	$T = 61$
Conduct Problems	$T = 67$
Anxiety	$T = 44$
Depression	$T = 63$
Somatization	$T = 50$
Atypicality	$T = 57$
Withdrawal	$T = 47$
Attention Problems	$T = 73$

ADAPTIVE SCALES

Social Skills	$T = 40$
Leadership	$T = 43$

VICTOR

Victor, as noted in the previous chapter, produced a classic BASC set of findings for a child with ADHD symptomatology. He was evaluated in a publicly funded psychology clinic.

Name of Child: Victor Thorpe
Chronological Age: 5 years 9 months

Tests Administered

Differential Ability Scales—Preschool Form (DAS)
Kaufman Survey of Early Academic and Language Skills (K-SEALS)
Bracken Basic Concept Scale—Revised (BBCS-R)
Developmental Test of Visual–Motor Integration (VMI)
Motor-Free Visual Perception Test—Revised (MVPT-R)
Achenbach Child Behavior Checklist (CBCL)
Achenbach Teacher Report Form (TRF)
Behavior Assessment Scale for Children (BASC)

Parent Rating Scales—Preschool (BASC-PRS-P)
Teacher Rating Scales—Preschool (BASC-TRS-P)

BASC Structured Developmental History—Parent Interview Format
Conners' Parent Rating Scale—Revised (CPRS-R)
Structured Interview for the Diagnostic Assessment of Children
    (SIDAC)
Teacher Interview

Referral Information

Victor Thorpe is a 5-year, 9-month-old kindergartener referred to the UGA School Psychology Clinic by his parents and his teacher for concerns about his ability to learn basic academic concepts, such as numbers and letters, his high level of activity, and his inability to focus on academic tasks. Victor's family pediatrician recommended that his parents obtain a full psychological evaluation to screen for attention-deficit/hyperactivity disorder (ADHD) and a possible learning disability.

Family Background

Victor's father is a herdsman for a dairy farm and his mother works as a secretary. He has one sibling, a sister Jessica (age 12), with whom he gets along well. The family lives on the farm. Victor's paternal aunts, uncles, and grandparents all live nearby, and he sees them often. His mother's parents live in a nearby state, and he is able to visit with them fairly frequently.

Developmental and Medical History

Weighing 9 pounds, 12 ounces at birth, Victor was the healthy product of a planned, full-term pregnancy and normal labor and delivery. He was slightly jaundiced at birth but did not require bilirubin lights. His mother had taken infertility drugs prior to his conception but had discontinued them before becoming pregnant with Victor.

Victor's mother reports that he was a colicky baby. However, he slept through the night much earlier than most babies.

His parents recalled that Victor was early or on time to reach developmental milestones. Indeed, they said that he was able to hold his head up on the day they brought him home from the hospital, and he crawled, walked, and talked early as well (and that he has remained "a talker"). With the exception of chicken pox, he has not experienced any serious illnesses, injuries, or ear infections. His parents did note, however, that Victor complains of head-aches frequently.

Victor is a very deep sleeper and continues to experience nightly enuresis. His parents try to wake him up at night to use the bathroom but are often unable to rouse him fully. Both parents and pediatrician are confident that he will "grow out of it."

His parents reported no family history of mental illness, but they did mention learning-related problems: Victor's paternal great-aunt had mental retardation, and his father recalled having difficulty learning the alphabet and that his mother insisted that he be held back in second grade. In addition, his father acknowledged a lifelong problem sitting still and added that he shares Victor's difficulties with getting to sleep and focusing on book work.

For the most part, Victor has good adaptive skills. He keeps his room clean, is very well-mannered, and is able to dress and bathe himself. He is not yet able to tell time.

His parents reported some difficulty with Victor's fine and gross motor skills. He is not yet able to catch a ball or tie his shoes, although he is able to ride a bike. His teacher also reported that he has a difficult time writing his letters, coloring, or drawing.

Educational History

Victor is currently attending kindergarten at Bonaire Elementary School. Victor's teacher, Ms. Brooks, reported that he is having trouble putting his letters together, learning his numbers, and recalling basic concepts. He does not know most of his numbers (though he is able to count from 1 to 6 fairly consistently), is unable to retain information over even short periods of time, and cannot focus on the task at hand. As a result of these weak areas, his problem continues to worsen. Both his teacher and his parents reported that his performance is very inconsistent. Currently, his teacher makes several modifications for Victor: She has him sit near the board during copying work; either she or her paraprofessional aide give him one-on-one attention for most written work; and she shortens most projects for him, since he is unable to complete the same length of work as the other children.

He can write his own name and spell the first two letters of particularly common words, such as *mommy* and *daddy*, but his parents reported that when they work with him at home on letters or numbers, he is often unable to retain information from one day to the next.

Both his kindergarten and preschool teachers have expressed concerns about Victor's heightened activity level. His current teacher reports that he is always on the run, talks excessively, is unable to stay seated for any period of time, and frequently interrupts class activities. In preschool, Victor had trouble sitting still during group activities and had to sit separate from the group, in a taped-in square area, to establish the boundaries by which he was to abide. When this separate seating arrangement became a long-term placement, his mother objected to his constant separation from the group.

Victor is the youngest child in his class. His parents have considered holding him back a grade, but his teacher has expressed some reticence to take this action, although she also expressed great concern about Victor's readiness to move to first grade next year. There is no aide available in first grade to give Victor the one-on-one attention he is receiving in her class. In addition, she feels that Victor has not mastered basic concepts necessary to succeed in first grade.

Behavioral Observations

Victor presented as a highly likable, happy, 5-year-old who is eager to work with a new friend and separates easily from his parents. He was mischievous before, during, and after testing, preferring to play hide-and-seek with the examiner than participate in testing. He has a very winning habit of crinkling his face up and smiling impishly when he is trying to avoid an unpleasant or boring activity. Because he is so creative, friendly, and happy in his efforts to escape testing, he does not present as oppositional or defiant even when he is trying to reverse the course of activities.

It was difficult to keep his attention on the testing, even when a token economy was introduced. He did not link performance on the task with the receipt of a reward and did not seem bothered by success or failure on most items. In fact, he had a very optimistic approach to most tasks, believing that he had gotten them correct even when he hadn't. This is not unusual for children of his age, however. Victor's inability to focus on the task at hand or sustain attention for even small lengths of time caused him to miss many items he would otherwise have gotten correct. For example, on a test of visual–motor integration in which he was asked to copy geometric forms, Victor simply scribbled on some items that he was able to copy on a subtest of a later test. In addition, he was often impulsive in choosing the answer and frequently had to change his first answer. As the problems became more difficult, he was less likely to notice that his first choice was incorrect.

Test Results and Interpretation

Cognitive Achievement

DIFFERENTIAL ABILITY SCALES (DAS)

The DAS was administered to Victor in order to measure his overall cognitive functioning. The DAS is an individually administered test of intelligence consisting of six "core subtests" as well as diagnostic tests. The core subtests, which measure somewhat different domains of cognitive ability, are used in the calculation of the General Conceptual Ability (GCA) score, an estimate of overall intelligence. On the DAS, Victor achieved a GCA score of 90, placing him in the average range of functioning and at the 25th percentile of the population. On the Verbal Cluster, Victor achieved a standard score of 106, placing him in the average range and at the 66th percentile of the population for verbal abilities. On the Nonverbal Cluster, Victor achieved a score of 83, placing him in the low-average range and at the 13th percentile of the population. Victor's Verbal Cluster score was significantly higher than his Nonverbal Cluster score, indicating that his verbal abilities are more developed than his nonverbal reasoning and visual–motor skills.

Victor did best on tasks that could be verbally mediated, that required more automatic processing abilities, and that had few visual or motor requirements. For example, he did very well on Naming Vocabulary, a test that measures expressive language abilities and required him to verbally name pictured items. In the nonverbal domain, he did best on the Picture Similarities task, where he had to match cards to pictures by identifying a shared feature. However, he often talked himself through the task, saying the shared feature aloud. He commented that he had a game like this at home. On another task, Pattern Construction, where he had to replicate a visual design using blocks, he was easily discouraged, saying "I can't do that one," even on relatively easy items. This task measures visual–motor integration and nonverbal reasoning skills that are not as easily mediated by verbal abilities.

Victor demonstrated a relative weakness on the Early Number Concepts subtest. Although he was able to identify general quantitative similarities (e.g., matching the size of buckets with similarly sized shovels), he had more difficulty matching numbers with specific quantities and was often unable to identify numerals. In addition, he frequently asked when he could take a break, attended poorly during this half of the test, and made careless and random errors. His poor attention on this subtest may have been due to his desire to escape a task he found both difficult and unrewarding.

KAUFMAN SURVEY OF EARLY ACADEMIC AND LANGUAGE SKILLS (K-SEALS)

The K-SEALS measures basic skills and concepts necessary for academic success and is meant as an early screener for specific skills deficits. On the K-SEALS, Victor obtained an Early Academic and Language Skills composite of 97, placing him in the average range and at the 42nd percentile of the population. His overall score is consistent with his GCA score on the DAS.

On individual subtests of the K-SEALS, Victor evidenced similar strengths and weaknesses as on the DAS. His Vocabulary subtest score of 110 placed him in the high end of the average range and at the 60th percentile of the population. His score of 84 on the Number, Letters, and Words subtest placed him in the low-average range and at the 14th percentile of the population. These scores are consistent with the strength in verbal abilities and weakness in early number concepts he evidenced on DAS. For the most part, Victor was unable to identify lower-case letters and to correctly identify numbers above 5. However, he was able to subtract 9 – 4 = 5 successfully. It was unclear how much this success was due to chance or whether his earlier failures were due to a lack of attention. It is likely that a relative deficit in some of this basic knowledge is aggravated by his attentional problems.

In terms of language, Victor achieved a standard score of 87 in the Expressive Skills domain, placing him in the average range and at the 19th percentile of the population. He achieved a standard score of 95 in the Receptive Skills domain, placing him in the average range and in the 37th percentile of the population. These scores combine both items from the Vocabulary subtest and the Numbers, Letters, and Words subtest. They are meant to provide information about a child's ability to understand spoken language versus his or her ability to produce meaningful language. Victor's inability to identify certain letters and numbers contributed to lower scores on each of these domains. In general, Victor's spoken and receptive language appear to be better developed than these scores reflect.

BRACKEN BASIC CONCEPT SCALE—REVISED (BBCS-R)

On the BBCS-R School Readiness composite, Victor achieved a scaled score of 7, placing him in the low-average range and at the 16th percentile of the population. The School Readiness composite measures basic knowledge of colors, sizes, numbers/counting, letters, comparisons, and shapes.

Results indicate that Victor knows all of his colors and most of his shapes and letters. In contrast to his performance on the K-SEALS, Victor was able to identify most letters (the exceptions were *m* and *i*). However, his performance on the numbers/counting subtest was consistent with the K-SEALS in that he was not able to consistently identify numbers or count higher than 5. He also did poorly on a task requiring him to identify and discriminate relative sizes of objects and was inconsistent on one that required him to visually discriminate various objects in terms of their similarities or differences.

DEVELOPMENTAL TEST OF VISUAL–MOTOR INTEGRATION (VMI)

Victor was administered the VMI to measure his capacity for integrating and coordinating his visual–perceptual and motor (finger and hand) abilities. On the VMI, Victor achieved a standard score of 66, placing him in the very low range and at the 1st percentile of the population. Victor did not finish most items on this test due to early failure at replicating the designs. He scribbled on some items, and the examiner believed he might not have been trying very hard. Nonetheless, this low score indicates the possible presence of significant problems with visual–motor integration. Corroborating this test score was his teacher report that Victor has difficulty both writing and drawing, does not enjoy coloring as much as other children his age, tends to use only single colors, and has great difficulty replicating pictures without guidance.

MOTOR-FREE VISUAL PERCEPTION TEST—REVISED (MVPT-R)

The MVPT-R is similar to the VMI in that it requires the child to match visual designs with an array of choices that contain the same design pattern. It can be used to determine whether a child has difficulty visually discriminating among shapes and symbols, while controlling for fine motor skills.

Victor achieved a standard score of 67 on this test, placing him well below average and at the 1st percentile of the population. Although he did well on early test items, he appeared to be guessing on most items on the second half of the test. He showed no basic pattern of success or failure. Along with Victor's low scores on the VMI, his low scores on this task suggest that he may have difficulties in accurately perceiving complex visual stimuli. He also appears to have deficits in his development of the fine motor skills necessary to replicate such patterns.

Social–Emotional Adjustment

PARENT REPORT

Victor's parents interact warmly with each other, display a great deal of affection for him, and describe him as a very social, engaging, and lovable child. His mother remarked, "Victor has never met a stranger." According to his parents, Victor is always happy, very talkative, and often mischievous. The family lives on a farm, so Victor has few opportunities to play with neighborhood children. However, his parents assert that he has many friends at school. His mother and father report average to high scores on the BASC-PRS Preschool Social Skills scales ([M] T score = 66; [F] T score = 57), suggesting that Victor is more socially well adjusted than most children his age. Similarly, both parents report high scores on the Adaptability scales of the BASC-PRS ([M] T score = 61; [F] T score = 61), suggesting that Victor easily adapts to new situations and demonstrates little negative emotionality.

Although he is more active than his sister was at this age, his parents expressed no concerns about behavioral problems at home. His mother and father believe strongly in a common front on disciplinary sanctions, and these usually involve Victor being sent to his room for minor infractions and a spanking for more serious misbehavior. Victor typically reacts quite emotionally to punishment, and his parents described him as melodramatic in this regard.

His parents reported that Victor is easily overstimulated in play, has difficulty calming down for sleep at night, and has trouble sitting still for academic exercises. His mother said that the more tired he becomes, the more "wound up" he gets—until he just collapses from exhaustion. Victor's heightened level of activity can be fatiguing for his mother. She describes him as much more active than his sister, always pushing his boundaries and testing for consequences. Both of his parents report clinically significant elevations on the BASC-PRS Attention Problems scale ([M] T score = 73; [F] T score = 73). His mother reported that he "almost always" is easily distracted and that he "often" has a short attention span, gives up easily when trying something new, and has trouble concentrating. His father reports that he "often" is easily distracted and "almost always" has a short attention span and trouble concentrating. He did not report that Victor gives up easily, however. His parents did not report elevations on the Attention Problems scale of the Achenbach Child Behavior Checklist ([M] T score = 54; [F] T score = 56). On the Conners' Parent Rating Scale—Revised, his father reported elevations on the ADHD index (T score = 68) and on the Global Index: Restless—Impulsive (T score = 65) that approached clinical significance. His father reported elevations on the Cognitive Problems–Inattention scale (T score = 67) and on the Hyperactivity scale (T score = 65) that approached clinical significance. Although his mother reported somewhat similar patterns of behavior, she did not report elevations on these scales. His mother reporter lower scores for the Cognitive Problems–Inattention scale (T score = 60) and did not report elevations on the Hyperactivity scale.

TEACHER REPORT

As noted, both Victor's preschool and kindergarten teachers expressed significant concerns about his heightened level of activity and inattentiveness. His
kindergarten teacher reported that Victor is fidgety and restless most of the
time, that he runs around more than most kids, finds it difficult to play quietly, cannot remain seated or stop moving around, and talks excessively. She
also reported that Victor is often unable to complete assigned work, that he
often blurts out answers without waiting his turn, that in play he moves
quickly from activity to activity, and that he has trouble waiting his turn in
group activities. According to her report, Victor often does not appear to be
listening, has difficulty following directions, finds it difficult to finish school
assignments, often loses things he needs, is forgetful, and needs repeated re-
minders to stay on task.

On the Achenbach TRF, his teacher noted clinically significant elevations
on the Attention Problems scale (T score = 84). On the BASC, she noted clinically significant elevations on both the Attention Problems scale (T score =
78) and on the Hyperactivity scale (T score = 83). Although the teacher also
reported elevations on the Atypicality scale of the BASC-TRS, it is not believed
that this score is demonstrative of problems in this area.

STRUCTURED INTERVIEW FOR THE DIAGNOSTIC ASSESSMENT
OF CHILDREN (SIDAC)

The SIDAC consists of a list of questions to which parents and teachers answer
yes or no to indicate the presence of symptoms relating to DSM-IV diagnosis.
Only the questions relating to attention deficit/hyperactivity disorder were administered. According to the DSM-IV, the criteria for determining a significant
problem are six symptoms positively endorsed in the category of inattention
and/or six symptoms positively endorsed in the combined categories of
impulsivity/hyperactivity.

DSM-IV Items Endorsed		
Item	Mother	Teacher
Inattention	6	9
Impulsivity	1	6
Hyperactivity	5	1

DSM-IV Diagnosis: Attention-deficit/hyperactivity disorder, combined type
(314.01)

Summary and Recommendations

Victor Thorpe, a 5-year, 9-month-old male, was referred by his parents and his teacher for concerns about delays in his acquisition of basic concepts, such as numbers and letters, and his high activity level. Victor is a socially well-adjusted, pleasant, polite, and engaging little boy who demonstrates a high level of adaptive skills and no internalizing symptoms such as depression or anxiety.

According to both parent and teacher reports, Victor is exhibiting symptoms of hyperactivity, impulsivity, and inattention, which in their number and intensity, are sufficient to warrant a diagnosis of attention-deficit/hyperactivity disorder, combined type (314.01). Victor's poor attention span, difficulty staying focused in school, and inability to remain seated for any significant length of time are significantly impairing Victor's ability to acquire basic academic concepts and, without intervention, will likely result in increasing behavioral problems.

Victor's cognitive functioning is in the average range, with a significant disparity between his performance on verbal tasks versus nonverbal reasoning tasks. He had particular difficulty with subtests that required manipulation of objects, replication of visual patterns, visual–motor integration, and more sustained attention. He did better on nonverbal reasoning tasks that could be mediated verbally.

Victor's verbal skills are well developed and firmly within the average range. However, he is lagging behind other children his age in his acquisition of basic skills, particularly numbers. He performed inconsistently on tasks of letter recognition, with the Bracken results suggesting adequate knowledge and the K-SEALS results suggesting problems in this area. On the other hand, his performance on tasks requiring knowledge of specific numbers and numerical quantities was consistently lower than average for his age range on three different exercises that measured this ability.

The following recommendations outline an integrated plan of intervention.

1. As noted, Victor is exhibiting symptoms of hyperactivity, impulsivity, and inattention, which in their number and intensity, are sufficient to warrant a diagnosis of attention-deficit/hyperactivity disorder, combined type (314.01). Victor's parents appear to be doing an excellent job of managing his heightened activity level at home. However, his inattention, heightened activity, and impulsivity are causing functional impairment in his academic progress. It is recommended that Victor's parents consult with his pediatrician regarding medication to treat his symptoms.

2. Victor's performances on a task of visual–motor integration and his performance on a task of visual–perceptual integration suggest significant problems with visual perception and/or visual–motor integration that should be investigated further. It is recommended that Victor's parents obtain a thorough vision screening to rule out poor eyesight. It is also recommended that Victor's visual–perceptual integration and his fine motor skills be evaluated fully by an occupational therapist trained to detect specific problems in this area. If such problems are apparent, they are likely playing a significant causal role in Victor's current academic delays.

3. Victor is evidencing a pattern of academic performance that may be indicative of an emerging learning disability. However, because of his young age, it is not possible to make this diagnosis at this time. It is strongly recommended that Victor receive a full psychological reevaluation in a year's time to monitor for the emergence of a learning disability.

4. It is recommended that Victor receive one-on-one intervention at school to remediate his deficits in basic knowledge of number and letters. For instance, his teacher might use flashcard drills to help Victor rehearse basic letter and number recognition.

5. It is recommended that Victor receive additional tutoring in these skills after school to complement in-school exercises.

6. It is recommended that his teacher continue to utilize accommodations already in place, such as shortened work assignments, one-on-one attention, repetition of directions, and moving Victor's desk closer to the front of the classroom.

7. Children with attention-deficit/hyperactivity disorder often require more consistent reinforcement for sustained mental effort. It is recommended that Victor's teacher systematically increase the use of both tangible (stickers, gold stars, etc.) and intangible (verbal praise) reinforcements for Victor, when he has succeeded in achieving a specific target goal, such as completing an assignment or remaining seated for a set period of time.

Psychometric Summary

Differential Ability Scales (DAS)

The DAS is an individually administered intelligence test consisting of six "core subtests" as well as achievement and diagnostic subtests. Only the core subtests are used in the calculation of the General Conceptual Ability (GCA) score, an estimate of overall intelligence. The DAS core subtests are also used to calculate cluster scores for verbal abilities, nonverbal reasoning, and spatial abilities.

The following composite standard scores have a mean of 100 and an SD of 15. Scores of 85–115 are considered to be within the average range and reflects 68% of the general population.

Domain	Standard scores	Percentile	90% Confidence interval
Verbal Cluster	106	66	97–114
Nonverbal Cluster	83	13	76–92
General Conceptual Ability	**90**	**25**	**84–96**

The following subtest T scores have a mean of 50 and an SD of 10. Scores of 40–60 are in the average range.

Domain	T scores
Core subtests	
Verbal Comprehension	48
Picture Similarities	46
Naming Vocabulary	59
Pattern Construction	40
Early Number Concepts	39
Copying	40
Diagnostic subtests	
Recall of Objects, Immediate	62
Recall of Objects, Delayed	54

Bracken Basic Concept Scale—Revised (BBCS-R)

The BBCS-R is an individually administered test for children ages 2 years, 6 months, to 7 years, 11 months, designed to assess basic knowledge of general concepts such as position, self and social awareness, quantity, and time. In addition, a school readiness cluster assesses knowledge of colors, numbers, shapes, and comparisons. The battery yields scaled scores for subtests having a mean of 10 and an SD of 3, where scores of 7–13 are within the average range. Total Test and School Readiness composite standard scores are also calculated; these have a mean of 100 and an SD of 15. Standard scores of 85–115 are considered to be within the average range and reflect 68% of the general population.

Subtests	Scaled scores	Percentile
School Readiness cluster	7	16
Self/Social Awareness	8	25
Quantity	7	16
Time/Sequence	10	50

Kaufman Survey of Early Academic and Language Skills (K-SEALS)

The K-SEALS is an individually administered, nationally normed measure of children's language (expressive and receptive skills), pre-academic skills (knowledge of numbers, number concepts, letters and words), and articulation. The K-SEALS has three separate subtests: Vocabulary; Numbers, Letters, and Words; and the Articulation Survey.

The items on the Vocabulary and Numbers, Letters, and Words subtests are organized into two language scales: the Expressive Skills scale and the Receptive Skills scale. The items on the Numbers, Letters, and Words subtest are further organized into two early academic scales for children ages 5 years to 6 years 11 months: the Number Skills scale and the Letter and Word Skills scale. All items on the Vocabulary and Numbers, Letters, and Words subtests are combined to produce a composite called the Early Academic and Language Skills composite.

Standard scores have a mean of 100 and an *SD* of 15. Scores of 85–115 are considered to be within the average range and reflect 68% of the general population.

Domain	Standard score	Confidence interval	Percentile rank
Vocabulary	110	101–118	75
Numbers, Letters and Words	84	78–91	14
Articulation Survey	Good (19/20)		
Early Academic and Language Skills Composite	97	91–103	42
Expressive Skills	87	80–95	19
Receptive Skills	95	87–103	37
Number Skills	83	74–95	13
Letter and Word Skills	83	77–90	13

Behavior Assessment System for Children—Parent Rating Scales (BASC-PRS)

The BASC-PRS is a questionnaire that is filled out by parents in order to assess the behavioral problems, emotional difficulties, and social competence of their children. The BASC-PRS yields T scores with a mean of 50 and an SD of 10. Scores above 70 are considered to be indicative of significant problems.

	T scores	
Domain	Mother	Father
Hyperactivity	58	52
Aggression	39	39
Externalizing Problems composite	**48**	**45**
Anxiety	47	42
Depression	39	39
Somatization	49	37
Internalizing Problems composite	**43**	**36**
Atypicality	37	41
Withdrawal	29	33
Attention Problems	73	73
Behavioral Symptoms Index	**48**	**47**

On the Adaptive scales, scores below 30 are considered significantly low.

Adaptability	61	61
Social Skills	66	57
Adaptive Skills Composite	**65**	**60**

Behavior Assessment System For Children—Teacher Rating Scale (BASC-TRS)

The BASC-TRS is a questionnaire completed by teachers rating adaptive skills and behavioral and emotional problems of students. The BASC-TRS yields T scores with a mean of 50 and an SD of 10. Scores above 70 are considered to be indicative of significant problems.

Domain	*T* scores
Hyperactivity	83
Aggression	57
Conduct Problems	50
Externalizing Problems composite	**71**
Anxiety	50
Depression	45
Somatization	43
Internalizing Problems composite	**45**
Attention Problems	78
Atypicality	74
Withdrawal	41
Behavioral Symptoms Index	**69**

On the Adaptive scales, scores below 30 are considered significantly low.

Adaptability	44
Social Skills	42
Adaptive Skills composite	**42**

Developmental Test Of Visual–Motor Integration (VMI)

The VMI is a developmental sequence of geometric figures that requires the child to copy each design exactly as it appears. The VMI measures how effectively the child can integrate and reproduce what he or she sees, using fine motor skills. The VMI yields a standard score with a mean of 100 and an *SD* of 15. Scores of 85– 115 are considered to be within the average range and reflect 68% of the general population.

Standard score	66
Percentile	1

Structured Interview for the Diagnostic Assessment of Children (SIDAC)

The SIDAC consists of a list of questions to which parents and teachers answer yes or no to indicate the presence of symptoms relating to DSM-IV diagnosis.

Only the questions relating to attention-deficit/hyperactivity disorder were administered. According to the DSM-IV, the criteria for determining a significant problem are six symptoms positively endorsed in the category of inattention and/or six symptoms positively endorsed in the combined categories of impulsivity/hyperactivity.

DSM-IV Items Endorsed		
Domain	Mother	Teacher
Inattention	6	9
Impulsivity	1	6
Hyperactivity	5	1

Achenbach Child Behavior Checklist—Parent Form (CBCL)

The Achenbach CBCL is a questionnaire completed by parents regarding the behavioral and emotional problems of their children. The CBCL yields T scores with a mean of 50 and an SD of 10. Scores of 67–70 are considered borderline significant; a score above 70 is indicative of significant problems.

T scores		
Domain	Mother	Father
Withdrawn	50	50
Somatic Complaints	61	56
Anxious/Depressed	50	50
Social Problems	50	50
Thought Problems	50	50
Attention Problems	54	56
Delinquent Behavior	50	50
Aggressive Behavior	50	50
Internalizing composite	49	40
Externalizing composite	47	46
Total composite score	**49**	**48**

Achenbach Teacher Report Form (TRF)

The TRF is a questionnaire completed by teachers regarding the behavioral and emotional problems of students. The TRF yields T scores with a mean of 50 and an SD of 10. Scores of 64–70 are considered to be borderline significant. A score above 70 is clinically significant.

Domain	*T* scores
Withdrawn	50
Somatic Complaints	50
Anxious/Depressed	55
Social Problems	65
Thought Problems	58
Attention Problems	84
Delinquent Behavior	57
Aggressive Behavior	66
Internalizing composite	51
Externalizing composite	64
Total composite score	**68**

Conners' Parent Rating Scale—Revised (CPRS-R)

The CPRS-R is a widely used rating scale using five factors that can help identify behavioral problems in children and adolescents. The most highly loaded symptoms from the factor scales yield the Conners' Hyperactivity Index.

The CPRS-R yields *T* scores with a mean of 50 and an *SD* of 10. Scores of 56–60 are considered borderline. Scores of 61–65 are considered to represent possible significant problems. Scores of 66 and above are considered to represent significant problems.

	T scores	
Domain	Father	Mother
Oppositional	44	44
Cognitive Problems/Inattention	67	60
Hyperactivity	65	48
Anxious–Shy	43	41
Perfectionism	40	39
Social Problems	64	46
Psychosomatic	50	55
Conners' ADHD Index	68	54
Conners' Global Index: Restless—Impulsive	65	58
Conners' Global Index: Emotional Lability	44	44

(continued)

Domain	Father	Mother
Conners' Global Index: Total	59	54
DSM-IV Inattentive	59	53
DSM-IV Hyperactive—Impulsive	61	53
DSM-IV Total	61	49

The next case, Darin, exemplifies the process of identifying individuals with low general cognitive ability who have a higher risk for psychopathology (Pearson & Amman, 1994; AAMR, 1992). Darin's risk status is expressed via the indication of significant attention problems in the absence of hyperactivity. The full report of his findings follows.

UNIVERSITY CHILD GUIDANCE CLINIC
PSYCHOLOGICAL EVALUATION

Name: Darin   *Grade*: Kindergarten
Age: 7 years   *Gender*: Male

Assessment Procedures

> Wechsler Intelligence Scale for Children—Third Edition (WISC-III)
> Kaufman Brief Intelligence Test (K-BIT)
> Woodcock–Johnson Test of Achievement—Revised (WJ-R)
> Peabody Picture Vocabulary Test—Third Edition (PPVT-III)
> Scales of Independent Behavior—Revised (SIB-R)
> Behavior Assessment System for Children (BASC):
>
>> Parent Rating Scales (PRS)
>> Teacher Rating Scales (TRS)
>> Structured Development History (SDH)
>
> Interview: Mother, Teacher, and Child

Reason for Referral and Background Information

Darin, a 7-year, 4-month-old kindergartner, was initially evaluated because of persistent concerns regarding his inability to master basic letter and number skills, his lack of concentration, and increased active behavior. At that time, he was referred by his mother. The goal of this 1-year reevaluation is to assess Darin's progress with implementing the recommendations made previously and to plan future interventions.

According to Mrs. Waxman, Darin continues to demonstrate difficulty learning basic letter and number skills. She stated that his performance improves when "hands-on" activities are employed, adding that he has difficulty "paying attention" and "can't sit still."

Mrs. Waxman reported that Darin has received weekly individual tutoring since his initial evaluation. Additionally, she indicated that his current kindergarten teacher works with him regularly on a one-on-one basis. Mrs. Waxman also stated that Darin has continued to receive speech therapy.

Darin currently resides with his parents and 14-year-old brother. Mr. and Mrs. Waxman are employed, and Mrs. Waxman provides primary care for the children during after-school hours. Darin currently attends a kindergarten classroom in a public elementary school.

Darin's mother reported that she experienced academic difficulties during her school years and received education services from second through seventh grades. She stated that she had difficulty reading and often "mixed up letters and numbers." Darin's maternal grandmother confirmed this information. Mrs. Waxman also reported that her husband experienced academic challenges while in school and sometimes still has difficulty reading. Additionally, Mrs. Waxman stated that Darin's older brother has received a dual diagnosis of attention-deficit/hyperactivity disorder and a reading disability.

Educational History

According to Mrs. Waxman, Darin is presently enrolled in his second year of a full-day kindergarten program. She reported that Darin attended day care beginning at age 3 and continuing through age 4. She indicated that the day care provided a structured, educational environment. She also stated that Darin was enrolled in a public prekindergarten program at age 5. She indicated that Darin does not demonstrate any awareness that he is not achieving at the same level as his peers.

Darin's kindergarten teacher, Mrs. Ehrhardt, reported that he is experiencing difficulties in several areas. She stated that he "is functioning on the bottom level of my class in reading, competing with 5-year-olds." Darin can add and subtract, but he "struggles with patterning and other higher level tasks" and "learns best with frequent rote memorization." However, she added that his "skill mastery is inconsistent." Darin "appears to learn best when using manipulatives" and is successful at memory games that include a visual cue. Further, Darin has difficulty "completing work due to distractions" and he "requires keying back constantly." She added that he "has difficulty following oral directions concerning games or assignments, but after viewing other students, is able to copy them." Mrs. Ehrhardt expressed that "Darin often appears unaware or concerned that he is not on the same level with others" (an observation also made by his mother). She added that he "rarely asks for help, would prefer to sit quietly rather than ask, has never refused to work, and is always totally cooperative."

Social and Developmental History

A Structured Developmental History was completed as part of the parent interview in April 1998 to elicit additional information about areas of concern for Darin. Mrs. Waxman reported that Darin was born 2 or 3 weeks early, following an uncomplicated pregnancy and normal delivery. At birth, Darin weighed 6 pounds, 12 ounces. Most subsequent developmental milestones were reportedly achieved within expected age limits. However, Darin received a diagnosis of enuresis and encopresis in April 1998. At the time of this reevaluation (March, 1999), these difficulties had been remediated for approximately 1 month. A physical examination revealed that Darin has a light heart murmur. Available medical history did not reveal instances of serious illness or injury. Routine hearing and vision screening completed in August 1997 did not reveal significant impairment.

Mrs. Waxman reported that Darin has been enrolled in speech therapy since September 1997 to remediate a severe articulation disorder and a mild language disorder. Darin's speech therapist, Mrs. Niekamp, reported that his speech is characterized by many substitutions and omissions of sounds. She stated that his language weakness is the result of poor grammar skills and that his vocabulary and pragmatics were judged to be within normal limits.

Test Behavior and General Observations

For the purpose of this reevaluation, Darin was evaluated over a period of 1 day at the University of Georgia School Psychology Clinic. He attended the clinic with his mother, father, and brother. Darin willingly accompanied the examiner to the testing room, was responsive to the examiner's attention but was initially tentative to engage in conversation. As the test proceeded, he increasingly engaged in conversation, and rapport was established. Darin had a pleasant disposition, smiling and laughing easily. He was cooperative and worked diligently throughout the assessment, though he had to be consistently redirected. When items became challenging to him, he would turn his back to the examiner and face the wall. He would also gaze at the ceiling, out the window, or put his head down on his crossed arms. He often whispered to himself while attempting to solve a problem. Due to Darin's possible lack of attention, it is difficult to determine whether his test results are a valid measure of his ability.

Test Results and Interpretations

Intelligence

Cognitive ability was assessed using different instruments. On the first, the Wechsler Intelligence Scale for Children—Third Edition (WISC-III), Darin achieved scores in the moderately below-average to significantly below-average range. Specifically, he obtained a Full Scale IQ of 69, which is comprised of a Verbal IQ of 70 and a Performance IQ of 73. Darin performed fairly consistently throughout this administration of the WISC-III. He demonstrated a relative strength on the Object Assembly subtest and seemed to perform better on tasks requiring spatial ability. Overall, Darin's performance on this administration of the WISC-III was equal to, or exceeded, that of about 2% of the individuals in his age range. There is a 90% chance that his "true" Full Scale score is included in the 66–75 range. (A psychometric summary of scores is included at the end of this report.)

The Kaufman Brief Intelligence Test (K-BIT) was administered as a second and comparative measure of intellectual ability. On this administration, Darin achieved a score of 65 on the Vocabulary scale and a score of 58 on the Matrices scale. The scores on these scales combined to yield a composite score of 58. Darin's performance on his administration of the K-BIT was equal to, or exceeded, that of about 0.3% of individuals in his age range. Darin performed consistently throughout this administration of the K-BIT. His scores were in the significantly below-average range.

Overall, these two measures of intellectual ability indicate that Darin is currently functioning at a level that is moderately to significantly below average. He appears to have well-developed spatial skills compared to his skills on tasks that require verbal and language ability. However, it should be emphasized that comparative strengths are relative to his own performance, and the scores attained on all subtests were in the moderately to significantly below-average range.

Achievement

In order to assess achievement capabilities, the Broad Reading and Broad Mathematics scales of the Woodcock–Johnson Test of Achievement—Revised (WJ-R) were administered. Darin yielded scores in the average to moderately below-average range. On this administration, Darin achieved a score of 74 on the Broad Reading scale and a score of 86 on the Broad Mathematics scale. These scores are slightly elevated in comparison to Darin's scores on the intelligence measures. However, they indicate that Darin is reading at a level that is moderately below average, compared with children in his age range. His scores on the Broad Mathematics scale indicate that he is performing math skills at a level that is average, compared with children in his age range. The results of this measure are consistent with reports made by Darin's teacher regarding his performance in school, and with results on the Scales of Independent Behavior—Revised (SIR-R) to be discussed in an upcoming section.

The Peabody Picture Vocabulary Test—Third Edition (PPVT-III) was administered to assess Darin's receptive (hearing) vocabulary skills. On this test, Darin achieved a score of 71, which is in the moderately below-average range. His performance was equal to, or exceeded, that of about 3% of individuals in his age range.

Overall, these measures of achievement indicated that Darin is currently functioning at a level that is moderately below average in reading and average in math. These reports are consistent with reports made by Darin's teacher regarding his school performance.

Behavioral and Social–Emotional Functioning

PARENT REPORT

An interview with Mrs. Waxman revealed continued concern regarding Darin's mastery of basic skills and his ongoing difficulty with focusing his attention. Although these problems are reportedly interfering with his academic functioning, they are not creating behavioral problems in the home setting.

Behavioral ratings were obtained from Mrs. Waxman using the Behavior Assessment System for Children—Parent Rating Scales (BASC-PRS). On this measure, Mrs. Waxman indicated that Darin's internalizing and externalizing behaviors are within normal limits. However, her scores on the Hyperactivity scale and the Attention Problems scale indicated that Darin may be experiencing some problems in these areas. Her ratings of Darin's Adaptive Skills, including Social Skills and Leadership, were in the average range.

Behavioral ratings using the BASC-PRS were obtained from Mr. Waxman, who indicated that Darin's internalizing and externalizing behaviors are within normal limits. However, Mr. Waxman's scores on the Attention Problems scale indicate that Darin may be experiencing some problems in this area, as Mrs. Waxman's scores also indicate. His ratings of Darin's Adaptive Skills were in the average range, like his wife's.

The Scales of Independent Behavior—Revised (SIB-R) were administered to assess Darin's ability to perform the daily activities required for personal and social sufficiency. The SIB-R measures motor skills, social interaction and communication skills, personal living skills, and community living skills. This administration of the SIB-R yielded a Broad Independence composite of 95, which indicates that Darin's adaptive skills met or exceeded 36% of individuals in his age range. This score is in the average range for Darin's chronological age.

TEACHER REPORT

Darin's kindergarten teacher, Mrs. Ehrhardt, submitted a letter specifying the difficulties Darin was experiencing in school. The difficulties she described were consistent with those indicated by Mrs. Waxman and included learning difficulties, inconsistent performance, and difficulty maintaining attention.

Behavioral ratings were obtained from Mrs. Ehrhardt using the Behavior Assessment System for Children—Teacher Rating Scales (BASC-TRS). On this instrument, Mrs. Ehrhardt rated Darin as having clinically significant elevations on the Attention Problems scale, the Learning Problems scale, and the School Problems Composite. Additionally, her ratings of Darin indicated some evidence of withdrawal.

Overall, these behavioral and social–emotional measures indicate that Darin is experiencing attention problems, learning problems, and withdrawal in the school environment. Mr. and Mrs. Waxman's ratings indicate that Darin is also experiencing difficulties with attention at home, and Mrs. Waxman's ratings suggest that Darin may be experiencing difficulties with hyperactivity at home. Finally, these measures indicate that Darin's adaptive skills are in the average range for individuals his age.

SPEECH PATHOLOGIST

Behavioral ratings were obtained from Ms. Niekamp, using the BASC-TRS. She rated Darin as experiencing some difficulty with attention; her ratings on the remaining scales were within normal limits.

Summary

Darin Waxman is a 7-year, 4-month-old boy who was referred for an evaluation of potential areas of learning difficulty. Persistent difficulties with mastery of basic letter and number skills, as well as difficulty maintaining attention, were specific areas of concern.

Assessment of general intellectual ability indicates that Darin is currently functioning in the moderately below-average to significantly below-average range. Additionally, Darin's performance on an academic achievement measure yielded scores in the average to moderately below-average range. His performance on the academic achievement measure was slightly elevated compared to his performance on intelligence measures. However, both intelligence measures and academic achievement measures indicate that Darin is functioning at a level that is below average compared to children in his age range. Darin's performance on adaptive measures were within normal limits. Behavioral and social–emotional measures indicate that Darin is experiencing difficulties with learning, attention, and withdrawal in the school environment. Additionally, these measures indicate that he is experiencing difficulties with hyperactivity and attention at home.

Diagnosis

Axis I: 314.00 Attention-deficit/hyperactivity disorder, predominantly inattentive type
Axis II: V71.09 Borderline intellectual functioning
Axis III: None
Axis IV: Educational problems
Axis V: GAF = 50 (current)

Recommendations

1. Darin requires school-based interventions to address his learning and attention difficulties. Darin's parents are advised to explore and consider the variety of services that may be available to them and Darin, to begin in September 1999.
2. Darin's parents may wish to share the results of this evaluation with Darin's teacher and his speech therapist to aid in his educational planning.

3. Darin should continue speech therapy, as advised by his therapist, for remediation of articulation and language disorders.
4. Darin may benefit from continued individual tutoring to promote attainment of basic skills. Integration of the following strategies may be beneficial to Darin's attainment of these skills.
5. Call on Darin when he is most likely to be able to respond successfully and reward him enthusiastically.
6. Darin may benefit from some of the following strategies to help increase his memory:
   - Encourage him to question any directions, explanations, and instructions he does not understand. Reinforce his efforts by assisting, congratulating, and praising him.
   - Ask him to paraphrase directions, explanations, and instructions soon after hearing them.
   - Use simple, concise sentences to convey information to him.
   - Ask him to serve as a classroom messenger. Give him a verbal message to deliver to another student, a teacher, etc. As he demonstrates success, increase the length of the messages.
   - Review the schedule of the morning and afternoon activities with him and have him repeat the sequence. Increase the length of the sequence when Darin is successful.
   - Instruct him to engage in game activities that require concentration, beginning with games that use a limited number of symbols and gradually increasing the number of symbols as he demonstrates success.
   - At the end of the school day, ask him to recall three activities in which he engaged during the day. Gradually increase the number of activities Darin is asked to recall as he demonstrates success.
   - After a field trip or special event, ask him to recall the sequence in which the activities occurred.
   - After reading a short story, ask him to identify the main characters, the sequence of events, and report the outcome of the story.
   - When reading a story to him, on occasion stop to ask questions about the plot, main characters, events in the story, etc.
   - Provide visual cues when giving Darin auditory instruction.
   - Use multiple modalities (e.g., auditory, visual, tactile, etc.) when presenting directions, explanations, and instructional content.
   - Assign a peer tutor to engage in short-term memory activities with him (e.g., concentration games, following directions, etc.).

- Ask him to practice repeating information to increase his short-term memory skills (repeating names, telephone numbers, dates of events).
- Teach him to learn sequences and lists of information in segments (e.g., telephone numbers are learned in clusters—706, then 542, then 8711, etc.).
- Reduce visual distractions by isolating the information that is presented to him (e.g., cover other information on the page, expose only a portion of a picture at a time, etc.).
- Tell him what to listen for before providing auditory information.
- Reward Darin for his effort and success in any of the aforementioned activities.

7. Darin may benefit from some of the following strategies to help increase his attention and concentration:
   - Follow a less desirable task with a more desirable task, making the completion of the first necessary to perform the second.
   - Give directions in a variety of ways to increase the probability of understanding (e.g., if he fails to understand verbal directions, present them in visual form).
   - Make directions as simple and concrete as possible.
   - Reduce directions to steps by giving him each additional step only after completion of the previous step.
   - Try various groupings to determine the situation in which he can concentrate most easily.
   - Reinforce him for beginning, staying on, and completing tasks.
   - Maintain physical contact with Darin while talking to him (e.g., touch his hand or shoulder).
   - Provide shorter tasks that do not require extended attention in order to be successful. Gradually increase the length of the tasks as he demonstrates success.
   - Seat Darin close to the source of information.
   - Enthusiastically reward Darin for his effort and success in any of the aforementioned tasks.

8. Play therapy may be beneficial for Darin. It would allow him an appropriate opportunity to explore and express his feelings and develop coping strategies related to his learning and attention difficulties.

Psychometric Summary

Wechsler Intelligence Scale for Children—Third Edition (WISC-III)

The WISC-III is an individually administered clinical instrument for assessing the intellectual ability of children ages 6 years–16 years, 11 months. The child's performance on 12 subtests is summarized in an overall intelligence score called the Full Scale standard score. The WISC-III also yields scores for Verbal and Performance scales. Verbal activities include defining words, answering factual as well as commonsense questions, and doing arithmetic problems without pencil and paper. Performance activities include putting together puzzles and picture sequences, making designs with blocks, and pointing out missing parts of a picture.

The following subtest scores have a mean score of 10 with an *SD* of 3; scores of 7–13 are considered average.

Subtest	Standard score	Subtest	Standard score
Information	6	Picture Completion	4
Similarities	6	Coding	2
Arithmetic	6	**Picture Arrangement**	6
Vocabulary	2	Block Design	6
Comprehension	3	Object Assembly	10
(Digit Span)	7	(Symbol Search)	5

The following composite scores have a mean of 100 with an *SD* of 15. Scores of 85–115 are considered average.

Composite score	Standard score	90% Confidence bands	Percentiles
Verbal Score	70	66–77	2
Performance Score	73	69–82	4
Full Scale score	**69**	**66–75**	**2**
Factor scores			
Verbal Comprehension	69	65–77	2
Perceptual Organization	80	75–89	9
FD (Third Factor)	81	76–91	10
Processing Speed	67	64–80	1

Kaufman Brief Intelligence Test (K-BIT)

The K-BIT is a brief, individually administered measure of verbal and nonverbal intelligence for children, adolescents, and adults ranging in age from 4 to 90 years. The individual's performance on three subtests is summarized in an overall intelligence score called the IQ Composite. The K-BIT also yields scores for Vocabulary and Matrices scales. Vocabulary test items include verbally identifying pictured items and providing a word in response to two clues. Both parts of the vocabulary subtest measure word knowledge, verbal concept formation, and fund of information. Matrices items include choosing which option goes best with a stimulus picture. The matrices subtests measure nonverbal reasoning, flexibility in problem-solving strategies, and ability to handle several variables simultaneously.

The following subtest and composite scores have a mean of 100 and an *SD* of 15. Scores of 85–115 are considered average.

Subtest	Standard score	Percentile rank
Vocabulary	65	1.0
Matrices	58	0.3
Composite	**58**	**0.3**

Woodcock–Johnson Tests of Achievement—Revised (WJ-R ACH)

The WJ-R ACH is an individually administered achievement test containing various subtests. The subtest scores are combined into composite scores: Broad Reading, Broad Mathematics, Broad Written Language, and Broad Knowledge. The WJ-R ACH yields standard scores with a mean of 100 and an *SD* of 15. Scores of 85–115 are considered average.

Domain	Standard scores	90% Confidence bands	Percentiles
Letter–Word Identification	75	72–78	5
Passage Comprehension	78	74–82	7
Broad Reading	**74**	**72–76**	**4**
Calculation	82	78–86	11
Applied Problems	99	94–104	47
Broad Mathematics	**86**	**82–90**	**18**

Peabody Picture Vocabulary Test—Third Edition (PPVT-III)

The PPVT-III is an individually administered, untimed, norm-referenced, wide-range test. Each item consists of four black-and-white illustrations arranged on a page. The child's task is to select the picture that best represents the meaning of a stimulus word presented orally by the examiner. The PPVT-III has a standard score mean of 100 and an SD of 15. Standard scores of 85–115 are considered to be average.

Standard score	Percentile
71	3

Scales of Independent Behavior—Revised (SIB-R)

The SIB-R is a measure of adaptive behavior, or the ability to perform daily activities required for personal and social sufficiency. In this version of the scale, adaptive behavior is measured in four domains: Motor Skills, Social Interaction and Communication Skills, Personal Living Skills, and Community Living Skills. The combination of these domains forms the Broad Independence Composite.

The SIB-R provides standard scores with a mean of 100 and an SD of 15. The domain scores are used to determine an overall adaptive behavior composite. Scores of 85–115 are considered average.

Domain	Standard scores	90% Confidence bands	Percentiles
Motor Skills	106	101–111	65
Social Interaction and Communication Skills	91	86–96	27
Personal Living Skills	88	84–92	21
Community Living Skills	96	92–100	40
Broad Independence composite	**95**	**93–97**	**36**

Behavior Assessment System for Children—Parent Rating Scales (BASC-PRS)

The BASC-PRS is a questionnaire that is filled out by parents in order to assess the behavioral problems, emotional difficulties, and social competencies of their children. The BASC-PRS subscales and composites yield T scores with a mean of 50 and an SD of 10. On the Clinical scales, scores of 65–70 are indicative of some difficulty; scores above 70 are considered significant problems. On the Adaptive scales, scores below 30 are considered significantly low.

Domain	T scores (mother)	T scores (father)
Clinical scales		
Hyperactivity	68	49
Aggression	42	42
Conduct Problems	41	41
Externalizing Problems composite	**50**	**43**
Anxiety	38	34
Depression	43	36
Somatization	41	39
Internalizing Problems composite	**38**	**32**
Atypicality	45	40
Withdrawal	57	57
Attention Problems	66	61
Behavioral Symptoms Index	**51**	**41**
Adaptive skills		
Adaptability	53	36
Social Skills	49	45
Leadership	48	50
Adaptive Skills composite	**50**	**43**

Behavior Assessment System for Children—Teacher Rating Scales (BASC-TRS)

The BASC-TRS is a questionnaire completed by teachers rating adaptive skills and behavioral and emotional problems of students. The BASC-TRS yields T scores with a mean of 50 and an SD of 10. On the Clinical scales, scores of 60 and 70 indicate some difficulty; scores above 70 are considered significantly high. On the Adaptive scales, scores below 30 are considered significantly low.

Domain	T scores (teacher)	T scores (speech pathologist)
Clinical Scales		
Hyperactivity	46	46
Aggression	41	41
Conduct Problems	47	43
Externalizing Problems composite	**44**	**43**
Anxiety	45	41
Depression	46	43
Somatization	55	42
Internalizing Problems composite	**48**	**40**
Attention Problems	71	60
Learning Problems	72	Unscorable
School Problems composite	**72**	**Unscorable**
Atypicality	49	47
Withdrawal	67	55
Behavioral Symptoms Index	**50**	**45**
Adaptive skills		
Adaptability	65	65
Social Skills	43	36
Leadership	40	Unscorable
Study Skills	42	Unscorable
Adaptive Skills composite	**47**	**Unscorable**

PSYCHOLOGICAL EVALUATION (CONFIDENTIAL)

Subject: DeShayne M
DOB: 8/13/87
Exam Date: 12/15/98
Chronological Age: 11 years 4 months
Date of Report: 11/18/98
Examiner: M. Markus, PhD

Tests and Procedures

Clinical Interview
Mental Status Exam
Wechsler Intelligence Scale for Children—Third Edition
Wide Range Achievement Test–3
Bender Visual–Motor Gestalt Test
Trail Making Test, Parts A and B
Clock Drawing Test
Controlled Oral Word Association Test
Test of Memory and Learning (verbal subtests only)
Human Figure Drawing
Kinetic Family Drawing
Revised Children's Manifest Anxiety Scale
BASC: Structured Developmental History
BASC: Parent Rating Scale—Child
BASC: Self-Report of Personality—Child
Collateral Interview with Mother

Background Information and Reason for Referral

DeShayne was referred for psychological evaluation by her mother, who complained that DeShayne has poor working habits at school, does not listen at home or school, does not behave, and seems to care about nothing in her life. The mother wants to know, in more detail, what is "wrong" with DeShayne and to obtain treatment, if indicated.

History and Development

DeShayne currently resides with her mother, a 14-year-old brother, and the mother's fiancé. DeShayne's mother stated that the father is a crack addict and that she divorced him in 1993. He has not visited DeShayne in the past year. The mother reported that DeShayne had a very close relationship with her father and cried a lot when he first separated from the family in 1991. The maternal grandparents are deceased. The father's current location is unknown, and he provides no financial or emotional support.

DeShayne is reported to participate in family relationships and to get along appropriately with her brother. The mother finds spending time with DeShayne and teaching her to cook the most enjoyable aspects of rearing her but complains about her lack of listening, poor attention span, and talking back. The mother has extremely high aspirations for DeShayne, wanting her to become a doctor or lawyer. The mother is in charge of discipline in the home and employs spanking, lecturing, and removal of privileges.

The mother reported a relatively uneventful pregnancy, with the exception of abnormal weight gain, hypertension, and the use of beer and amphetamines during the pregnancy. DeShayne was born via C-section to a 25-year-old mother, subsequent to a full-term pregnancy. Mild jaundice was evident, and both mother and child were kept in the hospital for 7 days. The mother could not recall developmental milestones. However, she did report some problems with toilet training, and bedwetting occurred until the age of 8. At 3 months, the mother reports that DeShayne's eyes would oscillate in a pendulum-like fashion, and up until the age of 3 to 4 years, occasionally she would pass out and fall on the floor. When older, she began to describe feeling sensitive to light before she would pass out. She would awaken with headache and nausea. She was evaluated by a local pediatric neurologist, who diagnosed her as having postural hypotension with migraines. She has had no episodes for the past 3 years. She takes no medication for these difficulties but does take Hismanil to control allergies. No special problems were noted in the early years, other than colic and some difficulties with feeding. She has had no childhood illnesses but does have hay fever, sinus problems, reflux, excessive urination, and the other problems, as noted above. She is being followed by Dr. Sanborn for these problems. The mother noted that DeShayne complains of all kinds of physical pains and that she "has always been that way." The mother appears to pamper her daughter in response to these complaints.

DeShayne has a history of extensive ear infections and a current vision problem, requiring glasses. She has never undergone psychological or psychiatric testing or therapy. Family health history is positive for cancer, hypertension, cardiovascular disease, "nervousness," and drug abuse. DeShayne has no special difficulties relating to, or playing with, other children, but is reported to have a short attention span, lack self-control, seem unhappy most of the time, hide her feelings, overreact to problems, be uncomfortable meeting new people, and require an extraordinary amount of parental attention. Adaptive behavior is developing appropriately for age. She has some difficulty with reading and math and receives poor grades, but she has never been evaluated for special education.

Observations, Test Behaviors, and Interview

DeShayne was brought to the evaluation session by her mother. She is tall, relative to age, and her weight is proportionate to her height. She was dressed appropriately in a sports jersey with jeans and tennis shoes and spoke freely and easily with the examiner. She was oriented appropriately for her age. Speech was soft but basically within normal limits for rate, volume, and articulation. She showed no flight of ideas, disorganized speech, or pressured speech. Her mood was sad and her affect labile in conversation. Thought was appropriate in content and processing. Language appears to be mildly delayed, relative to her other skills, and intellectual function appears to be average, but she does have difficulties with attention and concentration as well as poor judgment and little insight into her difficulties. She has no complaints regarding sleeping, eating, or other vegetative functions.

DeShayne reported that she resides with her mother, stepfather, and brother, that she gets along well with other family members, and that her mother takes very good care of her. She stated that she does have some difficulties with her mother being too controlling and telling her what to wear and other things in her life. She does not get along well with her stepfather, stating that they argue a lot and that he punishes her too much. She is quite sad about the loss of the relationship with her father; she does not know where he is and has not seen him in the past 2 to 3 years. She stated that she really misses him and does not know why he does not contact her. At this point in the interview, DeShayne began to cry softly and said that she thinks about her father a lot, misses him, and would really like to see him .

DeShayne was noted to be quite distractible and mildly impulsive during the evaluation . Nevertheless, she wanted to do well and interacted appropriately with the examiner at all times. Her efforts and cooperation indicated that her performance has provided valid indications of her current levels of cognitive and affective function.

Test Results and Interpretation

Assessment with the Wechsler Intelligence Scale for Children—Third Edition (WISC-3) indicated a Verbal IQ of 83, a Performance IQ of 107 and a Full Scale IQ of 93. On the WISC-3, this level of performance falls within the average range of skills, exceeding 32% of children at her age. The 24-point discrepancy between the Verbal and Performance IQs is quite significant, however, indicating that her verbal skills (including language development, verbal reasoning, and verbal memory) are in the low-average range at about the 13th percentile, while her performance or nonverbal reasoning and spatial abilities falls in the average range, exceeding 68% of children at her age. Her performance was highly consistent within these two areas of function, with the exception of a weakness in the area of verbal reasoning. Assessment of verbal

172

memory, using the Test of Memory and Learning, indicated significant verbal memory deficits, particularly on those tasks that are most attention-dependent. When given clear associations and meaningful stimuli to recall, DeShayne performed at an average level. On rote recall tasks that require intensive attention and concentration, she performed at a level below her low-average Verbal IQ.

Assessment of basic academic skills in reading and writing indicated standard scores that are commensurate with her current levels of intellectual functioning. She earned a standard score of 90 in reading and 101 in arithmetic.

On measures of neuropsychological functioning, numerous minor errors were noted. She tends to perform more poorly on neuropsychological measures that require verbal and other language-related functions. For example, her performance was within the normal range on Trail Making, Part A, but was notably impaired on Part B, which involves language. Her responses on the Controlled Oral Word Association Test showed substantial problems with language fluency as well, and she performed extremely poorly, relative to her age mates. A very mild constructional dyspraxia was seen, and her Clock Drawing Test was relatively poorly executed.

In addition to these neuropsychological deficits, a variety of affective and behavioral difficulties were observed. Her projective tests were replete with indications of anxiety. On an objective measure of anxiety, DeShayne's score suggests that she attempted to present herself in an extremely positive light, reporting no anxiety or any other distressing symptoms and responding in an extremely socially desirable pattern. On the more broadly based Self-Report of Personality, her score again indicated denial of any form of anxiety. She seems to use repression as a defense mechanism, which is likely responsible for her numerous somatic complaints. Despite her attempt to present herself in as positive a light as possible, she gave clear indications of the presence of significant depressive symptomatology. One of her highest scores was on the attention problems scale. The behavior rating scale completed by the mother indicated substantial problems with aggressive behavior as well as conduct-related problems. DeShayne has more somatic complaints than 99.9% of girls her age and fewer skills in adaptability and leadership than 99% of children her age. Some disturbances in the mother–child relationship are also evident.

DeShayne presented with a comprehensive and complex set of symptoms that is consistent with the presence of multiple psychiatric disturbances that will require the coordination of treatment between a knowledgeable child psychotherapist and the current family physician. DeShayne meets the diagnostic criteria for the presence of attention-deficit/hyperactivity disorder, primarily inattentive type; a major depressive disorder; and a somatization disorder. This particular complexity of this constellation of symptoms will necessitate, almost certainly, psychopharmacological intervention if it is medically safe for her at this time. The family physician should be consulted regarding the implementation of psychopharmacotherapy with an antidepressant, if medically appropriate. If the antidepressant is ineffective in assisting with DeShayne's behavioral and mood control, then the psychostimulants might be considered; however, these decisions will need to be made by the family physician. Individual psychotherapy is almost certainly warranted, and the family has been referred to Maria Evans as an appropriately experienced and licensed child therapist. The mother reports that an appointment has been set at this time.

DeShayne has many difficulties related to the abandonment by the father as well as her use of repression as a defense mechanism and the conflicts within the family. These areas, as well as her significant conduct problems, need to be a focus of therapy. Although she does not qualify for a diagnosis of conduct disorder at this time, she is certainly developing in that general direction. It is perhaps optimistic that she has developed the level of depression that is currently seen, which makes it more likely that her behavior will improve once her emotional symptoms are brought under control. A fairly lengthy period of individual psychotherapy should be anticipated.

DeShayne exhibits characteristics that are commonly associated with a specific learning disability (attention problems, Verbal IQ significantly lower than Performance IQ). However, despite some problems with grades, basic achievement skills are intact relative to intellectual level, and there are no problems that would necessitate substantial changes in her school placement; however, a variety of accommodations for her attention-deficit/hyperactivity disorder may be appropriate through the schools and her disorder should be considered in any disciplinary plans put forth by the school. This report should be shared with the school's Section 504 coordinator and appropriate accommodations developed at school in consultation with the school psychologist.

DeShayne's DSM-IV diagnosis is as follows:

Axis I: 314.00 Attention-deficit/hyperactivity disorder, primarily inattentive type
316.22 Major depressive disorder, single episode, moderate
300.81 Somatization disorder
Axis II: No diagnosis

Axis III: Postural hypotension with concurrent migraine, by history, in full remission

Axis IV: Moderate, problems with primary support group, conflicts with mother, divorce, abandonment by father

Axis V: Global Assessment of Functioning
Current: 51
Best in last 12 months: 61

M. Markus, PhD
Psychologist

Additional Psychometric Summary

Revised Children's Manifest Anxiety Scale T Scores

Total Anxiety	$T = 40$
Physiological Scale	$T = 53$
Worry/Oversensitivity	$T = 35$
Social Concerns	$T = 36$
Lie Scale	$T = 71$

BASC: Self-Report of Personality T Scores, General Norms

CLINICAL SCALES

Attitude to School	$T = 42$
Attitude to Teacher	$T = 53$
Atypicality	$T = 46$
Locus of Control	$T = 59$
Social Stress	$T = 54$
Anxiety	$T = 57$
Depression	$T = 61$

ADAPTIVE SCALES

Relations with Parents	$T = 39$
Interpersonal Relations	$T = 53$
Self-Esteem	$T = 57$
Self-Reliance	$T = 51$

BASC: Parent Rating Scale T Scores, General Norms

CLINICAL SCALES

Hyperactivity	$T = 52$
Aggression	$T = 85$
Conduct Problems	$T = 98$
Anxiety	$T = 57$
Depression	$T = 46$
Somatization	$T = 91$
Atypicality	$T = 59$
Withdrawal	$T = 69$
Attention Problems	$T = 84$

ADAPTIVE SCALES

Adaptability	$T = 19$
Social Skills	$T = 34$
Leadership	$T = 28$

BASC FORUM: A RESOURCE FOR PROFESSIONALS

BASCforum.com is an online discussion center where members can observe or participate in conversations regarding use of the BASC and other issues relating to psychological practice. Additional resources and information regarding the BASC and BASC ADHD Monitor are also available at this web site.

The BASC Forum is designed to be a resource for qualified professionals to exchange ideas and information, locate research, and ask questions. Initially started to support users of the BASC and BASC ADHD Monitor, the central discussion center has evolved into a forum where members can discuss issues they face in their daily practice. Membership is free of charge, but users must be certified psychologists or psychiatrists, or graduate students in these fields, to participate.

The BASC Forum has several goals:

- To provide a resource where professionals can discuss their work with colleagues from around the world
- To answer questions and offer support for users of the BASC and BASC ADHD Monitor
- To provide members a comprehensive library of research involving the BASC

- To give BASC users a site where they can ask questions of, and receive information from, the authors and developers of the BASC

Resources found on the BASC Forum include the central discussion center, an extensive research bibliography for the BASC and BASC ADHD Monitor, frequently-asked questions regarding these assessments, client profiles, and an Ask the Authors option where posted questions are answered by Drs. Cecil Reynolds and Randy Kamphaus. Topics of discussion range from "conduct disorder versus emotional handicap" to "unusual scores with the WJ-III" to "Asperger's and central auditory processing."

The forum is monitored to ensure that postings maintain a professional tone and focus, but postings are not edited or approved by the host web site, operated by AGS. The forum moderator is Dr. Mark Daniel, Director of Product Development for AGS.

History of the BASC Forum

The BASC Forum was released for beta testing in May 2000. It was introduced to the psychological community at the annual convention of the American Psychological Association held August 4–8, 2000, in Washington, DC. The response was immediate. By the end of September, there were more than 400 regular users visiting the site.

Since its introduction, the forum has continued to change and evolve. New discussion groups, such as the Clinicians' Corner, have been added in response to user requests. The Ask the Authors section allows members to post specific questions about using and interpreting the BASC and BASC ADHD Monitor. Drs. Kamphaus and Reynolds reply to questions posted at this site within 7–10 working days. Their answers are made available to all forum members. The forum accepts bibliographical entries and case studies for posting on the site. Other changes may be requested for consideration by the site administrators.

At the time of this publication, the BASC Forum had more than 1,000 registered members.

Participation in the BASC Forum

To visit the BASC Forum, use the URL *http://www.bascforum.com/*. Any site visitor may view general information, including the research bibliography, frequently-asked questions, and biographical information about the BASC authors. To gain access to the discussion center, users must register at the site. There is no charge for participation in any area of the BASC Forum.

From the BASC Forum home page, click on "Discussion Center Login." The login page has an option for new users to fill out a registration form online. In order to maintain the high level of professionalism in the discussion center, all members are asked to provide information regarding their certification, license types, and professional affiliations. Graduate students in psychology may also register at the site. New members receive verification and password information via e-mail within 3–5 business days of submitting their registration requests.

Membership in the BASC Forum is free of charge. The site is designed to be easy to navigate and load with any standard of Internet connection. For more information about the BASC Forum or for assistance with registration, contact AGS at 1-800-328-2560.

CHAPTER 5

Clinical Profiles
and Validation Research

Clinical findings for special populations are sometimes of dubious value. Such profiles are based on the often questioned assumption that existing diagnostic systems possess adequate validity (Kamphaus & Frick, 2002). At best, classification schemes have been useful for describing the behavior of a small number of children with the most deviant behavior problems by use of the DSM-IV (American Psychiatric Association, 1994) or the classification of "emotional disturbance" included in the Individuals with Disabilities Education Act (IDEA; Public Law 105-17; latest regulations are published in the Federal Register, 64(121), June 24, 1999). While the DSM system and many of its diagnoses are not supported by large numbers of validity studies, the IDEA classification of emotional disturbance is even less substantiated (Kamphaus & Frick, 2002).

The critiques of categorical-based diagnostic systems are legion, but a few well documented problems are of particular concern. For example, children who are just beneath the diagnostic threshold for some DSM-IV diagnoses (e.g., ADHD) are nevertheless significantly functionally impaired (Scahill et al., 1999). Specifically, they have difficulty adjusting in school and home settings. Children who exhibit significant functional impairment but do not meet diagnostic standards have been labeled "subsyndromal" by Cantwell (1996).

In addition, categorically based diagnostic systems assume that many child problems (symptoms, from a medical model view) are not continuously distributed in the population. This premise is likely false. Numerous recent studies using latent-class analytical techniques have shown that behavior problems that comprise the core diagnostic symptoms of ADHD, depression, and conduct disorder are distributed continuously, not categorically, among children (Hudziak et al., 1998; Hudziak, Wadsworth, Heath, & Achenbach, 1999; Neuman et al., 1999). In effect, then, the DSM and other systems create cut scores for continuous distributions that may not demarcate substantial differences in quality of life. A similar situation would occur in the case of mental retardation if rigid cut scores were used. It would be inappropriate, for example, to say that children with composite IQs of 70 function at a very different cognitive level than children with scores of either 68 or 72. Many behavioral problems seem to be distributed like IQ scores, with the exception that the distributions are skewed. Hence, a child who is one or two symptoms short of a conduct disorder or depression diagnosis may also exhibit significant behavioral problems in need of treatment, just as the child with the 75 IQ will likely need specialized interventions or modifications as well. Only considerable additional research devoted to the validity of cut scores will reveal the utility of categorical diagnoses for behavioral problems. Until such time, the assumption that children's behavioral problems are categorically organized appears to be highly questionable.

We provide these brief caveats regarding categorical diagnoses so as to caution the reader against interpreting this chapter as either an endorsement of such systems or as an argument that profiles for clinical samples have particular utility for making diagnostic or treatment decisions. On the contrary, we think that the BASC scales are best conceptualized as continuously scaled measures of psychological constructs that are supported, in many cases, by decades of research investigating constructs such as depression, conduct problems, and anxiety. BASC results indicate the *presence* and *severity* of problems that are also measured by the DSM or other systems that use the constructs of *depression, anxiety, hyperactivity,* and *inattention*. Therefore, because the BASC results do not indicate the presence or absence of a DSM disorder, per se, comparisons of profiles to clinical populations are of limited value. We also do not reify either the BASC results or the DSM criteria when conceptualizing cases. Both of these traditions—the psychometric and the categorical—are somewhat orthogonal, and the relationship among the two requires further research.

We find that it is also difficult to generalize profile information to the individual case. Individual children may have results that are quite different from the BASC profile for ADHD, for example, and yet have ADHD. Lewin

(1931) aptly noted, long ago, the problems of generalizing group results to the individual:

> The concepts of average child and average environment have no utility whatso- ever for the investigation of dynamics. . . . An inference from the average to the particular case is . . . impossible. (cited in Richters, 1997, p. 199)

The same inferential problem, from the sample of children with ADHD to the individual child with ADHD, holds true: The individual child's case formulation may be quite different from that of the clinical sample.

Ponder, if you will, the question of why it is *the number* of symptoms of depression that carriers the burden of diagnosis of depression and not *the interaction* between the presence of symptoms and their relative severity. Scales such as the BASC can accommodate such interactions, but diagnostic typologies rarely can. For example, on the BASC, a child may show consistently elevated scores that fall into the clinically significant range on the Depression subscale and be identified by the severity and frequency of this narrow set of symptoms. Likewise, a child may show elevated scores only into the at-risk range but of the multiple scales still be identified by the BASC Internalizing composite, even though one subscale (such as anxiety, depression, somatization, and withdrawal) is at 70 or above. Discrete typologies cannot accommodate such children as easily as can a clinician with clear, objective, developmentally sensitive data.

We now review data for a variety of clinical populations. Special applications to traumatic brain injury and posttraumatic stress disorder populations are reviewed in Chapter 7.

When children or youth match a model or an average profile or clustering associated with carefully derived known diagnostic groups, of course the probability of the child having the syndrome in question rises considerably. However, to reiterate our crucial point, the child for whom there is no clear match to a known clinical sample may still have any one of many disorders and may still be in dire need of diagnosis and treatment.

EMOTIONAL DISTURBANCE/INDIVIDUALS WITH DISABILITIES EDUCATION ACT

The Individuals with Disabilities Education Act (IDEA), reauthorized in 1997, essentially provides a diagnostic system for use by schools that seeks to create a standard for determining if a child is eligible for special education and/or related services. According to the law and its associated regulations, "emotional disturbance" is defined as:

> (4) Emotional disturbance is defined as follows:
>> (i) The term means a condition exhibiting one or more of the following characteristics over a long period of time and to a marked degree that adversely affects a child's educational performance:
>>> (A) An inability to learn that cannot be explained by intellectual, sensory, or health factors.
>>> (B) An inability to build or maintain satisfactory interpersonal relationships with peers and teachers.
>>> (C) Inappropriate types of behavior or feelings under normal circumstances.
>>> (D) A general pervasive mood of unhappiness or depression.
>>> (E) A tendency to develop physical symptoms or fears associated with personal or school problems.
>> (ii) The term includes schizophrenia. The term does not apply to children who are socially maladjusted, unless it is determined that they have an emotional disturbance. (*Federal Register*, March 12, 1999, Section 300.7, p. 12423)

As is evident from this definition, there is considerable room for variation in its application. The definition is likely to be applied in very different ways due to differences in local and state policies and regulations, geographical differences in the epidemiology of child problems, and social/cultural factors, among others. Therefore, our advice for using the BASC as part of the special education qualification process is necessarily generic. The BASC is well suited to providing evidence of the presence, longevity, and severity of child behavioral problems, but local factors must be considered when making decisions regarding qualification for special education services. Furthermore, the BASC (or any other scale, for that matter) should not be the sole source of information used for qualification purposes, per se, especially in light of the fact that the qualification decision is mandated to be a multidisciplinary process. Our strategy for using the BASC in such work follows.

First, BASC scales may be used to identify problems that have "one or more of the following characteristics," as shown in Table 5.1. This table is not exhaustive; it merely highlights scales that may be particularly relevant. It is conceivable that many of the scales will be relevant in some cases.

The rationale for including these selected scales is that (1) they may have relevant item content, (2) they were part of a profile for a relevant clinical population (e.g., children with depression, autism, etc.), or (3) other research

TABLE 5.1. BASC Scales That May Be of Value for Documenting "Emotional Disturbance" Forms and Scales

IDEA problem area	TRS	PRS	SRP
Interpersonal relationship problems	Social Skills Aggression Withdrawal Adaptability Learning Problems	Social Skills Aggression Withdrawal Adaptability	Social Stress Interpersonal Relationships Attitude to Teachers Relations with Parents
Inappropriate behavior or feelings	Anxiety Aggression Atypicality Withdrawal Social Skills Learning Problems	Anxiety Aggression Atypicality Withdrawal Social Skills	Anxiety Atypicality, Social Stress
Unhappiness or depression	Depression Learning Problems	Depression	Depression Sense of Inadequacy
Physical symptoms or fears	Anxiety Somatization Learning Problems	Anxiety Somatization	Anxiety Somatization
Inability to learn	Any clinical scale	Any clinical scale	Any clinical scale
Schizophrenia	Atypicality Attention Problems	Atypicality Attention Problems	Atypicality
Autism and pervasive developmental disorders	Withdrawal Attention Problems	Withdrawal Attention Problems	Atypicality Sense of Inadequacy

has found the scale to be predictive of school adjustment (e.g., the Adaptability scale). The Atypicality scale is included for schizophrenia because it is often elevated in these students. It also has many other interpretations, as we have cautioned throughout this volume, and it is not exclusively indicative of psychotic disturbances (see discussion in Chapter 2).

Second, the criterion of "marked degree" is answered by the use of norm-referenced T scores. We suggest that Clinical or Adaptive scores in the at-risk range may designate an impairment of this magnitude. Scores of 60 and above on Clinical scales and 40 or below on Adaptive scales would meet this standard. These scores reflect problems that are one standard deviation from the mean and may signify the presence of a DSM-IV disorder, as was demonstrated in some studies of ADHD and other disorders common to childhood (Kamphaus & Frick, 2002). Using scores in the at-risk range also allows us room to err in the direction of including more false positives than false negatives, which is a commonly accepted practice to ensure that children who need to be served are not overlooked.

Third, the criterion of "long period of time" will require multiple BASC administrations at various time points. Typically, the BASC is used as part of a prereferral screening assessment process in schools. Consequently, if a child is followed through this process, he or she will undergo a prereferral BASC, an assessment of response to prereferral intervention BASC (TRS or PRS or both), and a BASC completed at the time of assessment to determine qualification for special education as a case of emotional disturbance. To some, this number of administrations will seem excessive, but sound statistical precedent suggests that three assessments are the minimum required to obtain a stable trend (as noted elsewhere in this volume). Information on the length of time a student has exhibited the identified behavioral and/or affective symptoms or feelings will also be obtained from sections of the SDH and should be a routine part of the clinical interview of the student and the collateral interview with the parent (using the structured format provided by the SDH). This procedure provides strong information for the initial diagnosis and placement decision regarding status as an "ED" student, and follow-up BASC rating scale and self-report data can be gathered as the clinician monitors progress and assesses the need for continued placement and treatment of a student as emotionally disturbed.

The BASC has the advantage of providing objective data on the criteria of IDEA for the ED realm. Objective data regarding behavior and emotions are always necessary, even when interview and projective data have been carefully collected. The BASC is developmentally sensitive in multiple ways (see Chapter 1), providing clear normative reference points for levels of severity across age, and it covers the full breadth of areas that qualify a student for a classification of ED.

IDEA withholds eligibility for services from students who are "socially maladjusted," unless they have another form of emotional disturbance. The purpose of this exclusion is to limit services to students who are affected by an emotional disorder that is not characterized primarily by conduct or deportment problems. The Conduct Problems scale was included in the BASC specifically to assist in this process. Students who show elevated scores on the Conduct Problems scales of the TRS and/or PRS and/or the Sensation Seeking scale of the SRP, but no other scales, most often will not qualify as ED due to their presentation as socially maladjusted or having a conduct disorder (see the current DSM for criteria) as a sole diagnosis. The Aggression scale may also show elevated scores for these students, but this result is usually insufficient to qualify them for ED services if their only other elevated scores are on the Conduct Problems or Sensation-Seeking scale.

Essentially, we are laboring with imperfect diagnostic criteria of emotional disturbance and with variable group decision-making processes. In this context, the BASC is best used to document presence, severity, and longevity of problems. These three IDEA criteria, however, are the crux of determining the presence of emotional problems that require specialized services. The "effects" of these problems of academic progress are outside the realm of the BASC, with one exception. The Learning Problems scale of the TRS serves as one indicator of the presence of learning problems, especially when considered with other academic achievement measures. The BASC also provides assistance with objective evaluation and implementation of the ED exclusionary criteria.

ATTENTION-DEFICIT/HYPERACTIVITY DISORDER

Much of the latest BASC research has focused on the assessment and diagnosis of clinical populations, such as those with attention-deficit/hyperactivity disorder(ADHD). Studies by Vaughn, Riccio, Hynd, and Hall (1997) and Doyle et al. (1997) have clarified the role that BASC parent and teacher ratings can play in the diagnosis of ADHD. Doyle et al. (1997) concluded that the BASC PRS and the CBCL were roughly equivalent for the diagnosis of ADHD, combined type. In addition, they stated a preference for using the BASC due to the rational derivation of its scales. Vaughn et al. (1997), on the other hand, found BASC PRS and TRS, and CBCL and TRF results to differ significantly for cases of ADHD, predominantly inattentive type. These authors again noted equivalence between the two systems for the diagnosis of combined type, although the authors suggest that "the CBCL may not be as accurate when diagnosing ADHD:CT children without externalizing disorders" (p. 356). Regarding the diagnosis of combined type, they concluded, "When discriminating among ADHD:PI children, however, the BASC scales are more accurate" (p. 356). Numerous research studies of the use of the BASC with clinical populations are underway by researchers who have no vested interest in supporting the BASC. These studies undoubtedly will add much to our clinical understanding of the functioning of the BASC with a variety of populations.

An interesting dissertation study by Johnson-Cramer (1998) used the SDH to make a differential diagnosis of ADHD for 9- to 12-year-old boys, with and without ADHD, who had histories of low birth weights. The sample was drawn from an original population of 704 children with low birth weight who were followed longitudinally. The researcher used the SDH, Conners' Teacher Rating Scale, and Conners' Continuous Performance Test and studied the validity of each to make the ADHD diagnosis. In order to include the SDH in analyses, she created "scales" with raw scores. She then created two composites: one comprised of the Development, Medical History, Friendships, Behavior/Temperament, Adaptive Skills, and Educational History portions of the SDH; and the other of Development, Friendships, Behavior/Temperament, and Educational History.

Correlations between SDH scales and physician diagnoses were very high, above .80, for Development, Educational History, Friendships, and Temperament. Of greater interest were the findings that the SDH was significantly related to DSM-IV diagnosis; relatively little variance was contributed by the Conners' Teacher Rating Scale; and the Conners' Continuous Performance Test contributed nothing to the prediction of ADHD. Furthermore, a model including the SDH and both Conners' scales produced a correct hit rate of 84%, whereas use of the SDH alone produced a nearly identical hit rate of 81%. The Educational History, Temperament, and Friendship domains of the SDH contributed most to differential diagnosis.

Based on these findings, the author then surveyed school psychology students to assess their perceptions of the utility of the SDH and other procedures for ADHD diagnosis. She found that the SDH was rated highest for determining treatment recommendations. She concluded: "If only one assessment is chosen, the structured developmental history from the Behavior Assessment System for Children by Cecil R. Reynolds and Randy W. Kamphaus is recommended in the clinic setting for case conceptualization" (p. xii).

Yet another interesting investigation of the utility of the BASC PRS for making the diagnosis of ADHD was conducted with a large sample of 309 children with the disorder who were drawn from a community sample of 7,231 children in grades 1–4. Ostrander, Weinfurt, Yarnold, and August (1998) used optimal discriminant classification tree methods to identify PRS scales that differentiate children with ADHD from the general population, and the optimal *T* scores for making this differentiation. They found the Attention Problems scale to be exceedingly efficient for making a diagnosis of ADHD, whether combined or inattentive type. They concluded:

> The high degree of accuracy (97%) shown by the BASC Attention scale in correctly classifying nonspecific ADHD implies that this scale is nearly pathognomic for a parent endorsement of ADHD. . . . The BASC Attention scale clearly offers a promising means for a relatively comprehensive, economical, and accurate identification of children with ADHD. (p. 668)

Ostrander et al. (1998) reported that a cut score of $T > 59$ on the Attention Problems scale correctly classified 88% of their cases of ADHD. Moreover, they found that the addition of other measures did not improve significantly the classification rate. Their findings, however, are provocative in that they did not find the Hyperactivity scale to be as useful. This scale may be extremely useful, however, for assessing the emotional self-regulation problems so commonly associated with a diagnosis of ADHD, as shown next.

Still another concern of clinicians is the greater frequency of application of diagnoses of bipolar disorder, juvenile bipolar disease, early onset mania, and similar labels in cases of ADHD. Typically, studies by Biederman and colleagues (1999) are cited as empirical support for this practice. The value of this line of research for highlighting the potential existence of bipolar disorder in children is unquestionable. Nevertheless, the rapidity with which this research is applied in the forms of diagnosis and somatic treatment is alarming. We propose great caution in the application of these compelling but preliminary findings when using the BASC. We agree with the point of view expressed by Hechtman (1999):

> Current criteria based primarily on adult populations modified with relatively little systematic empirical data are clearly not very specific and therefore over inclusive. This over inclusiveness has serious consequences for children and their families. These patients are given a serious lifelong diagnosis that carries with it considerable stigma, morbidity and, at times, treatment with potentially hazardous side effects. The diagnosis should therefore not be made lightly, and should require strong, sound evidence. On the other hand, it is clear that some patients with ADHD who have marked labile and/or irritable mood and significant temper outbursts may benefit from mood stabilizers. Such treatment can be given without labeling these youngsters as bipolar or manic for life. (p. 3)

Some of the BASC scales (such as the Hyperactivity, Depression, and Adaptability scales) may be particularly useful for assessing the degree of emotional lability and manic-like activity levels associated with ADHD or other disorders. In fact, a study by Nelson, Martin, Hodge, Havill, and Kamphaus (1999) found the Externalizing composite of the BASC TRS (of which Hyperactivity, Aggression, and Conduct Problems scales were components) to be highly related to the temperament variable of negative emotionality, defined as "intense crying or anger in response to frustration (e.g., in response to rules imposed by parents), prolonged emotional upset due to changes in plans, and a general tendency toward irritability" (p. 697).

Nelson et al. (1999) collected parent ratings of their children's temperament at age 5 and compared them to teacher ratings of the same children at age 8. Using latent variable path analysis with partial least squares estimation, they found negative emotionality to be (1) a very strong predictor of the TRS Externalizing composite and (2) a substantial predictor of the TRS School Maladjustment composite. These findings suggest that the TRS Externalizing composite and its component scales may be a sensitive indicator of the negative emotionality that is associated with bipolar disorder (whether or not one labels the symptoms *bipolar*).

The adaptive behavior of children with ADHD may also need to be targeted specifically for intervention, even though the Social Skills and related Adaptive Skills scales may not be pathognomic for the disorder. Nelson et al. (1998; see Chapter 7) also found the Adaptive Skills scale to be related to early temperament, thus raising the possibility that adaptive skills may be a pernicious problem for children with ADHD. Research with the Vineland Adaptive Behavior Scales has shown that adaptive skills, in general, are more impaired for children with ADHD, relative to their IQ scores, than for comparison groups of children with mental retardation and pervasive developmental disorders (Stein, Szumowski, Blondis, & Roizen, 1995). Stein et al. (1995) hypothesize that associated adaptive behavior deficits are a major contributor to poor prognosis for some children with ADHD.

A study using the Minnesota Test of Affective Processing found that a subset of children with ADHD had social skills deficits, marked delayed processing of affective information, and more affective decoding errors (Hutchinson, 1999). However this same study found that a subgroup of children with ADHD did not have social skills deficits, as measured by the BASC. Two important implications regarding social skills deficits and emotional dysregulation in children with ADHD seem apparent when these results are considered in relation to previous findings. First, a significant number of children with ADHD may not have social skills deficits. Second, the presence of social skills deficits warrants aggressive and long-term intervention that addresses their chronicity and underlying basic affective processing difficulties.

LEARNING DISABILITIES

A clear trend emerges on the TRS and PRS scales for children who have received school-based classification as learning disabled (LD). Scores in the average or at-risk range of the Learning Problems scale of the TRS are the most logical and sensitive indicators of the presence of academic difficulties. From Table 5.2 of clinical samples, however, it is clear, that this scale is not specific to cases of LD. It could be said that this scale would identify any child with academic problems, whether the problems are related to mental retardation or conduct disorder. The ubiquity of elevations on the Learning Problem scale indicates that this scale functions similarly to any measure of academic achievement (reverse scored), in that academic difficulties may be reflected therein.

Another trend for children with learning disabilities is an elevated score on the Attention Problem scales. Given that inattention has always been linked to academic difficulties (Kamphaus & Frick, 2002), this correlation is also anticipated. As is the case with the Learning Problems scale, the Attention Problems scale is nonspecific to LD but perhaps specific to ADHD, as alluded to earlier.

A noteworthy finding for children with LD is the lack of comorbid problems and general lack of scale elevations, beyond the indications of academic difficulties and inattention. This profile is consistent with the literature, which suggests that the behavior problems of children with LD are diverse: Many children have normative behavior in most domains, while some children have significant behavior problems. Taken together, these BASC results from many samples suggest that the TRS and PRS scales for children with LD will show general indications of the core deficits associated with the disorder and a lack of co-occurring symptomatology for most cases but frank symptomatology for a smaller number of cases. In these latter cases, careful social–emotional assessment is crucial to identify the full range of behavior problems that a child may exhibit.

CONDUCT DISORDER

As is evident from Tables 5.2–5.4, symptoms of conduct disorder (CD) rarely are present in isolation from problems such as depression. Consequently, it is unlikely that BASC TRS and PRS ratings will identify large numbers of children who are solely "socially maladjusted," without evidence of comorbid emotional disturbance. This result is due to the prevalency of comorbidities for children with conduct problems and not to any characteristic of the BASC (Kamphaus & Frick, 2002). It is conceivable that some of these "emotional" symptoms may be of a transient nature for a child with CD. This transience is easy to assess by using the previously discussed procedure of taking multiple ratings at various time points. However, when the Conduct Problems scale shows elevation, either in isolation or with Aggression and/or Sensation-Seeking scales, as the only comorbid elevations, than conduct disorder is a highly probable diagnosis.

TABLE 5.2. TRS: Mean T Scores of Clinical Groups

Scale	Conduct disorder[a] (combined)	Behavior disorder[a] (special education) Child	Behavior disorder[a] (special education) Adolescent	Depression[a] (combined)	Emotional disturbance (special education)[a] (combined)	ADHD[a] (child)	ADHD, predominantly inattentive type[b] (child)	ADHD, combined type[b] (child)	Learning disability (special education)[a] Child	Learning disability (special education)[a] Adolescent	Mild mental retardation (special education)[a] Child	Mild mental retardation (special education)[a] Adolescent	Autism[a] (combined)
Hyperactivity	61	61	60	53	63	61	51	63	56	55	55	56	57
Aggression	64	64	63	57	64	59	48	59	55	54	52	54	48
Conduct Problems	71	63	66	65	60	58	49	55	53	53	50	51	52
Anxiety	59	57	55	53	58	57	57	56	54	55	56	53	47
Depression	59	62	56	62	63	59	52	58	55	52	57	54	53
Somatization	60	52	56	53	55	53	54	51	51	53	55	56	52
Attention Problems	58	60	61	55	62	63	64	64	57	57	59	54	62
Learning Problems	60	57	60	52	64	61			60	62	61	57	59
Atypicality	56	59	57	57	63	57	56	61	53	52	60	56	70
Withdrawal	57	60	57	55	56	59	51	59	56	52	62	55	75
Adaptability	42	38	—	42	35	41			44	—	41	—	44
Social Skills	44	45	42	46	41	43			49	46	43	41	37
Leadership	44	42	42	44	41	42			47	45	39	37	35
Study Skills	42	41	39	43	37	39			44	44	37	40	35
Composite													
Externalizing Problems	67	64	65	59	63	60	50	60	55	55	53	54	53
Internalizing Problems	61	59	57	57	60	57	56	56	54	54	57	55	51
School Problems	59	59	61	54	64	62	59	60	60	60	61		
Adaptive Skills	42	40	40	44	38	40	45	45	39	39	36		
Behavioral Symptoms Index	62	63	61	57	65	61	56	55	58	56	58		
Age	13	8	13	13	10	8			9	14	8	13	10
Gender	F14/M57	F37/M149	F20/M78	F20/M13	F3/M14	F20/M48			F79/M186	F45/M181	F44/M44	F10/M114	F1/M18
N	71	186	98	33	17	68	265	226	88	24	19	13	10

[a]Reynolds & Kamphaus (1992); [b]Vaughn, Riccio, Hynd, & Hall (1997).

190

TABLE 5.3. PRS: Mean *T* Scores of Clinical Groups

Scale	Conduct disorder[a] (combined)	Behavior disorder (special education)[a] Child	Behavior disorder (special education)[a] Adolescent	Depression[a] (combined)	Emotional disturbance (special education)[a] (combined)	ADHD[a] (child)	ADHD, predominantly inattentive type[b] (child)	ADHD, combined type[b] (child)	ADHD, combined type[c] (child)	Learning disability (special education)[a] Child	Learning disability (special education)[a] Adolescent	Mild mental retardation (special education)[a] Child	Mild mental retardation (special education)[a] Adolescent	Autism[a] (combined)	Acute lymphocytic leukemic[d] (combined)
Hyperactivity	63	62	64	66	66	68	55	74	66	56	58	60	56	68	51
Aggression	67	64	62	69	63	63	54	65	63	54	57	50	50	50	50
Conduct Problems	73	68	75	80	62	63	52	62	59	52	56	52	52	50	47
Anxiety	51	48	53	57	53	50	52	53	58	51	53	44	53	44	52
Depression	61	62	58	73	65	62	59	66	66	54	56	53	55	49	54
Somatization	49	50	50	55	55	49	48	54	57	50	50	50	51	53	54
Atypicality	57	58	58	67	59	55	55	61	63	54	54	62	61	67	51
Withdrawal	55	52	55	60	57	50	52	51	50	51	55	55	58	57	51
Attention Problems	59	61	63	64	66	66	72	72	65	58	63	61	60	64	57
Adaptability	32	37	—	26	33	37			38	46	—	41	—	38	45
Social Skills	42	41	39	37	38	41			44	47	46	40	38	34	46
Leadership	42	41	39	41	37	43			50	45	45	35	38	32	43
Externalizing Problems	70	67	70	76	66	67	54	70		55	59	55	53	57	50
Internalizing Problems	54	54	54	64	60	55	54	60		52	53	49	53	48	54
Adaptive Skills	40	38	38	37	34	39				45	45	37	37	32	44
Behavioral Symptoms Index	63	63	63	72	67	65		57	59	57	58	60	54		
Age	13	8	14	13	10	8				9	14	8	13	10	
Gender	F8/M32	F17/M70	F9/M35	F14/M15	F5/M11	F16/M36				F56/M132	F29/M116	F25/	F10/M16	F0/M16	F13/M16
N	40	87	44	29	16	52				188	145	63	26	16	34

[a]Reynolds & Kamphaus (1992); [b]Vaughn, Riccio, Hynd, & Hall (1997); [c]Barringer (2000); [d]Shelby, Nagle, Barnett-Queen, Quattlebaum, & Wuori (1998).

TABLE 5.4. SRP: Mean *T* Scores of Clinical Groups

Scale	Conduct disorder (combined)	Behavior disorder (special education)		Depression (combined)	Emotional disturbance (special education) (combined)	ADHD (child)	Learning disability (special education)		Mild mental retardation (special education) (combined)
		Child	Adolescent				Child	Adolescent	
Attitude to School	56	50	55	56	55	54	51	51	52
Attitude to Teachers	55	53	55	56	55	53	51	50	50
Sensation Seeking	59	—	57	54	56	—	—	53	49
Atypicality	55	54	53	55	56	54	51	50	50
Locus of Control	54	53	51	58	57	54	51	50	53
Somatization	55	—	52	53	51	—	—	49	51
Social Stress	53	55	50	56	59	54	50	49	53
Anxiety	51	51	47	52	53	52	48	46	51
Depression	54	55	51	59	60	53	52	51	55
Sense of Inadequacy	53	56	52	56	56	55	53	52	57
Relations with Parents	44	46	48	38	49	50	49	49	53
Interpersonal Relations	46	43	48	43	37	49	50	49	46
Self-Esteem	49	48	53	46	49	49	50	50	50
Self-Reliance	49	48	48	45	50	50	49	51	51
Composite									
School Maladjustment	58	52	57	57	56	54	51	52	51
Clinical Maladjustment	54	54	51	56	57	54	50	49	52
Personal Adjustment	46	45	49	41	45	49	49	50	50
Emotional Symptoms Index	53	55	50	57	59	53	50	50	54
Age	13	9	13	13	11	8	9	14	10
Sex	F15/M60	F19/M77	F3/M26	F20/M13	F3/M10	F22/M32	F48/M112	F46/M106	F15/M22
N	75	96	29	33	13	54	160	152	37

All data from Reynolds & Kamphaus (1992).

192

The BASC's assessment of conduct disorder is consistent with prior research in other ways. For example, the primary symptoms appear on the Externalizing composite in the form of elevated Conduct Problems, Aggression, and Hyperactivity scale scores, thus producing an Externalizing/Internalizing split on the PRS. Given the disruptive nature of such problems, it is not surprising that teachers would often identify co-occurring learning and attention problems as well.

The BASC preschool forms may be of particular value for the assessment of CD due to the differing prognoses of early-onset and late-onset CD, with the former having a significantly poorer prognosis. In addition, identifying consistent types of aggression problems early in development is also important. The Conduct Problems scale of the PRS and TRS are well suited to identifying the onset of CD in middle school and high school. At the early elementary grades and preschool ages, however, externalizing problems can still be assessed in lieu of conduct problems. The Aggression and Hyperactivity scales of the preschool and elementary age forms allow for the assessment of early-onset CD-related symptoms. Such symptoms may not indicate the eventuality of a CD diagnosis, but they clearly indicate substantial risk for disruptive behavior problems that lay on the spectrum of CD, oppositional defiant disorder, or ADHD, combined type.

Hence, although a formal diagnosis of CD, based on elevations on the Externalizing composite of the BASC, cannot and should not be made at ages 2, 3, 4, or 5, such a score should trigger careful and consistent monitoring and/or presumptive treatment. Such monitoring and treatment are necessary, given the amount of research indicating that these problems typically do not spontaneously resolve themselves when they appear early in development. In fact, it has been shown that the early and untreated presence of aggression in childhood places individuals at significant risk for important adult outcomes, such as unemployment (Kokko & Pulkkinen, 2000).

A program evaluation study by Conoley et al. (2001) showed that solution-focused family therapy was effective for reducing aggression in four case studies of children, ages 7 to 9, diagnosed with conduct disorder. Their $N = 1$ design with four replications used the BASC PRS, a treatment manual, and a treatment integrity measure. The interventions lasted from two to five sessions. The therapists were advanced doctoral students with limited to no experience using solution-focused family therapy. The intervention showed evidence of effectiveness, using a variety of outcome measures, with three of the four families (see Table 5.5). The PRS results as well as other measures clearly detected changes in the children's levels of aggression and conduct problems in response to this short-term intervention.

TABLE 5.5. Selected PRS Results of the Conoley et al. (2001) Investigation of the Effectiveness of Solution-Focused Family Therapy with Four Cases at Pretest, Posttest, and 3-Month Follow-up

	Todd			Arnie		Jim			Marla		
	Pre	Post	Follow-up	Pre	Post	Pre	Post	Follow-up	Pre	Post	Follow-up
Clinical scales											
Aggression	64	64	53	68	47	74	62	60	73	60	63
Conduct Problems	57	50	50	74	60	54	64	47	56	56	51
Composite Scales											
Externalizing	71	71	64	68	53	72	69	61	60	52	60
Internalizing	64	66	58	49	45	72	62	65	51	44	44
Behavior Symptom	84	82	73	58	49	82	73	74	60	50	60
Adaptive Skills	42	45	47	50	47	23	35	35	40	38	34

DEPRESSION

Even our prepublication research with the BASC revealed that the Depression scale would be elevated for many clinical samples. Moreover, as shown for the PRS and TRS, cases of depression are often complex and associated with co-occurring problems. In fact, some our results led us to believe that there may be some referral bias in cases of depression, in that children with depression were more likely to be referred if they had significant behavioral problems. Repeatedly seeing elevations on the Depression scale for many samples led us to wonder about the meaning of these high scores.

Our current conclusions are that the Depression scale is extremely valuable for assessing general distress in children and adolescents. In psychometric terms, it could be considered a good measure of "general psychopathology" akin to the g assessed by IQ tests. This conclusion is based on our factor analytic experience with the BASC, which showed that this scale loaded significantly on both the Externalizing and Internalizing constructs (Reynolds & Kamphaus, 1992). Often, children and adolescents with depression will externalize these uncomfortable feelings by acting out. Boys, in particular, become aggressive and engage in rule-breaking behavior. It is not surprising, then, that high Depression scores are seen for samples of children with conduct disorder, depression, and, in some cases, ADHD, because the scale also strongly reflects the much discussed concept of negative affectivity in the adult literature.

Based on our data, the Depression scale score can have a range of meanings, depending on its scale elevation. For some children, the Depression scale could be revealing general distress or unhappiness that is insufficient to warrant a diagnosis of depression, per se. Scores of 55, 60, or even 68 could fall into this category. In addition, scores of this magnitude could occur for children with LD, ADHD, CD, or even those with a previous diagnosis of depression who are currently asymptomatic. As noted, when communicating results of these children to parents or others, we have even suggested renaming the scale as one of "distress" or "unhappiness" so that caregivers do not equate the scale with the diagnosis.

Scores of 61, 68, or 80 in other children will signify the presence of clinical depression, as defined by the DSM-IV criteria. How does one know this? We suggest that the child's (or adolescent's) symptoms be compared against the DSM-IV criteria when a Depression scale score of 60 or higher is obtained on the SRP, TRS, or PRS. If the child meets these criteria, then a diagnosis of depression is warranted, regardless of the presenting problem or prior diagnoses (except, of course, in the case or rule-outs), whether they be CD, ADHD, etc. We have found that depression often co-occurs with other problems, as is consistent with the findings in the literature regarding comorbidity (Kamphaus & Frick, 2002). We believe that the Depression scales of the BASC are highly useful because they serve as sensitive indicators of a construct ranging from mild or transient emotional distress to clinical depression with vegetative symptoms and suicidal ideation. Checking the BASC items against DSM-IV criteria is greatly facilitated by using the BASC computer scoring option, which pairs the items sorted by scale with the items' associated responses.

ACUTE LYMPHOCYTIC LEUKEMIA (ALL)

A study of child survivors of leukemia revealed primarily internalizing problems, attention problems, and adaptive skills deficits (Shelby, Nagle, Barnett-Queen, Quattlebaum, & Wuori, 1998) (see Table 5.3). Shelby et al. (1998) studied 34 child survivors of cancer between the ages of 6 and 17 who had terminated treatment an average of 4 years 7 months earlier after averaging 2 years 9 months in treatment. The child sample did not differ from the normative mean on these scales and composites; the adolescent sample, however, revealed significantly more problems on the BASC PRS.

The authors cite prior research that indicates that internalizing problems and social competency deficits are more common among child survivors of leukemia. Attentional difficulties have been found in other studies. Although the mean scores for the BASC scales are not particularly high, the proportion of the sample scoring in the at-risk and significant *T* score ranges was relatively high (e.g., 38% of the sample for the BSI).

CULTURAL/LINGUISTIC GROUPS

While again acknowledging substantial within-group differences as a major methodological concern, we now report data related to cultural group similarities and differences. The previously described study by Kamphaus et al. (2000) noted that BASC parent and teacher ratings produced consistent and meaningful gender differences across four cultural groups, and that cultural group differences were far less consistent and interpretable. It was also noted that parents tended to rate their children more severely than teachers rated them. These findings suggest that teachers rating children who are from different cultural backgrounds than their own are likely to express less negative response sets.

Murphy (2000) tested this hypothesis by investigating response sets for 77 Anglo and 10 African American teachers who rated 42 Anglo and 22 African American special education students. This study is particularly germane because it included children who are typical of those for whom BASC TRS ratings are obtained in the schools. Murphy's findings were revealing: African American and Anglo teachers did not differ in their ratings of African American special education students; Anglo teachers, however, rated Anglo students as having significantly more externalizing problems than African American teachers rated them. Murphy (2000), while acknowledging the limitations of her study, concluded that "educators tend to view and report student behavior equitably for Caucasian and African American students in the assessment process for emotional and behavioral disorders" (p. 20).

Additional evidence that teacher ratings are fairly accurate measures of child behavior is available. Consider the following findings:

- Traits that are considered stable were rated consistently by teachers over a 2- to 8-week interval (Reynolds & Kamphaus, 1992). A study of three clinical samples produced median test-retest values of .89, .91, and .82 for preschool, child, and adolescent levels.
- Different teachers rated the same child similarly (Reynolds & Kamphaus, 1992). Thirty children were rated by two teachers within a few days of one another. Interrater coefficients were variable, ranging from a low of .53 for Social Skills to .94 for Learning Problems. Most Clinical scales had adequate reliabilities, such as Aggression .71, Anxiety .82, Attention Problems .68, and Learning Problems. 94.
- Teacher internal consistency coefficients were higher than those for either parent or adolescent self-reports (Reynolds & Kamphaus, 1992).
- Teacher ratings were better able to diagnose the subtypes of ADHD

than classroom observations by independent observers (Lett & Kamphaus, 1997). The TRS was significantly better than the SOS at differentiating nondisabled, ADHD, combined type, and ADHD, combined type, plus conduct problem groups with about a 70% accuracy rate.

- Teacher ratings were significantly associated with adjustment to school (Thorpe, Kamphaus, Rowe, & Fleckenstein, 2000).
- Teacher ratings of elementary school children were predictive of adjustment six years later (Verhulst et al., 1994).

We are simultaneously intrigued by the nonstatistically significant finding from Murphy's study that African American teachers rated African American children (mean $T = 62$) as having more externalizing problems than Anglo children (mean $T = 53$). Taking all findings together (i.e., parents rating children more severely than teachers, Anglo teachers rating Anglo children more severely than African American children), it appears that *the better known the child is to the rater, the more severe the ratings*.

This proposition is supported by Malgady and Constantino's (1998) study of Hispanic patients diagnosed by Anglo and Hispanic clinicians. Anglo clinicians made fewer diagnoses of Hispanic patients than did Hispanic clinicians. One of the theories offered by the authors was that the Anglo clinicians do not have enough familiarity with the cultural and linguistic background of these individuals to identify accurately the severity of their symptoms. Of course, this theory will require an extraordinary accumulation of evidence, given the absence of a "gold standard" for children's actual behavior. Considerable evidence is mounting.

DEVELOPMENTAL DISABILITIES AND AUTISM

BASC results for children with autism and mental retardation are strikingly similar in that some of the core deficits of these disorders are clearly reflected in prepublication research findings. Specifically, the core deficits of behavioral peculiarity and immaturity are measured by the Atypicality scale, and the adaptive behavior and social skills deficits are measured by the Adaptive Skills scale. In addition, the academic problems associated with both disorders are measured by the Learning Problems scale of the TRS.

Differential ratings of parents and teachers were seen in cases of children with autism: Teachers tended to rate children with autism as having more significant atypicality, withdrawal, and social skills problems than the parents rated their children (Reynolds & Kamphaus, 1992). This result is not surprising, given teachers' opportunities to observe children in a larger social milieu of peers than is typically available to parents. It appears that the well-documented pattern of impaired social functioning in children with autism is likely to be reported by both parent and teacher ratings, but more so with teacher ratings.

CONCLUSIONS

In this chapter, we have attempted to review research findings that can serve as guideposts for the assessment of children with disabilities—a daunting task, indeed, given the inherent weaknesses of current diagnostic systems. In fact, there is more evidence of reliability associated with psychometric scales, such as the BASC, that represent many child problems and adaptive competencies on a continuum.

Although diagnosis is a necessary part of assessment practice, we should not let our efforts to make a diagnosis distract us from other significant findings that warrant treatment, prevention, or further evaluation using other methodologies. In working with an adolescent who has a long criminal record and is diagnosed with CD, for example, there may be a tendency to pay less attention to adaptability deficits and depression symptoms, as assessed by the BASC or a similar measure. However, it could be true that the depression problems and emotional dysregulation are causing the adolescent as much problem in daily functioning as the CD symptoms—and, in some cases, may be a *cause* of the CD symptoms. In our view, diagnosis is merely one assessment goal, and identification of problems and assets, regardless or whether or not they contribute to a diagnosis, is a coequal goal.

CHAPTER 6

BASC ADHD Monitor and Student Observation System

In this chapter the role of diagnosis is secondary to two BASC components that are particularly important for the design and evaluation of treatment programs, especially in the school and pediatric settings. We begin first with the ADHD Monitor, which is designed for use in both pediatric and school settings, then turn to the BASC SOS, which is a key component for the evaluation of behavior change in the classroom.

BASC ADHD MONITOR

The BASC ADHD Monitor fills a unique role in the assessment of children who are diagnosed with ADHD. Administering the Monitor is the second step in an assessment regimen that is designed to enhance treatment planning and evaluation by thoroughly evaluating the primary symptoms of ADHD on a continuing basis. Attention problems and hyperactivity constitute the core symptoms used by the DSM-IV to define the ADHD syndrome (Kamphaus & Frick, 2002). Problems in one or both of these areas are used to differentiate the three subtypes: ADHD, predominantly inattentive type; ADHD predominantly hyperactive–impulsive type; and ADHD, combined type.

Components of the original BASC system serve as the first step in the comprehensive assessment of children suspected of having ADHD (see also Chapter 7). The BASC evaluates a broad sampling of child behavior in order to identify the full range of child problems, especially those that mimic the symptoms of ADHD. If the initial administration of the BASC reveals an elevation on the Attention Problems (see Chapter 5) and/or Hyperactivity scales, the diagnosis of ADHD becomes a possibility. Of greater importance, however, is using the BASC Teacher, Parent, and Self-Report Forms to rule out co-occurring problems (Kamphaus & Frick, 2002). This process of ruling out other problems is particularly central to determining a valid diagnosis of ADHD, with which so many comorbid disorders occur, and given that other disorders (e.g., childhood depression) may appear to be ADHD. In fact, the use of narrow-band scales of inattention or hyperactivity may often result in overdiagnosis of ADHD (see Chapter 7).

The narrowly focused Monitor is designed to assess an expanded range of attention problems and hyperactivity symptoms in a time-efficient and practical manner. This additional detail allows the clinician to refine the diagnosis of ADHD and, of greater importance, to design a comprehensive treatment program aimed at reducing the core behavioral problems of inattention and hyperactivity. The Monitor also provides Internalizing and Adaptive Skills scales that further encourage comprehensive treatment planning and evaluation of treatment effectiveness by allowing clinicians to easily include these important constructs in the treatment plan.

The BASC and BASC ADHD Monitor represent a coordinated multiple-step assessment system that allows the clinician to proceed from referral for ADHD to diagnosis, treatment design, and treatment evaluation with greater ease and precision. In order to achieve these objectives, the Monitor utilizes information provided by parents, teachers, and a classroom observer to assess the following constructs.

Component	Scales
Parent Monitor	Attention Problems
	Hyperactivity
	Internalizing Problems
	Adaptive Skills
Teacher Monitor	Attention Problems
	Hyperactivity
	Internalizing Problems
	Adaptive Skills

BASC SOS	Response to Teacher/Lesson
	Peer Interaction
	Work on School Subjects
	Transition Movement
	Inappropriate Movement
	Inattention
	Inappropriate Vocalization
	Somatization
	Repetitive Motor Movements
	Aggression
	Self-Injurious Behavior
	Inappropriate Sexual Behavior
	Bowel/Bladder Problems

Few tests for children are designed in a manner that facilitates the repeated collection and dissemination of information to treatment providers (Kratochwill et al., 1999). The Monitor is designed to meet the unusual practical demands dictated by the need for the repeated assessment of the core symptoms of ADHD. The original BASC is quite sensitive to behavioral changes in individual children, and it can be used repeatedly to evaluate treatment effects (Conoley et al., 2001), particularly if a child is found to have multiple problems (e.g., ADHD, depression, anxiety, and conduct disorder) that cannot be assessed fully by the Monitor. In the case of ADHD and its subtypes, however, the Monitor is constructed so as to allow clinicians to evaluate treatment with greater focus and time efficiency.

The BASC ADHD Monitor is designed to:

1. Provide accurate and frequent feedback to the prescribing physician. The physician and other health-care workers need accurate information in order to adjust dosage and to ensure that a child is receiving the most helpful psychotropic regimen. Information about the effects of medication on hyperactivity, attention problems, internalizing problems, and adaptive skills deficits can aid the physician in making crucial medical treatment decisions.

2. Ensure that the ongoing assessment of ADHD problems is efficient, timely, and cost-effective. Given the multiple time demands on parents, teachers, and health-care workers, asking them to complete lengthy or unnecessarily complex rating scales that are not specifically targeted to the needs of the child with ADHD is counterproductive. Accordingly, the Monitor is brief yet provides coverage of four important symptom domains that affect the functioning of the child with ADHD: attention problems, hyperactivity, internalizing problems, and adaptive skills.

3. Provide coordinated instruments that allow for input from multiple informants. Teacher, parent, and clinician observations are all relevant to the treatment process, and communication among these individuals is crucial for effective treatment (Bender, 1997). Each Monitor form is designed to meet the specialized needs of each of these informants.

4. Emphasize the assessment of specific behavioral outcomes in order to demonstrate accountability for services. Increasingly, the effectiveness of child services is being challenged, thereby creating the need to assess outcomes. The Monitor assesses the DSM-IV criteria for ADHD and includes items that are written in clear behavioral terms. In addition, the Monitor software is designed to produce output that gives providers and administrators a clear indication of response to treatment. The Monitor is designed to provide clinicians with the information needed to adjust treatment whenever response to intervention is not optimal.

5. Link assessment to treatment planning and evaluation. The Monitor is designed to be practical enough to be considered central to the treatment process. Heretofore, physicians and other clinicians typically have had difficulty acquiring the feedback needed to adjust treatment. The selection of items and scales, test length, scoring and reporting systems, graphical output, and other Monitor characteristics were all guided by the need to provide information relevant to treatment.

ADHD Monitor interpretation may require several forms, depending on the instrument(s) used, the theoretical orientation of the clinician, the evaluation questions posed, and other factors. It is also important to keep in mind that the Monitor is designed to create and evaluate treatment plans. Therefore, interpretation of the scales as diagnostic devices is of considerably lesser importance.

The initial step in evaluating Monitor results is asking whether or not significant change has occurred in response to treatment. For the parent and teacher Monitors, four questions are generally posed:

1. Is treatment affecting symptoms of inattention?
2. Is treatment affecting symptoms of hyperactivity?
3. Is treatment affecting internalizing symptoms?
4. Is treatment affecting adaptive skills?

The questions related to change are parallel for the SOS, where one may be assessing change at either the item or scale level (discussed later in this chapter). Keep in mind that changes in scores may show deterioration in some areas, not just improvement. For example, as a child's symptoms of overactivity and inattention come under control, comorbid symptoms of depression may become more prominent, causing scores on the internalizing dimension to elevate.

Even if a significant change in T scores is apparent, there are additional questions to consider:

1. Which scales have changed?
2. Is there a temporal (and potentially causal) relationship between treatment delivery (or lack thereof) and the observed change?
3. Is the change of "clinical significance"? In other words, regardless of the amount of T-score change, are parents and/or teachers reporting change that is adequate to reduce functional impairment in their eyes?

In our view, establishing the temporal relationship between T-score change and delivery or withdrawal of treatments is of greatest importance. It is our experience that this relationship is assessed, all too often, via the speculation or supposition of the clinician. We propose that a better way to draw as conclusion regarding the relationship between treatment and behavior change is to conduct repeat assessments until the correlation is clear. For example, one could see a reduction in attention problems subsequent to the first month's administration of medication. While this change represents a hopeful sign, this pretest–posttest methodology is probably insufficient to draw a definitive conclusion. A third set of Monitor ratings, a few months later, showing the same trend, and a set of ratings reflecting the presence of more symptoms when the child is not taking medication (e.g., in the summer months) would provide more assurance that the conclusion that medication is having an effect is warranted. We often find that an additional brief assessment clarifies our conclusions to a much greater extent than prolonged theorizing based on more limited data.

Administration of the BASC often precedes that of the ADHD Monitor. There is, however, one important area of interpretive overlap between the BASC PRS and TRS the ADHD Parent and Teacher Monitor forms. A T-score baseline for treatment evaluation can be obtained from either set of measures. Two administration scenarios are most likely:

1. A clinician may administer either or both of the BASC parent and teacher forms (PRS, TRS) during the initial diagnostic evaluation. The obtained T scores for the Hyperactivity, Attention Problems, Internalizing Problems, and Adaptive Skills scales can be entered into the BASC ADHD software

and be used as the baseline against which subsequent administrations of the ADHD Monitor will be compared.

   2. A clinician may administer either or both of the BASC ADHD Parent/ Teacher Monitor forms during the initial diagnostic evaluation. The obtained *T* scores for the Hyperactivity, Attention Problems, Internalizing Problems, and Adaptive Skills scales can then be used as the baseline against which subsequent administrations of the ADHD Monitor forms will be compared.

   It is important to establish a *T*-score baseline in a timely fashion, regardless of the method used, during the evaluation phase and prior to implementation of treatment. The ADHD Monitor *T* scores for parent and teacher rating scales serve as the most reliable indicator of behavioral change over time (see Kamphaus & Reynolds, 1998).

STUDENT OBSERVATION SYSTEM

Functional Behavioral Assessment with the SOS

The SOS addresses some of the shortcomings inherent in the use of classroom observation techniques. Specifically, the SOS was developed as a practical means of utilizing a momentary time sampling procedure that adequately samples the full range of a child's behavior in the classroom (Reynolds & Kamphaus, 1992). Several characteristics of the SOS exemplify this effort:

1. Both adaptive and maladaptive behaviors are observed (see Reynolds & Kamphaus, 1992).
2. Multiple methods are used, including clinician rating, time sampling, and qualitative recording of classroom functional contingencies.
3. A generous time interval is allocated for recording the results of each time sampling interval (27 seconds).
4. Operational definitions of behaviors and time sampling categories are included in the BASC manual (Reynolds & Kamphaus, 1992).
5. Interrater reliabilities for the time sampling portion are high, which suggests that independent observers are likely to observe the same trends in the child's classroom behavior (see Lett & Kamphaus, 1997).

   These characteristics of the SOS have contributed to its popularity as a functional behavioral assessment tool. It is crucial, for example, to have adequate operational definitions of behaviors that, in turn, contribute to good interrater reliability. Without such reliability, clinicians will never know if their observations are unique, perhaps influenced by their own biases or idiosyncratic definitions of behavior.

It is central to the validity of such observations that they have a simultaneous capacity to account for a child's adaptive skills in the classroom. It is only by doing so that a clinician is able to identify which behaviors should be targeted for instruction and/or intervention, and which for strengthening.

Specifically, the BASC SOS, Parts A, B, and C (and other components) can contribute to the functional assessment of behavior from multiple perspectives:

- Behavior *frequency*. Part A assesses frequency via ratings of "never observed," "sometimes observed," and "frequently observed." Part B assesses frequencies by category of behavior problem, and PRS and TRS ratings tally the frequency of behavior problems.
- Behavior *duration*. Part B ratings quantify percentage of time engaged in a particular behavior by category.
- Behavior *intensity*. Part A ratings of "disruptive," Part B ratings of frequency by category, cover this aspect.
- *Antecedent events to behavior*. Part C requires descriptions of teacher position, behavior, and other contextual variables that precede misbehavior.
- *Consequences of behavior*. Part C requires descriptions of teacher behavior, peer behavior, and other variables subsequent to misbehavior.
- *Analysis of behavior across settings*. SOS observations are made at various times of day and in different classroom settings. The PRS may be used for the assessment of behavior in the community and home environments.

Other components of the BASC, such as the PRS and TRS, may also be used as part of a functional behavioral assessment paradigm. Given the time-consuming nature of observations, however, it may be more practical to collect teacher ratings from classrooms where an observation is not practical and parent ratings in order to assess differences across settings. Observations are central to the ongoing classroom problem-solving and consultation process that is frequently concerned with the ongoing assessment of a child's behavioral adaptation in school as is discussed next section (additional functional behavioral assessment guidance can be obtained at *http://www.air.org/cecp/ fba/problembehavior/strategies.htm#direct*).

Monitoring with the SOS

The SOS is the one component of the BASC ADHD Monitor that may be applied to all children, regardless of their diagnosis or classification. In fact, we know of school districts that use the SOS and Monitor software to evaluate progress toward IEP objectives, assess effects of prereferral intervention, and assess the effectiveness of various special education programming decisions. Some have used the SOS to assess the impact of social work or other services on classroom behavior. Perhaps more than any other BASC component, the SOS was specifically designed to serve the behavioral intervention and evaluation process in the classroom. We now discuss possible scenarios and examples of applying the SOS.

Medical Effects

Mary's parents are opposed to the use of medication with their child, in spite of the fact that numerous behavioral (e.g., psychotherapy, play therapy, token economy, etc.) and educational interventions (e.g., peer tutor, after-school tutor, summer school, preferential seating, etc.) have failed. The SOS may help such reluctant parents gauge the effects of pharmacological interventions on their child's classroom behavior in a manner that they perceive as more objective than teacher ratings.

In this hypothetical example, an independent, perhaps even case blind, observer will take SOS observations prior to the administration of somatic therapy, at two or more points after initiation of somatic therapy (perhaps in as few as 2 to 4 weeks after the initiation of a medication such as methylphenidate, which reaches therapeutic levels rather quickly), and whenever dosage or medication is changed. The BASC Monitor software then graphs Part B (momentary time sampling) results which can be shared with parents, physician, and other service providers and caregivers. Specific behaviors from Part A can be graphed as well, but we would expect individual behaviors to be less reliable indicators of change overall.

In this scenario it is crucial to establish a link between somatic therapy and behavior change. In order to do so, the SOS should be administered concurrently with changes in regimens. We find that the 15-minute time sampling is adequate for this purpose, based on our experience and the fact that interobserver reliability did not differ for 15- or 45-minute observations (Lett & Kamphaus, 1997). In addition, those children receiving a variety of medications, such as psychostimulants, anxiolytics, antidepressants, and antipsychotics, require careful monitoring to determine the effects of these drugs on classroom behavior.

IEP Objectives

Part A was designed specifically to enhance the development of IEP objectives. Behavior noted in Part A can then be tracked via repeated Part A ratings and any changes graphed by Monitor software. Statisticians who have expressed concern about the overreliance on significance testing have noted that graphing is a powerful alternative method for data analysis. We have noted how convincing a graph can be for teachers, parents, and others.

We suggest, however, that clinicians administer Part B prior to completing Parts A and C, because the vigilance required to complete the momentary time sampling ensures careful observation—which, in turn, leads to a more accurate, ongoing rating of the behavior intervention plans.

Finally, since three data points are advised to establish a reliable trend line, we recommend that, as a minimum, observations be collected at the outset of the school year (after the child has had a month to adjust to teachers, peers, etc.); at a midpoint, when it may be convenient to adjust intervention (certainly March or April of the academic year would be too late), and just prior to the annual evaluation of IEP goals.

Prereferral Intervention

The evaluation of prereferral intervention can occur in the same framework advised for the annual evaluation of IEP objectives, but on a shorter timetable. Again, a minimum of three data points are advised, even if the intervention is designed to be brief (e.g., 1 or 2 months). Consider the following example:

Shane, a victim of physical abuse by his mother, has been placed in foster care for 3 months. During this time period, his mother is receiving treatment, and he is receiving routine counseling sessions at school for the first time. Shane also has a school history of distractability and truancy. His truancy could be tracked by event recording during this time period, and his classroom behavior could be assessed by the SOS during monthly intervals. SOS results could be of some additive value in assessing the value and effects of the foster-care placement and counseling on his classroom behavior.

School-Wide Interventions

While recognizing the impracticality of using the SOS on a large scale, we do think that it could be used for sampling purposes. For example, one or two children from each classroom, deemed to be at risk for aggression, could be sampled to evaluate the effects of the school's violence prevention program.

Good evaluation data are crucial for such programs, given that some evidence of iatrogenic effects has been noted.

The SOS is designed specifically for classroom-based intervention. SOS results should not be considered when evaluating home-based intervention, unless home- and school-based interventions are linked. For example, a home-bound reinforcement program could be used to improve behavior at school.

As noted, the frequency of classroom behavior problems is assessed by the SOS. Consequently, SOS results from Parts A and B can be used to identify behaviors in need of intervention. Specifically, any behavioral problem that is exhibited, and any adaptive skill that is not exhibited, become potential candidates for intervention. Within these groups, problem behaviors of higher frequency can be given priority for intervention. Analogously, low-frequency adaptive skills also become targets for intervention.

The SOS is unique among Monitor components in that it allows clinicians to prioritize behaviors for classroom-based intervention. The SOS also measures the "bothersomeness" of a child's behavioral problems via the disruptive category in Part A. Often, these children display a number of behavioral problems, making it difficult to prioritize behaviors for intervention (Schwanz & Kamphaus, 1997). Ratings of disruptiveness can be used to identify behaviors that should be targeted first for treatment.

SOS Training and Administration

Although for most part, the SOS is easy to administer and score, there are some "tricks" for becoming fluent with its administration. First, we suggest beginning with Part B, the momentary time-sampling procedure. If for no other reason, this sampling procedure "forces" vigilance on the part of the observer, as already noted. SOS users will find that completing Part B first gives them a rich compendium of information upon which to base Part A ratings and Part C qualitative information.

Part B Administration

When arranging the observation session, several procedures are helpful to remember. First, with the SOS there is typically no need to select target behaviors to observe because the Part B categories provide the selection of target behaviors and require broad observations. It is conceivable that a new category of behavior will be necessary in some cases, and space is available for including such a category.

Second, focus on aspects of observation that enhance the likelihood of minimal disruption and valid data collection. For example, schedule the observation period at a time of day and in a class where problems are known to be of concern to teacher or parent so that target behaviors can be observed. In addition, the examiner may also want to use the SOS in a class where problems are not present, particularly at the high-school or middle-school level.

Given concerns about "strangers" in the classroom, the observation process can be conducted in a manner that minimizes disruption by using an observer who already works in, or is familiar at, the school; or by having the unfamiliar observer introduce him- or herself to the teacher ahead of time, in the presence of the students. The observer is advised to observe the classroom, in general, for a few minutes before beginning the official timing for Part B. This delay will allow the students to settle down somewhat—which, in turn, will allow the observer to obtain a more accurate sample of the child's typical classroom behavior.

Third, develop a timing mechanism that enhances examiners' comfort level with the 30-second momentary time samplings and the 3-second observation periods. Many observers simply check their watch in order to time the intervals for observation and coding. Others make an audiotape that "beeps" at the beginning and end of each 3-second observation. Still other creative ways of timing the observation periods are probably available. The timing procedure is best developed by practicing with the BASC SOS training videotape (for availability, contact the publisher, AGS, at *agsnet.com* or *bascforum.com*, or telephone 800-328-2560).

Fourth, be aware that there are 30 columns on the SOS Part B page for making checkmarks to indicate the presence of a behavior. Half of the columns are white, and half are shaded blue. The shading was included to help observers mark all categories within the same observation period. We have noted that some new users find this shading confusing in that they think they should use only the white columns. *Both* sets of columns are needed in order to have space for 30 observations.

The BASC manual (Reynolds & Kamphaus, 1992) instructions for the SOS should be read carefully before using any part of the SOS, including Part B. Only the BASC manual includes all of the operational definitions of the behaviors that are coded for Parts A and Part B.

Completing Part A

The observer's rating of individual behaviors for Part A is easily accomplished after using Part B. The same behaviors that were previously coded by category for Part B are now coded individually for Part A.

We are often asked if there is a numerical value for discriminating between the rating categories of *sometimes*, *often*, *almost always*. There is no
such value. In order to allow clinicians to consider the importance of local
context and culture, we opted to forego assigning an arbitrary value in favor
of allowing and encouraging clinicians to use their knowledge to rate
the items. This same lack constraint in the BASC TRS and PRS results in
satisfactory-to-high reliability and validity indices (see Reynolds & Kamphaus,
1992). All such ratings on all our rating scales are impressionistic, and for
good reasons: The impressions are developed in context and have heuristic
and practical value.

Completing Part C

The final portion of the SOS is qualitative in nature and central to the role of
the SOS as a classroom consultation tool. The observer is cued to note
changes in teacher position and behavior change techniques that either pres-
age (antecedents) a child behavior of interest or immediately follow such a
behavior (consequences). This sequential analysis is especially useful for developing theories about the effects of a teacher on the child's behavior. By
gathering this kind of empirical information, the classroom consultant and
the teacher can work together to change maladaptive sequences of events and
to increase the frequency of adaptive sequences.

Sample Case: Norman

Norman is the subject of the BASC SOS training video (see *BASCforum.com* or
telephone 800-328-2560 for availability). He is a middle-school-age child who
was referred by his mother for consideration for special education placement
due to suspicion of ADHD. Norman, however, is doing quite well in school:
He earns A's and B's in all subject areas. He has never been retained nor has
he been referred for prereferral intervention by any previous teachers.

Norman's baseline SOS Part B results are shown in Figure 6.1. As can be
seen from viewing his behavior in the video and record given in Part B, he is
inattentive and overactive from time to time. These observations support his
mother's contention that he displays some symptoms of ADHD. His behavior,
however, was not rated by the observer as disruptive on Part A of the SOS.
Moreover, he responded well to teacher redirection and completed assigned
tasks as requested.

The same pattern of results was obtained using BASC PRS and TRS. He is

Part B - Time Sampling of Behavior

Directions: At the end of each 30-second interval, observe the child's behavior for approximately 3 seconds (for example, when the stopwatch reads 0:30-0:33). Then place a check mark (√) in the time column next to each category of behavior that occurred during that interval.

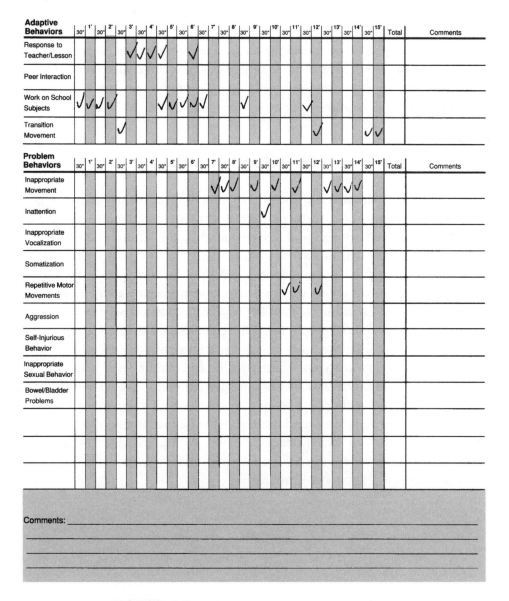

FIGURE 6.1. SOS Part B results for Norman.

somewhat inattentive and hyperactive at home and school, but his behavior is far more problematic at home. Teachers have consistently reported that they can manage him adequately at school, where little evidence of educational impairment has been found.

The SOS results for Norman will serve as a baseline, along with BASC ADHD Monitor parent and teacher ratings, against which his future behavior can be evaluated. Because of their time efficiency, these methods could be used again in a month or two to track his behavior and determine if it is consistent, worsening, or improving.

CONCLUSIONS

The BASC ADHD Monitor and the SOS fill unique needs when assessing children for the purposes of treatment. Neither of these instruments has received substantial research, though both are frequently used. Future research is necessary to establish their utility.

We have noted substantially more interest in the SOS in recent years. We think that this interest is due, in part, to the reauthorization of the Individuals with Disabilities Education Act in 1997, which prescribed usage of functional behavioral assessment strategies for children with disabilities. Another possible contributor to increased SOS usage was a consent decree in a court case in Alabama (*Lee v. Macon*), which advised the use of functional behavioral assessment measures and classroom observations as methods to be used as part of prereferral intervention programs. The goal of such programs, in many cases, is to prevent problems and thereby decrease participation in special education programs. The SOS appears to be perceived as an especially timely instrument, given that the need for replicable, practical, and relatively user-friendly observation systems is increasing.

CHAPTER 7

Applications in Prevention, Forensics, Pediatrics, and Program Evaluation

PREVENTION

Various components of the BASC are being utilized in longitudinal investigations to study the risk, onset, course, and progress of behavioral problems and psychopathology in childhood. Some studies have used the BASC as a measure of child outcomes or as the criterion variable of interest.

Nelson et al. (1999; also reviewed in Chapter 5) used the BASC TRS and PRS as outcome criteria to assess the predictive validity of early temperament. The temperament construct is commonly considered to represent a largely biological predisposition toward certain behavior patterns (Martin, 1988). If this is the case, then we could hypothesize that early temperament, as assessed by parent and teacher ratings in infancy or the preschool years, may serve as the building blocks for personality and later functional behavioral status. Nelson et al. (1999) used this logic to predict that preschool temperament would predict later functional behavioral status, as assessed by the BASC.

Their hypothesis was supported: Three temperament constructs (i.e., poor self-regulation of attention and motor behavior, adaptability, and negative emotionality) rated by parents when their children were 5, were sometimes associated with BASC TRS-C ratings at age 8. Negative emotionality, the most meaningful predicator of all four TRS-C composites was most highly related to the externalizing composite. Poor self-regulation of attention and motor control were related only to the school problems composite. The authors noted that the relationship between emotional intensity and externalizing problems, and between regulation of attention and school problems, are both

213

well supported by previous findings. Therefore, identification of problems early in development, via teacher ratings, may indicate early risk. These and related findings give considerable support to the advisability of early screening and targeted prevention. As teachers use the BASC TRS repeatedly, they become adept at completing the forms and commonly do so in about 10 minutes. A teacher can complete the BASC TRS-P for an entire class in about three hours—hours that can easily be spread over a 1- to 2-week period. There are few such efficacious approaches to screening for prereading-age children who are at high risk of developing behavioral and emotional difficulties. Once these at-risk youngsters are identified, a clinician (such as the school psychologist or a counseling psychologist) can review information on the child in more detail and determine whether further assessment is required, if an early intervention might be beneficial, or if the finding of high risk was a false alarm. Efforts to interrupt the early development of behavioral and emotional problems have high levels of long-term payoffs in the form of increased aversion of school failure (e.g., Meyers & Nastasi, 1999). Nevertheless, such efforts sometimes meet with resistance because the benefits may not be seen immediately. However, programs that identify high-risk children and subsequently employ targeted interventions may be far less expensive and more effective than system-wide programs targeted to all children. The BASC TRS-P and the PRS-P offer efficient screening for identification of high-risk children in the 2½- to 5-year age range.

CHAMPUS, the U.S. military civilian and retiree health-care system, began a longitudinal study of adolescents placed in residential treatment centers (RTCs) in 1997. The purpose of the study, under the direction of Dr. Richard Gaines, is to predict which adolescents referred for placement would actually benefit from the expensive RTC setting. Gaines (personal communication, 2001), reports that the BASC has been found to have "good predictive power" in this study, although details remain scant at this writing. We anticipate that the BASC will continue to be used in such contexts and that it will perform well due to its combination of rational, theory-driven, and empirical methods.

The BASC has also been used as a "basic" clinical science research tool, as exemplified in the studies by Kamphaus et al. (1997) and Kamphaus et al. (1999). The former study involved a cluster analysis of the TRS-C norming sample with the aim of developing a typology of child classroom behavior for the United States. The resulting seven-cluster typology may prove useful for the study of risk and protective factors in the context of research in developmental psychopathology. Briefly, the seven clusters identified were *well-adapted, average, disruptive behavior problems, learning problems, physical complaints/worry, general problems–severe*, and *mildly disruptive*. This study provides an estimate of the prevalence of these clusters in the U.S. classroom population and a description of their phenomenology (see Tables 7.1 and 7.2).

These analytic studies provide a method of classifying child behavioral adjustment into a finite number of types. In a sense, this process is akin to classifying weather phenomena, such as thunderstorm versus tropical storm versus sunny. As mentioned in Chapter 5, we currently have systems for classifying deviant behavior or psychopathology that do not allow us to study children on the cusp of significant problems or the transitions that take children on the cusp of normality into abnormality. It seems obvious to us that normal behavior is multidimensional and requires a taxonomy of its own. Psychology, especially the various clinical domains of the discipline, spends a grossly disproportionate amount of time and resources in the study of abnormal behavior to the exclusion of research on variants of normality. Further research on the dimensions and typologies of normal behavior is desirable and may well lead

TABLE 7.1. Mean *T* Scores by Scale for the Seven Cluster Solution (Total *N* = 1227)

Scales	Type						
	1	2	3	4	5	6	7
Externalizing							
Aggression	44.00	43.19	**67.83**	49.25	49.63	**69.56**	57.74
Hyperactivity	43.48	44.56	**66.29**	52.34	49.60	**69.92**	57.52
Conduct Problems	45.26	45.60	**65.37**	51.32	47.60	**71.31**	52.66
Internalizing							
Anxiety	45.88	44.80	54.39	52.32	58.40	**70.62**	47.28
Depression	44.48	44.55	**61.05**	51.79	55.30	**76.35**	50.28
Somatization	46.58	45.25	53.64	48.87	**64.99**	61.83	47.39
School Problems							
Attention Problems	40.99	49.18	**63.43**	60.77	49.22	**68.34**	52.50
Learning Problems	42.28	49.30	**62.90**	61.11	50.56	**65.56**	49.70
Other Scales							
Atypicality	45.12	46.22	58.91	55.09	49.41	**80.83**	50.26
Withdrawal	45.11	47.24	54.96	59.40	53.79	**69.38**	45.16
Adaptive Skills							
Adaptability	58.89	50.10	**37.26**	41.11	48.19	**32.54**	46.64
Leadership	59.02	43.38	41.85	**38.83**	49.99	41.60	50.72
Social Skills	58.81	44.34	41.16	**39.70**	51.89	42.33	47.43
Study Skills	**59.98**	46.39	37.97	38.35	51.06	**38.52**	47.92

Note. Values that differ from the mean by one standard deviation or more (regardless of direction) are printed in **boldface** type. Cluster 1 = well-adapted; cluster 2 = average; cluster 3 = disruptive behavior disorder; cluster 4 = learning disorder; cluster 5 = physical complaints/worry; cluster 6 = severe psychopathology; cluster 7 = mildly disruptive.

TABLE 7.2. Mean *T* Scores by Scale for the PRS-C Nine-Cluster Solution (Total *N* = 2029)

Scales	Type								
	1	2	3	4	5	6	7	8	9
Externalizing									
Aggression	47.68	51.88	53.13	**41.36**	44.26	48.68	52.70	**67.36**	64.60
Hyperactivity	45.66	54.69	51.62	**40.46**	42.80	50.99	49.21	**65.45**	62.85
Conduct Problems	46.07	52.19	51.76	**41.30**	43.84	50.19	49.81	**64.56**	62.98
Internalizing									
Anxiety	52.87	**59.13**	46.21	**42.31**	47.48	43.77	**59.79**	61.09	48.14
Depression	48.09	54.98	48.12	**39.76**	45.62	48.84	**59.96**	**72.52**	58.17
Somatization	50.36	**64.34**	46.81	**42.18**	45.89	48.39	51.44	**62.24**	49.97
Other Scales									
Attention Problems	**42.10**	51.69	51.16	**39.80**	45.65	**57.64**	52.12	**64.12**	61.42
Atypicality	48.43	**57.61**	46.72	**42.10**	44.98	49.38	50.92	**72.83**	54.16
Withdrawal	46.98	53.31	**42.87**	**42.78**	52.29	51.80	**62.96**	**59.11**	48.58
Adaptive Skills									
Adaptability	**57.29**	50.10	50.88	**60.78**	52.41	**41.25**	42.54	**35.68**	39.72
Leadership	**61.36**	50.83	53.26	**60.54**	47.51	**38.66**	44.51	40.67	45.40
Social Skills	**61.15**	51.74	49.70	**60.46**	49.89	**37.62**	45.83	**39.17**	41.00

Note. Values that differ from the mean by 7 points or more (regardless of direction) are printed in **boldface** type. Seven points represents the average standard deviation of scales within each cluster. Cluster 1 = adapted; cluster 2 = physical complaints/worry; cluster 3 = average; cluster 4 = well-adapted; cluster 5 = average, minimal problems; cluster 6 = attention problems; cluster 7 = internalizing; cluster 8 = general psychopathology-severe; cluster 9 = disruptive behavior problems.

us to a better understanding of deviancy and to improved interventions or possibly even new classes of interventions altogether.

In addition to classification, the research program reviewed above facilitate prioritization of various scales and composites of the BASC for purposes of prevention and intervention work. Out TRS cluster analytic studies clearly show that externalizing problems are the most salient (followed by adaptive skills) for determining behavioral adjustment in school. Internalizing problems are of considerably less significance (see Figure 7.1). Our prevention efforts related to school adjustment may be best directed toward externalizing problems and the promotion of adaptive skills development. The focus on externalizing problems is also consistent with our saliency ratings of BASC items, obtained from teachers and students (elementary and high school): Teachers and students consistently rated externalizing problem behavior as the most disturbing to them. Adaptive skills are nevertheless quite important for school adjustment, as demonstrated by two additional studies (Handfinger, 2001; Schwanz, 2001).

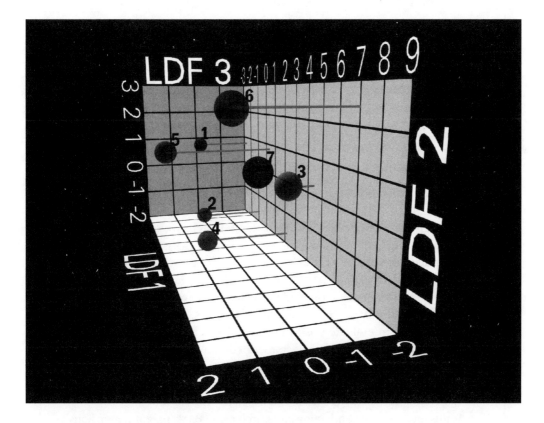

FIGURE 7.1. TRS-C seven-cluster solution represented in multidimensional space by three linear discriminant functions, where LDF 1 = Externalizing, LDF 2 = Adaptive Skills, and LDF 3 = Internalizing.

Merydith (2000) used the BASC TRS-A to assess the effects of violence prevention programs conducted in schools. Assistant principals were asked to nominate potential participants based on frequency of disciplinary referrals from teachers. Altogether, 18 students were referred for the intervention. Permission slips were mailed home to parents and guardians, of which 12 were returned. The students (7 female, 5 male) who participated were from grades 10–12 and had various educational classifications. Participant ethnicity consisted of 75% African American, 8% Caucasian, 8% Hispanic, and 8% Middle-Eastern. A control group was matched for educational placement, age, gender, and ethnicity. Frequency of disciplinary referrals was obtained by the assistant principals and attendance clerks and provided to the researchers. The control group was used only to review school records, not to administer pre- and posttests.

217

INTERVIEW 7.1

David A. Pineda, MD
Professor of Neurology and Neuropsychology
Universidad de Antioquia
Universidad de San Buenaventura
Medellín, Colombia

How do you use the BASC in your practice, research, and/or training activities?

We have used the BASC mainly in research on behavioral profiles of Colombian children and adolescents. Through this research, we have identified the normal clusters of different dimensions of conduct (social behaviors) in our young population. Also, we were able to calculate the prevalence of deviant conduct, such as ADHD/+H and ADHD/–H clusters. The cluster analyses showed, besides hyperactivity, inattention, and schooling problems, other probable clusters associated with ADHD, such as conduct problems, anxiety, and depression. It is also possible to evaluate positive or adaptive behaviors, using the BASC.

We used selected BASC dimensions as continuous criterion variables for grouping the sample in one study of language disorders in children with ADHD, with and without hyperactivity, and in another study on the neurological and neuropsychological characteristics of adolescents with conduct disorder.

At this time, we are conducting a research using BASC parent dimensions as quantitative continue traits (depend variables) in the lineal regression model for ADHD genetic markers (independent variables) of "Antioquian community" from Colombia. Initially we will search for dopamine D4RD7 (dopamine receptor) allele and DAT1 (dopamine protein transporter) mutations, and if someone tests positive, we will try to predict which dimensions of the conduct, measured with BASC parent, could be considered significantly as hereditary traits. We will compare these models with those obtained using the dimensions from SWAN-SNAP parent questionnaire.

In clinical practice the BASC has permitted us to relate the categorical diagnoses of the DSM-IV criteria (and other unidimensional questionnaires) to the behavior profiles obtained with BASC and thereby clarify the main problems on which to focus during the therapeutic sessions.

Please identify some of the outcomes of these activities.

We have calculated the structural reliability of the questionnaires for teachers and parents. Cronbach's alpha coefficient was .85 for the clinical scale (nine items) and .75 for the Adaptive scale (three items). A scale designed with four

(continued)

INTERVIEW 7.1 *(continued)*

items to assess (probably) ADHD (hyperactivity, attention problems, aggression, and conduct problems) showed an alpha coefficient of .82. Male children scored significantly higher than female (analysis of variance $p < .05$) in hyperactivity, conduct problems, and atypicality. Children of low socioeconomic status scored significantly higher than children of high socioeconomic status in most of the Clinical scale variables ($p < .05$) and lower in the three variables of the Adaptive scale.

Cluster analysis of six selected clusters found a prevalence of 61.6% for "normal" male children, with 14.8% showing higher adaptive capabilities, and 6.4% with deficient social skills; 8.6% had scores suggesting the possibility of ADHD, combined subtype, and 10.6% suggesting the possibility of uncontrolled temperament. "Normal" females showed a prevalence of 69.8%, with 18.9% obtaining higher Adaptive scale scores, 18.9% with high-risk scores on the Anxiety scale, and 13.2% scoring low leadership scale scores: 9.4% had scores suggesting the possibility of ADHD, combined subtype, and 1.9% of this group showed indications of multiple psychopathology with attention deficiency. In the total sample, 4% showed a possibility of ADHD type II (inattentive) and 14% of ADHD type I (combined).

Can you identify any particular strengths or weaknesses of the BASC, which others should consider in their work?

The main strength of BASC is its ability to delineate profiles of the different dimensions of behavior in children or adolescents grouped by categorical diagnoses. Another very important characteristic is its ability to identify positive and adaptive behaviors in normal and abnormal children and adolescents, which it is not possible with categorical systems and structured interviews.

The main weakness is the absence of more structured dimensions in the BASC self-report designed to obtain factors of conduct disorder and drug abuse, mainly for adolescents. Our clinical experience tell us that the self-reports are more reliable for detecting these problems in the earliest stages than are questionnaires for parents.

The researchers conducted small group training sessions for 50 minutes, once weekly, for 10 weeks. The results produced two significant findings. First, Externalizing Problems on the TRS-A were reduced significantly from a mean of 63 to 50, and School Problems from 57 to 52. Secondly, adaptive skills increased from 37 to 43. These improvements suggest that the TRS-A is sensitive to the effects of even brief intervention programs, such as the one implemented in this study.

Williford, Woods, and Shelton (2000) designed a preliminary study to test the effects of individualized service plans, parent and teacher training, classroom management consultation, direct classroom intervention, and child social skills training on the externalizing problems of preschoolers. Head Start children with externalizing T scores in the 93rd percentile or beyond were assigned to *assessment only* ($N = 16$) and *intervention groups* ($N = 28$). Most children were of African American heritage (82%) and 67% were male. Intervention group children received services over the course of 1 academic year. Numerous differences between BASC-TRS pre- and posttest ratings were observed. Significant reductions were noted on the BSI, Externalizing composite, Hyperactivity, and Attention Problems scales. The greatest reduction was observed on the Aggression scale, where the T score was 62.2 before intervention and 56.8 afterwards. Teachers also reported increased confidence in working with these children after intervention. Again, the TRS was shown to be sensitive to the effects of intervention.

FORENSIC APPLICATIONS

The BASC has many appropriate uses in legal and forensic settings. Under multiple U.S. Supreme Court rulings of the 1990s (e.g., see *Daubert v. Merrell Dow*, 1993; also see Reynolds, 2001b, 2001c), psychometric properties of tests used by forensic psychologists are crucial to consider when determining the admissibility of expert testimony based on test results. The BASC manual (Reynolds & Kamphaus, 1992) contains considerable information on the reliability of BASC scores and the standard errors of measurement of these scores, the availability of which is considered by judges in determining the issue of admissibility of testimony based in whole or in part on tests. The need for reliability in measurement to support the admissibility of testimony has been emphasized in the instructional materials designed for federal judges by the Federal Judicial Center (see Kaye & Freedman, 2000). The BASC manual, this book, and related literature on the BASC contain additional crucial data regarding the validity of the BASC as a measure of child and adolescent psychopathology and the ability of the BASC to discriminate among various diagnostic groups—additional considerations in determining admissibility. As we have noted throughout this work, the BASC has multitudinous clinical applications outside of the legal arena—a factor judges also view positively (Reynolds, 2001b, c). To the extent that judicial opinions are developed based on BASC results that are consistent with current literature, the choice of the BASC as a diagnostic instrument should bolster the arguments for admission of the expert's opinions.

Aside from the growing application of the Daubert standard for admissibility of expert testimony in federal and state courts, the BASC has other features to recommend it in forensic settings. One important factor for clinicians to consider in choosing instruments for forensic evaluations is the presence of scales designed to detect dissimulation (Reynolds, 1997). Dissimulation is the act of making oneself (or in the case of rating scales, the person being rated) appear dissimilar or different in some way from one's actual state. In the legal arena, individuals may have much to gain by appearing to have more or fewer problems than actually exist. Almost any behavioral or emotional disorder can be the subject of dissimulation. As Sattler (1998) notes in his extensive review, dissimulation, especially negative dissimulation or malingering, is difficult to identify. Objective methods are *de rigueur* for the accurate identification of dissimulation, although such a determination will ultimately be a decision made by the clinician on the basis of cumulative objective data and history (Reynolds, 1997).

The BASC rating scales (all levels of the PRS, TRS and the SRP-C and SRP-A) contain a key measure of dissimulation in the form of an F or Infrequency index. F indexes are sometimes referred to as "fake bad" scales because they detect exaggerated presentation of problems. Developed on the basis of two distinct parameters F indexes are composed of items with low overall levels of endorsement that have small–average intercorrelations. Thus, F index items are those least likely to be endorsed singly and even less likely to be endorsed in concert. The cluster of items on an F index does not define a particular symptom pattern or correspond to a particular form of psychopathology. When an F index is elevated, an exaggerated symptom pattern is often present; however, the reason for the exaggeration or overreporting of symptoms is indiscernible from the mere fact of elevation on the scale itself. The detection of patterns of negative dissimulation is crucial in settings where individuals may be motivated to present a false picture of the severity of their problems.

Even in cases involving children and adolescents, negative dissimulation is at issue in a variety of legal proceedings. Consider the following hypothetical scenarios, intended to be exemplary and not exhaustive.

An adolescent male with a history of minor vandalism was detained and charged with arson of an occupied building. He was referred by the judge of the juvenile court for a comprehensive psychological evaluation to assist the court in reaching a proper disposition in the case. As part of an evaluation, which also includes an extensive review of the young man's history, parent interviews, and a variety of psychological tests, BASC data were obtained, including a PRS from each parent, a TRS from two teachers, and the SRP-A. The judge was considering the prosecution's request for committing the young man to a secure facility for adjudicated delinquents until he reached the age of 18. The parents were arguing that their son was seriously mentally ill and should be placed in a local treatment facility instead. It was clear to all parties that this young man had serious behavioral problems; the court was interested in the nature and prognosis of his difficulties.

Josh's two TRS forms showed clinically significant elevations (70 or higher) on the Learning Problems, Aggression, and Conduct Problems scales, with an at-risk rating on the Attention Problems scale. F indexes on both TRS forms were within normal limits, indicating valid responding. On the two PRS forms obtained, both parents rated their son in the clinically significant range on the Atypicality and Depression scales; the mother also rated him in this range on the Anxiety scale. The Externalizing composite was a T of 50 and 60 for each parent. However, the F index on both PRS forms was elevated. On the SRP-A, Josh had clinically significant T scores on Atypicality and Sensation Seeking, with an at-risk T of 63 on the Anxiety scale. However, his F index was also elevated. Although the conclusions reached by the psychologist were based on additional interviews and other test data, the BASC results weighed heavily in reaching a formulation. The teacher ratings and Josh's history were consistent with a diagnosis of conduct disorder; however, the responses of the parents and Josh looked more like a form of psychotic disorder that would necessitate psychiatric treatment.

Given the consistent elevations on the F indexes by those with known motivations to malinger or engage in negative dissimulation, and the inconsistency in the cross-informant findings, the psychologist reached the conclusion that malingering was present in both child and parents. A diagnosis of conduct disorder was reported to the court, along with recommendations for implementation of empirically supported treatments associated with conduct disorder (e.g., see Hughes, 1999).

There are countless forensic circumstances when a parent might be motivated to engage in negative dissimulation about a child, and there are instances known to us where parents have induced their children to collude in such presentations (e.g., determining eligibility for social security disability income). We have seen this kind of behavior occur in personal injury litigation, where large sums of money change hands depending upon the nature and extent of the injuries suffered by a child or adolescent. Often children and adolescents who have brain injuries, other physical injuries, or are sexually assaulted will have significant behavioral and emotional changes that may or may not resolve over time. Most parents and their children present these changes in a forthright manner, but some do not (e.g., Binder & Rohling, 1996; Reynolds, 1997), and it is important to use rating scales and other measures that contain indexes designed to detect negative dissimulation.

Individuals may also be motivated to deny problems, although this scenario is less common in the forensic setting. Nevertheless, it is also important to be able to detect positive dissimulation or the denial of extant problems. Toward this end, the BASC SRP-A contains an *L* (Lie) or Social Desirability index. The *L* index is included in the SRP-A because of the propensity of adolescents to deny problems, even in clinical settings. Sattler (1998) notes that dissimulation is most likely to occur with children during the periods of older childhood and adolescence. Adolescents may well show elevations on the *L* index in a variety of forensic settings. For instance, in a juvenile proceeding, an adolescent may wish to appear supranormal to persuade a judge that the conduct bringing him or her to court was no more than a momentary lapse of judgment or a matter of having followed the bad example of a peer—just this one time. Adolescents may show elevations on the *L* index when attempting to mask alcohol or drug problems as well. Chapter 2 reviews additional validity indexes (*V* and Consistency) that may detect other patterns of invalid responding that are not typically purposeful patterns of dissimulation. However, due to the adversarial nature of the process, forensic settings tend to require a higher standard of defensibility. The use of scales, such as the BASC, that contain measures of response distortion is helpful to the forensic clinician.

Child Custody

The BASC has many applications in the context of conducting child custody evaluations. There is little more stressful, polemic, or anger-inducing experience than a child custody dispute. Psychologists are often involved in making recommendations to family courts on such issues. Specific training and supervised experience are strongly recommended for anyone engaging in this pre-

carious, litigious aspect of forensic practice. When courts decide custody issues, they generally have free reign to consider virtually any factor that might
impact what has become known as "the best interest of the child." Indeed,
this best-interest determination serves as the ultimate guidance to the court in
reaching a decision. Other factors to consider or emphasize in reaching a decision vary from state to state, but most include instructions in the state law
requiring judges to consider the wishes of the child (weighted by the child's
age); the relationship of the child to each parent; the child's adjustment to
home, school, and community; any special needs the child may have (e.g.,
various developmental, emotional, or behavioral disorders); some variant of
the construct of continuity of care; and a host of parent variables.

The BASC is an especially useful set of instruments for evaluating many of
these child variables. The entire process of using the BASC in child custody
evaluations would require a book of its own; however, it does have special
features that augur for its use in the child custody process. Aside from its
psychometric characteristics (e.g., large normative sample, reliability and validity data, etc.), the BASC is useful in determining the presence of emotional,
behavioral, and some developmental disorders in the context of a custody dispute, just as in its general application to clinical practice. Its strong normative
base also allows it to be interpreted as a measure of emotional and behavioral
maturity, which interests courts in weighing not only the child's wishes but
the amount of care required relative to the child's age.

In considering various aspects of the common legal instructions to the
courts regarding variables to consider in determining custody, the BASC offers some unique and efficacious contributions. For example, the *Uniform
Marriage and Divorce Act* instructs the court to consider "the interaction and
interrelationship of the child with his [or her] parent or parents." Commonly,
this relationship is considered by child custody evaluators, including psychologists, on a subjective basis, using interview and casual (or, on occasion,
more structured) observations (see Melton, Petrila, Poythress, & Slobogin,
1997). The BASC SRP contains a Relations with Parents scale that provides an
objective evaluation of the child's regard for the parents but also looks at the
child's feelings of being esteemed by the parents. During early research on
the development of the BASC, a group of experienced clinical psychologists
also recommended these items as measures of overall family adjustment (see
Reynolds & Kamphaus, 1992, p. 166). Clinically significant scores on the Relations with Parents scale by adolescents are also associated with antisocial behavior and delinquency (see Reynolds & Kamphaus, 1992, Tables 14.17 and
14.19)—factors that should also be considered by the evaluator. Although the
items on this scale do not differentiate the child's feelings about each parent,

they do provide an empirical measure of the relationship with the parents. Furthermore, the individual items can be used to distinguish the responses by parent in follow-up interviews with the child.

Using self-report personality scales and the child's response to the items as a means of generating good interview questions is a longstanding recommendation (e.g., see Koppitz, 1982, which also includes examples). As an example, one item on this SRP scale presents the stem, "I am an important person in my family." A child who responds "no" should be queried to understand whether the actions of the parents differed in the child's development of these feelings. Other items may provide direct information about the child's relationship with each parent when queried specifically for that detail (e.g., "I like to be close to my parents," "My parents listen to what I say," and "My parents don't think much of me.").

Additionally, the SRP-C and SRP-A contain a Locus of Control (LOC) scale that include many questions about how much control parents exert. A high score on LOC should alert the evaluator to query responses to such questions as "My parents blame too many of their problems on me," "My parents control my life," and "My parents expect too much from me." The various responses are easy to access because the BASC computer programs each contain an option that allows the examiner to print items grouped by scale for the TRS, PRS, and the SRP, along with the answer marked by the respondent. For those who prefer to use the hand-scored BASC, Appendix C lists items by scale for all the forms. Melton et al. (1997) emphasize clinical inquiry into the "child's depictions and conceptualization of relationship with each parent" (p. 502). Certainly the BASC and its scales should not be the sole means of such inquiry (additional interviews with collateral sources, evaluating approaches to discipline, etc., are also useful), but it does provide objective, quantifiable data and clear suggestions for follow-up queries.

The BASC PRS also offers a unique opportunity to look quantitatively at how each parent views the behavior of a child, in quantitative terms and the concordance of the views with each other and with various collateral sources. During custody evaluations, as in other evaluations, it is useful to obtain behavior rating scale data independently from each parent and from other sources who know the child well (e.g., a teacher). Once these data have been obtained and entered into either of the BASC computer-scoring programs, profiles can be generated and contrasted empirically for the ratings of each parent. The multi-informant report profiles each person's ratings of the child in addition to providing a table of T scores for each rater, testing the significance of the difference in the ratings for each subscale and composite score, and computing a similarity coefficient.

Figure 7.2 presents a comparison table from an actual case, where Rater 1 is the father and Rater 2 is the mother. This is typically the fourth page of the printout. In this case, the parents show a high level of agreement regarding their son's behavior; there is no significant difference in the ratings on any of the scales (see Figure 7.2, column 4), and the similarity coefficient is quite high at .83. The similarity coefficient on the BASC printout is a specialized co-efficient of correlation that considers shape (i.e., peaks and valleys) and eleva-tion or level of the overall profile. It has a range of values from −1.00 to +1.00, and is interpretable in a manner essentially consistent with that of co-efficients of correlation as a measure of shared variance.

T SCORE COMPARISON BETWEEN RATERS: General Norm Group

Scale	PRS-A Rater 1	PRS-A Rater 2	Significance Level
CLINICAL SCALES			
Hyperactivity	69	75	NS
Aggression	57	57	NS
Conduct Problems	66	62	NS
Anxiety	56	67	NS
Depression	50	55	NS
Somatization	64	64	NS
Atypicality	68	72	NS
Withdrawal	57	64	NS
Attention Problems	68	68	NS
ADAPTIVE SCALES			
Social Skills	46	46	NS
Leadership	43	45	NS

Composite	PRS-A Rater 1	PRS-A Rater 2	Significance Level
Externalizing Problems	67	67	NS
Internalizing Problems	58	64	NS
Behavioral Symptoms Index	65	71	NS
Adaptive Skills	44	45	NS

SIMILARITY COEFFICIENT

The Coefficient of Profile Agreement is computed on scale scores only and ranges from +1.0 (for prefect agreement between profiles) to −1.0 (for opposite profiles. Values close to +1.0 indicate that the two profiles are similar in both shape and level.

Similarity coefficient for Rater 1 and Rater 2: 0.82

FIGURE 7.2. BASC multirater PRS report form table showing high levels of agreement.

226

It is particularly noteworthy to the evaluator in a custody determination when parents show disagreement over the behavior of the child. In such instances, confirmation of any negative or positive biases will be important and often can be obtained by comparing each parent's ratings to the ratings of one or more teachers. The multi-informant report allows the contrast of a PRS with another PRS, the PRS with a TRS, or a TRS with another TRS (also see later section containing a case example of negative dissimulation).

Figure 7.3 presents another actual case showing mild-to-moderate disagreement on key aspects of the child's behavior. The father, Rater 1, sees the child as having a clinically significant number of behavior problems that are accented by problems with attention and unusual or atypical behaviors, the

T SCORE COMPARISON BETWEEN RATERS: General Norm Group

Scale	PRS-P Rater 1	PRS-P Rater 2	Significance Level
CLINICAL SCALES			
Hyperactivity	69	68	NS
Aggression	56	47	NS
Anxiety	55	45	NS
Depression	62	52	NS
Somatization	43	34	NS
Atypicality	63	37	.05
Withdrawal	51	59	NS
Attention Problems	80	69	NS
ADAPTIVE SCALES			
Social Skills	49	31	NS
Leadership	34	42	NS

Composite	PRS-P Rater 1	PRS-P Rater 2	Significance Level
Externalizing Problems	64	58	NS
Internalizing Problems	54	42	NS
Behavioral Symptoms Index	70	54	.01
Adaptive Skills	41	35	NS

SIMILARITY COEFFICIENT

The Coefficient of Profile Agreement is computed on scale scores only and ranges from +1.0 (for prefect agreement between profiles) to −1.0 (for opposite profiles. Values close to +1.0 indicate that the two profiles are similar in both shape and level.

Similarity coefficient for Rater 1 and Rater 2: 0.61

FIGURE 7.3. BASC multirater PRS report form table showing mild-to-moderate disagreement.

latter rarely seen by the mother. The parents may disagree for a variety of reasons: (1) the child, in fact, might behave quite differently with one parent than the other; (2) one parent may have a distorted, overly negative or overly positive view of the child; (3) one parent may be engaging in dissimulation for gain (e.g., "This child has numerous behavioral and emotional problems, and I am best suited to provide the special resources and special care he will require"), or (4) one of the parents (and sometimes both) may be ignorant of his or her child's actual behavior patterns. In making a custody recommendation, it is important to determine which explanation is likely to be the most accurate.

When children show large variations in their behavior with one parent, there are usually good reasons why, and discovering why is nearly always important. Clinical insights may be gleaned into the effectiveness of each person's parenting skills, ability to discipline appropriately, and capacity for tolerating the normal activity levels of children. Overly negative views of children can be detrimental to their development and instill poor expectations, while overly positive views may lead a parent to ignore real behavioral and emotional problems, again to the detriment of the child. Intentional distortion is virtually always seen as a negative indicator in a custody evaluation. All parties should put the child's best interest first, and this principle requires honest, cooperative interaction with the evaluator and the court. Parents who are less knowledgeable about their children may present special problems as well. Having each parent complete the BASC SDH independently helps to detect limited knowledge, as the two are compared to each other and to school and medical records. Often, a lack of knowledge reveals a lack of involvement in the daily care and routine of the child—another salient consideration for the court. Comparisons between TRS and PRS results are useful in this context as well.

The BASC thus has a number of features that provide assistance in formulating recommendations that have empirical support in custody proceedings. Experienced examiners, however, are aware that no single instrument or set of instruments—even those designed solely for use in custody evaluations—are sufficient for such decisions (e.g., see Melton et al.'s 1997 review of critiques of custody evaluation systems such as the ASPECT, BPS, PASS, and others).

Personal Injury

Outside of criminal casework, most forensic work performed by psychologists involves personal injury lawsuits. Behavioral changes are commonplace when children are injured in accidents, in cases of physical or sexual abuse, may suffer brain injuries. Adolescents, males in particular, are one of the two highest risk populations for traumatic brain injury. Emotional and behavioral changes post-TBI occur even in mild injuries (e.g., see Reitan & Wolfson, 2000). The primary diagnostic criteria for posttraumatic stress disorder (PTSD) and postconcussion disorder are changes in behavior (American Psychiatric Association, 1994). Behavior ratings thus have an integral role to play in evaluating "damages" in such cases and in establishing a diagnosis.

A brief example of a case wherein negative dissimulation or malingering in a personal injury case was strongly suspected may be instructive. This case involved a suit for damages associated with a motor vehicle accident in which a truck and car collided.

An 8-year-old boy was riding with his mother when they were struck by a concrete truck alleged to have run a stop sign. The child had a bruise on his right frontal skull region, just above the orbit of the eye. The mother described a brief loss of consciousness ("He seemed dazed and out of it for a few seconds and then started to cry"). Emergency Medical Services arrived within 15 minutes of the accident. The boy's Glascow Coma Scale was 15 (a perfect score) on examination at the scene, but his bruise had become prominent, making a small elevation of the skin (or "mouse"). He was transported to a local emergency room, where his neurological examination was reported as normal and a CT scan of the brain was negative. He was treated for a headache with Tylenol and released to his mother with standard TBI instructions for observation and a return to the emergency room if he became nauseous, dizzy, lethargic, or excessively sleepy. He continued to complain of headaches over several months, but follow-up neurological exams and a repeat CT at 2 weeks were normal, as was an EEG at 2 months after the accident.

In the lawsuit the mother claimed that Joey was subsequently "a different child," that his entire personality had been altered. She described her once happy, energetic, and accommodating son as moody and "hyper," displaying tantrums, crying episodes, and increasing aggression. School performance had not changed significantly when he was seen 15 months later for a neuropsychological examination related to the lawsuit filed on his behalf by the mother.

Cognitive testing revealed a young man with an average IQ doing average work in school. His scores on the Test of Variables of Attention (TOVA) were normal, but several mild neuropsychological deficits were seen on spatial and visual–motor integration tasks. He had a strength in his receptive language skills. However, the BASC PRS, completed by the mother, revealed substantial behavioral and emotional problems (see Figure 7.4 in which the father is

T SCORE COMPARISON BETWEEN RATERS: General Norm Group

Scale	PRS-C Rater 1	PRS-C Rater 2	Significance Level
CLINICAL SCALES			
Hyperactivity	38	76	.01
Aggression	39	73	.01
Conduct Problems	45	75	.01
Anxiety	44	63	.05
Depression	46	69	.01
Somatization	50	59	NS
Atypicality	42	59	NS
Withdrawal	44	50	NS
Attention Problems	42	71	.01
ADAPTIVE SCALES			
Adaptability	50	22	.01
Social Skills	51	27	.01
Leadership	39	37	NS

Composite	PRS-A Rater 1	PRS-A Rater 2	Significance Level
Externalizing Problems	39	79	.01
Internalizing Problems	46	68	.01
Behavioral Symptoms Index	38	77	.01
Adaptive Skills	46	25	.01

SIMILARITY COEFFICIENT

The Coefficient of Profile Agreement is computed on scale scores only and ranges from +1.0 (for prefect agreement between profiles) to −1.0 (for opposite profiles. Values close to +1.0 indicate that the two profiles are similar in both shape and level.

Similarity coefficient for Rater 1 and Rater 2: −0.77

FIGURE 7.4. BASC multirater PRS report form table showing severe levels of disagreement. Rater 1 is the father and Rater 2 is the mother.

Rater 1 and the mother, Rater 2). Fairly significant problems are seen in multiple domains.

The parents had been divorced for 2 years prior to Joey's accident; the father had standard visitation (he had Joey on the first, third, and fifth weekends of each month, from Friday at 5:00 P.M. until Monday morning, a 2-hour visit each Wednesday evening, 45 days in the summer, and alternate holidays). Since the father had consistent contact with Joey, he was also interviewed; he completed a PRS-C on Joey as well. The father's ratings (Rater 1 in Figure 7.4) differ markedly from the mother's. The father rated Joey as being well adjusted overall. The profile similarity coefficient for the profiles produced by the mother and the father was –.77, indicating staunch disagreement between the two, with near mirror-image profiles. The scaled scores obtained were statistically significantly different on nearly all scales as well (see third column of Figure 7.4).

If the father's description and ratings are accurate, there likely has been no behavioral change, and no lasting injury would be indicated. If the mother's ratings and descriptions are accurate, along with his prior unremarkable history, a significant brain injury, likely associated with fronto-temporal functioning, would be indicated. To assess which was more likely, cognitive findings were reviewed, along with the F index on each PRS-C, and a TRS-C was obtained from the teacher reported to know Joey the best. There were no cognitive findings associated with frontal or temporal damage. Memory and attention on actual performance tasks were normal (average), although the mother reported observations of problems in both areas. The F index on the mother's PRS-C was in the *extreme caution* range; on the father's, it was in the *acceptable* range. Joey's SRP-C showed at-risk findings on the Social Stress and the Depression scales but was otherwise normal in all respects.

The TRS-C showed no areas of clinically significant findings but did rate Joey as at risk on the Depression scale. As an empirical assessment of the level of agreement between the teacher's rating and each parent, a multirater report was generated for the TRS-C and each PRS-C. The similarity coefficient between the PRS-C completed by the father and the TRS-C was .79, whereas the coefficient between the mother's completed PRS-C and the TRS-C was –.61. These two similarity coefficients are obviously disparate and can be shown to be statistically significantly different as well.[1]

Based upon the overall findings of the examination, the history, and the incongruities noted above (also see Reynolds, 1997), the examiner concluded that the mother was misrepresenting her child's behavior, engaging in nega-

---

[1]To assess the statistical significance of the difference between any pair of BASC similarity coefficients, subtract each coefficient from 1, place the larger obtained value over the smaller obtained value, and divide—for example, $(1 - r_1)/(1 - r_2)$. This calculation produces a ratio of the residual variances in the profile. This ratio will approximate Student's T distribution. If this ratio of residual variances is equal to or greater than 2.02, you can be reasonably confident ($p \leq .05$) that the two similarity coefficients are different, meaning that the two profiles of ratings, taken as a whole, are different. Remember that a minimum of three profiles is necessary, A, B, and C. To contrast the similarity of A with C to B with C, compute similarity coefficients for A with C and B with C. The values of the coefficients will tell you which rater, A or B, is more like C. This is a measure of how similar the profiles are to each other. To determine if the profiles A with C and B with C are significantly different, taken as a whole, compute the ratio of residual variances, as given above. If they differ, then you can be confident that the profile produce by Rater A, taken as a whole, differs significantly from the profile provided by Rater B. This comparison takes into account the entire profile, not a single difference in scales or the lack of any difference on a specific scale.

tive dissimulation, for the purpose of financial gain. Had it been determined that Joey had suffered a TBI and the behavioral and emotional sequelae alleged by the mother, he would have received a substantial settlement, most likely placed into a trust for him. As his parent and managing conservator, the mother would have had access to these funds to use for Joey's benefit. Based upon the findings and conclusions of the neuropsychological examination, a much smaller monetary settlement was reached.

Posttraumatic Stress Disorder

Broad-band rating scales, as opposed to scales designed to assess symptoms specific to a disorder such as PTSD, are necessary with children and adolescents for several reasons: (1) "Children exposed to traumatic life events often exhibit symptomatology other than post-traumatic stress disorder" (Amaya-Jackson, 2000, p. 2766); and (2) children and adolescents are less predictable than adults in their presentation of symptoms and are likely to manifest problems secondary to traumatic life events that deviate from formal diagnostic criteria. Accurate differential diagnosis thus requires a review of a broad range of behaviors that goes beyond the specific diagnostic criteria for PTSD (Amaya-Jackson, 2000). This principle is true in relation to other disorders of children and adolescents as well (e.g., depression). Accurate diagnosis is not only crucial to designing proper treatment plans but to the litigation process as well, where diagnosis, causation, and prognosis are central determinants of the settlement.

As noted, the BASC has the advantage of dissimulation indexes, which are highly relevant in litigation proceedings. The use of all of the BASC components is encouraged in this context to assess the degree to which symptoms are evident and consistent (i.e., pervasive) across settings.

With respect to PTSD symptoms, the BASC PRS, TRS, and SRP have directly relevant scales. Once it has been determined that a child or adolescent has experienced a traumatic life event, the key factors to consider in reaching a diagnosis are degrees of arousal, avoidance, and reexperience. Arousal and avoidance (along with ancillary symptoms) can be assessed directly by the BASC but should also be covered in the interview. The assessment of traumatic reexperiences (e.g., nightmares, thought intrusion, reenactments) requires a clearly focused clinical interview with the individual and a very detailed history from a caregiver in order to establish a timeline of the symptoms detected.

BASC scales from the TRS and PRS that bear particular scrutiny under the arousal heading include all subscales of the Externalizing Problems composite: Aggression, Hyperactivity, and Conduct Problems. Children and youth lack the level of development of various coping mechanisms seen in adults and may not understand their feelings well. They often show aggression, over-activity, and even rule-breaking behavior as they act out the intense feelings experienced in response to the traumatic life event(s). Hyperactivity can be a direct result of increased arousal in otherwise normal children, whereas in the ADHD child, increased arousal may actually reduce the level of inappro-priate activity. On the Internalizing Problems composite, the Anxiety scale bears particular scrutiny in evaluating increased arousal. Children who experi-ence trauma and do not have many externalizing symptoms are at high risk for elevation on the Somatization scale as well. Under the School Problems composite, the Attention Problems scale also may denote increased arousal, as attention becomes difficult to maintain, and concentration wanes due to reduced energy. Learning problems, as indicated on the BASC subscale or otherwise, are a poor indicator of PTSD. Some children show improved school performance, as they throw all of their energy and attention into schoolwork to avoid thoughts of the trauma. Other children are overwhelmed by the traumatic stress to the point where they cannot function well academi-cally.

The PRS and TRS scales of Withdrawal and of Depression are the most in-formative regarding the avoidance seen in PTSD, although not for assessing the individual's penchant for avoiding stimuli associated specifically with the trauma or even thoughts of it. However, avoidance is often more pervasive in the behavior of traumatized children, leading them to withdraw from all their support systems and to experiencing the resultant secondary symptoms of de-pression.

The SRP assesses a variety of symptoms associated with PTSD. Self-esteem and self-reliance are often low in traumatized children, leading to restricted development of ego strength. SRP subscales (Sense of Inadequacy, Anxiety, Locus of Control, and Depression) will also address internalizing symptoms the child may not have expressed to others. However, it is important to keep in mind that *individual* children are not predictable in their manifestations of trauma, despite the trends that are evident among *groups* of traumatized chil-dren. Results of broad-based measures, such as the BASC, must be integrated with the history, the interview and observations of the child, and possibly with narrow-band scales that focus specifically on the traumatic event. Nega-tive findings on narrow-band trauma scales, however, do not rule out PTSD or other trauma-related responses in children.

The preceding discussion applies to children who undergo behavior and personality changes subsequent to physical injuries as well. Permanent physical injuries may force behavioral changes, and trauma-related changes are also likely to manifest following physical injury (e.g., see Amaya-Jackson, 2000).

Traumatic Brain Injury

Traumatic brain injury (TBI) is an all too common occurrence in children and adolescents, the latter being particularly susceptible to motor vehicle accidents and other perils of youth. TBI also occurs as a result of falls, injuries incurred in contact sports, fights, and a variety of unusual accidents. TBI is associated with many changes in cognitive, social, educational, behavioral, and emotional functioning (e.g., see Reynolds & Fletcher-Janzen, 1997, especially Chapters 7, 23, and 24). Even mild TBI can produce profound changes in personality, behavior, and the emotional aspects of the individual (Reitan & Wolfson, 2000). Changes in behavior and affect may be the only noticeable sequelae of a mild TBI. This outcome highlights the necessity of evaluating the behavior and personality of children and adolescents who sustain a brain injury.

In a litigation context, it is important to take a broad perspective of behavior following TBI and to use measures that include assessment of potential dissimulation (as previously noted). The BASC provides for each issue and contains scales that assess directly some of the most common or likely behavioral changes following TBI.

As documented over many decades, the most common behavioral changes following TBI (at all ages) are disturbances of attention and concentration and disruption of the inhibitory systems of the brain (Reynolds & Fletcher-Janzen, 1997; Riccio, Reynolds, & Lowe, 2000). The BASC TRS and PRS provide strong coverage of these areas. The Attention Problems scale provides a direct measure of the most common set of problems afflicting TBI children (ranging in age from 2½ to 19 years). Behavioral changes associated with disinhibition, often emphasized in TBI children (e.g., see Hartlage, 1989), are thoroughly covered on the Externalizing Problems composite scales. Unusual or odd behaviors that sometimes follow TBI are evaluated on the Atypicality scale.

The BASC Attention Problems, Learning Problems, and Conduct Problems scales have been demonstrated to correlate significantly with some neuropsychological performance measures (Riccio et al., 1994). Riccio et al. (1994) examined correlations between the BASC rating scales and performance on the Wisconsin Card Sorting Test (WCST). The WCST is a cognitive measure requiring rule induction and set-shifting on a novel problem-solving

234

task. These tasks are commonly considered to assess the integrity of frontal lobe functioning (e.g., Heaton, 1981), especially in children (e.g., Chelune & Thompson, 1987). The BASC Attention Problems scale was the most closely associated with the largest number of scoring alternatives on the WCST, including the perseverative errors score, often noted to be the best measure of frontal lobe functioning on the WCST. The Conduct Problems scale and the Learning Problems scale also showed good correlations with multiple scores on the WCST.

The BASC rating scales contain a number of items that are influenced strongly by TBI, including problems in frontal lobe or executive functioning, as noted above. Barringer and Reynolds (1995) used an expert approach to identification of BASC rating scale items for a frontal lobe/executive functioning scale, followed up by group comparisons. Barringer and Reynolds (1995) surveyed editorial board members of the three leading clinical journals in neuropsychology, *Archives of Clinical Neuropsychology*, *Journal of Clinical and Experimental Neuropsychology*, and *The Clinical Neuropsychologist*. Each board member was asked to rate each BASC PRS item according to the strength of its perceived association with frontal lobe functioning. Based on the obtained ratings, the items were ranked and a series of item analyses were performed, using the BASC standardization and clinical norm groups (Reynolds & Kamphaus, 1992). A set of 18 items that produced a highly reliable score (coefficient alpha of .84 on both the PRS-C and PRS-A) was then identified. Seventeen of the 18 items are common to the PRS-C and the PRS-A. These items are listed in Table 7.3 and may be used as a measure of frontal lobe and executive functioning. The content of the items is consistent with problems of attention and control as well as motivational issues. One of the major barriers to treating patients with frontal lobe injuries is their lack of motivation (sometimes referred to as amotivational syndrome) and a lack of awareness of behavioral changes or deficits (termed an *anosognosia*). These items can be readily located on the BASC computer printout or via the hand-scored forms.

Comparisons of various clinical groups on this scale showed high levels of discrimination. In the BASC standardization sample, the general norm group, had a mean *T* score of 48.4 on this scale. The BASC ADHD sample had a mean *T* score of 64.00 (1.4 *SD*'s above the total sample mean, and 1.56 *SD*'s above the normal sample), while children and adolescents with a diagnosis of conduct disorder earned a mean *T* score of 67.20 (1.72 *SD*'s above the total sample mean, and 1.8 *SD*'s above the normal sample). A sample of children with mental retardation had a mean *T* score of 60.1. Thus, the frontal lobe scale appears to be sensitive to organic conditions, with groups known to

TABLE 7.3. BASC PRS Items Associated with Frontal Lobe and Executive Functioning

PRS-C Item No.	PRS-A Item No.	
8	51	Cannot wait to take turn.
30	40	Throws tantrums.
34	77	Hits other children.
39	4	Forgets things.
40	80	Repeats one activity over and over.
41	70	Uses foul language.
43	8	Needs too much supervision.
44	115	Is a "self starter." (*reversed scoring*)
51	110	Is easily distracted.
64	92	Is easily upset.
67	55	Uses appropriate table manners. (*reversed scoring*)
78	103	Interrupts others when they speak.
86	99	Completes homework from start to finish without taking a break. (reversed scoring)
89	71	Changes moods quickly.
104	12	Begins conversations appropriately. (*reversed scoring*)
108	47	Completes work on time. (*reversed scoring*)
117	—	Adjusts well to changes in family plans. (*reversed scoring*)
118	45	Argues when denied own way.
—	67	Acts without thinking.

have frontal lobe impairment (ADHD and CD) scoring higher than a group with a more diffuse form of organic impairment.

Table 7.4 presents normative tables for the derivation of *T* scores for this scale for the PRS-C and the PRS-A. These *T* scores were based on the BASC standardization sample (see Reynolds & Kamphaus, 1992, for a detailed description) and used the same scaling methods described in the BASC manual. Consistent with our recommendations earlier (see Chapter 1), as well as Reitan and Wolfson's (2000) recommendations regarding demographic corrections and brain-injured persons, we have provided general norms data for this scale.

To use this table (7.4), locate the column under the correct form (PRS-C or PRS-A) that corresponds to the child's age group. Locate the child's raw score (the sum of the item scores, using reverse scoring as noted in Table 7.3). The corresponding *T* score is in the first column.

In addition to changes in observable behavior that can be rated objec-

TABLE 7.4. Normative Tables for the BASC PRS-C and PRS-A Frontal Lobe/ Executive Control Scale

	Raw scores			
T Scores	PRS-C ages 6–7	PRS-C ages 8–11	PRS-A ages 12–14	PRS-A ages 15–18
110			69–72	71–72
108			—	70
107			68	69
106	72	71–72	67	—
105	—	—	66	68
104	71	70	—	67
102	70	69	65	66
101	69	68	64	—
100	67–68	67	63	65
99	66	66	62	—
98	—	—	—	64
97	65	—	—	—
96	—	65	61	63
95	64	64	60	62
94	—	—	59	—
93	63	63	—	61
92	—	62	—	60
91	62	—	58	—
90	61	61	57	59
89	—	60	—	—
88	60	—	56	58
87	—	59	55	57
86	59	58	—	—
85	58	57	54	56
84	57	56	—	55
83	—	—	53	54
82	56	55	52	—
81	55	—	—	53
80	54	54	51	52
79	53	—	—	51
78	—	53	50	—
77	52	52	49	—
76	—	51	—	50
75	51	50	48	49
74	—	49	—	—
73	50	48	47	48
72	49	—	46	47
71	—	47	—	—
70	48	46	45	46
69	47	45	—	—
68	46	—	44	45
67	45	—	—	—
66	—	44	43	44

(continued)

TABLE 7.4. (continued)

	Raw scores			
T Scores	PRS-C ages 6–7	PRS-C ages 8–11	PRS-A ages 12–14	PRS-A ages 15–18
65	44	43	41–42	43
64	43	42	—	42
63	—	—	40	41
62	42	41	—	—
61	—	—	39	40
60	41	40	38	39
59	40	39	—	38
58	—	—	—	—
57	39	38	37	—
56	—	—	36	37
55	38	37	35	36
54	—	36	—	35
53	37	—	34	—
52	—	35	—	—
51	36	—	33	34
50	34–35	33–34	32	33
49	33	32	31	—
48	—	—	—	32
47	32	31	30	—
46	—	—	—	31
45	31	30	29	30
44	—	—	—	29
43	—	29	28	—
42	30	—	—	28
41	29	28	27	27
40	28	27	26	26
39	27	26	—	—
38	—	—	25	25
37	—	—	—	—
36	26	25	24	24
35	—	24	23	23
34	25	—	22	—
33	—	23	—	22
32	24	22	21	21
31	23	—	—	—
30	22	21	20	20
29	21	20	—	—
28	20	—	19	19
27	19	19	—	18
26	—	18	18	—
25	18			

tively by knowledgeable observers, changes in internal states are common in children with TBI. For example, depression may be induced as an organic problem following certain types and locations of TBI. The BASC SRP covers the primary areas of interest thoroughly and contains measures of dissimulation to detect over- and underreporting of symptoms. In all, we believe that the BASC has much to offer in the evaluation of any TBI child and a number of advantages in the litigation of such injuries.

Juvenile Certification

Another common area of forensic practice involves the issue of court certification of juveniles to stand trial as adults. The question of whether a juvenile should be transferred or waived to the adult court has become increasingly common (Melton et al., 1997). When juvenile judges make decisions in such matters, often referred to as certification hearings, the law gives them guidance in factors to consider, but it is ultimately a discretionary issue for the judge. In addition to considering the nature of the offense (e.g., whether it was a violent or otherwise aggravated offense) and the chronological age of the child, most states (not all; consult your state's juvenile or family code) instruct the judge to consider the relative maturity of the child and his or her amenability to treatment in the juvenile system.

The BASC is useful in evaluating both issues. Aside from its capacity to detect dissimulation or purposeful distortion, the BASC provides an objective means of establishing the presence or absence of a mental, emotional, or behavioral disorder. Once an accurate, objective diagnosis has been made, the consulting clinician is in a strong position to inform the judge regarding the availability of empirically supported treatments.

Since the BASC is a set of developmentally sensitive scales, with age- and with gender-based norms (which are important in establishing *relative* maturity levels), the issues of emotional maturity and behavioral maturity can be assessed by use of the PRS and the TRS. Obtaining teacher ratings is particularly important in such a context, since parents may be motivated to distort their responses in order to protect their child. The Adaptive Skills composites on the TRS and PRS are particularly good measures of maturity; low scores on these scales denote immature levels of development. However, all of the BASC scales are developmentally sensitive and deviations from normal the range of behaviors will be of interest.

The SRP has several features of special interest in certification evaluations. Two of the SRP Personal Adjustment composite scales, Self-esteem and Self-reliance, are, when combined, a good index of ego strength. Ego-strength scales are, in turn, good indicators of receptivity to, and ability to benefit from, treatment.

During the development of the BASC scales, 14 licensed clinical psychologists were asked to read all of the SRP items and sort them into discrete categories, which they created. These clinicians sorted the items that eventually became the Self-Reliance and Self-Esteem scales into one scale most often labeled Ego Strength. One may then combine these two scales into a content scale by averaging their *T* scores into a composite Ego Strength scale (content scales derived through expert analysis are common on many personality scales, most prominently the MMPI-2, which has more content than regular scales), as an aide in predicting the likelihood of a positive treatment response. The higher the score, the more optimistic the prognosis.

Three additional scales deserve special scrutiny in this context: Relations with Parents (RWP), Interpersonal Relations (INT), and Locus of Control (LOC). The RWP and INT scales are closely associated with a variety of research findings on resiliency. Resiliency comes from ego strength internally but also through the presence of support systems, most importantly in the form of family and peers. High scores on these two scales denote a resilient juvenile with strong support for change and improvement. A low score on LOC is a positive indicator, since such individuals tend to believe that they can control their own fate and are not simply unlucky or too easily overwhelmed by external factors, including their current circumstances or overbearing parents, teachers, or peers.

The BASC scales offer considerable assistance to the process of certification examinations. For additional components of this complex process, see Melton et al.'s (1997) overview.

Needs of Adjudicated Delinquents

The BASC is being utilized and researched at a variety of sites to identify the needs of adjudicated and incarcerated adolescents. In one such study, Stowers-Wright (2000) administered the SRP-A to 385 male juvenile offenders, 12–17 years old, to determine if there were patterns of mental health needs evident in this population. She hypothesized that at least a third of this population would have significant mental health problems. Her three-cluster solution identified about half of the sample as having mental health problems, comprised of two clusters, while one cluster did not report significant problems on any of the scales. The two "clinical" clusters differed primarily on the Attitude to Teachers and School scales. One cluster of adolescents reported significant problems in these areas, whereas the other did not. Both of the clinical clusters showed elevated scores on the Depression and Sense of Inadequacy scales, as well as other scales.

All three clusters displayed the same profile but differing levels on the Relations with Parents, Self-Esteem, and Self-Reliance scales, as shown in Figure 7.5. The similar shape of this adaptive scale profile for incarcerated adolescents appears meaningful. All of these adolescents essentially see themselves as having no lack of self-esteem. When experiencing adjustment difficulties, such as those in clusters 2 and 3, they feel that their relationships with parental figures are strained, they do not feel self-reliant, and yet their self-esteem remains intact. One potential implication of these findings is that these adolescents separate their feelings and self-perceptions along the lines of the SRP-A scales. Clearly, they can feel very capable in one area while reporting problems in another. Evidently, they require careful assessment of multiple domains, and any evident bravado does not rule out problems.

Stowers-Wright (2000) also notes that these findings are similar to those of previous investigations. Sorneson and Johnson (1996), for example, identified five clusters using the MMPI and Jesness inventories. They, too, identified a large cluster of incarcerated juveniles whom they described as free of emo-

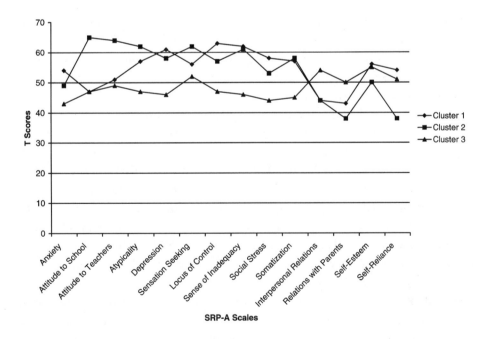

FIGURE 7.5. A graphic representation of the three-cluster solution of the SRP-A for adjudicated delinquents studied by Stowers-Wright (2000).

tional disturbance and another group with multiple elevations, as was the case for Stowers-Wright's cluster 1. Stowers-Wright's results, though still requiring validation, suggest that the SRP can play an important role in forensic settings.

The forensic circumstances described in this section are not intended to be exhaustive treatises on how the BASC can be applied in such forensic situations. They are given as examples, guided by our decade of experience with the BASC in forensic applications, our knowledge of the developmental process of the BASC itself, and the subsequent research reported in the literature. Many other forensic applications have been made; the BASC is useful in any context where diagnosis of childhood psychopathology, behavioral change, and prognosis are at issue.

THE BASC IN PEDIATRICS AND PEDIATRIC PSYCHOLOGY

Pediatric psychologists deal with a host of presenting problems, often centering around medical issues that include neurodevelopmental and genetic disorders, chronic serious medical conditions (such as juvenile leukemia and diabetes), and organ transplantation (e.g., see Goldstein & Reynolds, 1999; Olson, Mullins, Gillman, & Chaney, 1994). Many of these children and youth, especially those with chronic conditions, have problems of behavior and affect (e.g., see Fletcher-Janzen & Reynolds, in press; Goldstein & Reynolds, 1999; Olson et al., 1994; Whelan & Walker, 1997). Chronic dialysis, various cancer-related chemotherapies, and even asthma treatments can have iatrogenic effects on behavior and affect, including self-perceptions. Behavior rating scales and self-reports of feelings and perceptions are routinely included in psychological and neuropsychological exams, and the BASC is often recommended (e.g., Reynolds & Mayfield, 1999). Broad-based measures such as the BASC are useful at all levels of diagnosis in pediatric psychology.

An example of the variety of pediatric investigations that have used the BASC is provided by Bunke (1998), who found that children with poor coping strategies during medical procedures were more likely to have more externalizing, internalizing, and school problems, as rated by teachers on the TRS-C and the TRS-A. In addition, the teachers' ratings of these youth on the BASC Adaptive Skills composite were negatively correlated with poor coping strategies. These relationships are significant in light of the fact that they are correlations between teacher ratings of behavior and the children's self-reports of coping strategies, thus providing evidence that the BASC TRS results have implications for primary health care.

INTERVIEW 7.2

Michael Reiff, MD
Learning and Behavior Problems Clinic
Department of Pediatrics
Children's Hospital, Minneapolis

I am a developmental and behavioral pediatrician. As part of my clinical work I direct a multidisciplinary team that evaluates school-aged children for learning and behavior problems. I work clinically in a behavioral pediatrics service where we see children for evaluation and treatment of enuresis, encopresis, chronic headaches, pain syndromes, stress, tics, and other problems.

We use the BASC for most evaluation visits (always a parent, often a teacher, and, selectively a self). For evaluations we also use parent and teacher versions of the DSM-based scales that have been normed and validated. It is very helpful to compare and contrast the two. Subsequently, during follow-up visits, we often request a teacher BASC particularly for children with ADHD and comorbid conditions who are treated with medication but experience suboptimal performance or unexplained changes in functioning. BASCs have also become components of our a yearly routine visits

In our behavioral pediatrics program we request a parent BASC at intake, as a general screen. We find that the interviews can subsequently be much more focused and selective than if we did not have this information. We collect a systematic database on all patients and are hoping to do a project comparing clinical diagnoses with DSM scales, BASC reports, continuous performance tasks and individual clinical finding.

Strengths: We find BASC profiles to be extremely useful tools for developmental/behavioral pediatricians and trainees. They are very helpful in defining areas of high risk and helping to guide decision making regarding referrals to psychology.

Weaknesses: It is rare for us to find a "self" BASC on which at-risk or significant endorsements are made. Because of this, we have not found the child or self-report instruments to be particularly helpful with our patient population.

Other remarks: BASC reports are extremely helpful with many bio-psycho-social problems, including the "mostly medical" arena such as children with chronic medical illnesses. I would also encourage their use in primary care practices for the same purpose—providing help in making appropriate referrals for behavioral and mental health services.

(continued)

INTERVIEW 7.2 *(continued)*

Turf issues and billing considerations have been of some concern. I have found some psychologists concerned about and wary of the use of BASCs by medical providers. Obtaining reimbursement as a medical provider may also be an issue. In my institution physicians have been discouraged from billing for BASCs that have been administered, as this is an unusual kind of routine for medical office visits. I would speculate that this might be a similar situation in other institutions or offices.

The American Academy of Pediatrics Report on Diagnosis of ADHD

In May of 2000, the American Academy of Pediatrics (AAP) released a preview of their subsequent report on diagnosis of ADHD (AAP Committee on Quality Improvement, 2000). Noting that ADHD is a common problem and becoming increasingly a controversial one, the AAP (2000) recommended broad diagnostic work that is largely behaviorally based. For example, the AAP recommended the use of behavior rating scales in the following actions:

1. The assessment of ADHD should include information obtained directly from parents or caregivers, as well as a classroom teacher or other school professional, regarding the core symptoms of ADHD in various settings, the age of onset, duration of symptoms and degree of functional impairment.
2. Evaluation of a child with ADHD should also include assessment for co-existing conditions: learning and language problems, aggression, disruptive behavior, depression or anxiety. As many as one-third of children diagnosed with ADHD also have a co-existing condition. (AAP, 2000, p. 1)

In making these recommendations, the AAP appears to recognize the need, as we do and as others have noted (e.g., Goldstein, 1999), for a broad-based assessment of the behavior and affect of children suspected of having ADHD. However, the AAP COQI report (2000) in *Pediatrics* goes on to recommend *narrow-band* scales, such as the BASC ADHD Monitor, for *diagnosis* of ADHD. This is faulty thinking both logically and clinically. Narrow-band scales with a sole focus on ADHD symptoms (or other, similar, single-disorder scales) cannot assist in the determination of comorbid disorders and inevitably lead to over-diagnosis of the named condition. The recommendation for use of narrow-band scales in the possible case of ADHD contradicts other positions expressed

INTERVIEW 7.3

Robert A. Leark, PhD
Vice-President, Research amd Development,
Universal Attention Disorders, Inc.

How do you generally use the BASC in your practice?

The BASC is an integral component of any clinical work I do with children. Following a thorough history of the child, I use the BASC results to assist with the development or confirmation of clinical hypotheses. This is especially true for those children with sufficient reading skills. In these cases, the full complement of BASC assessments (self, teacher, and parent) becomes helpful in identifying converging areas of need through the consistent signs and symptoms of the child. Areas of discrepancy also become evident through the multirater model. These discrepancies are helpful in determining the areas of focus for treatment. For example, discrepancies between teacher and parent ratings of behaviors may lead to a better of understanding of the child's behavior in structured versus unstructured settings. Furthermore, the BASC scales (for all assessment modalities) help me determine what other collaborative assessments need to be completed, and they provide an objective method for assessing treatment outcomes. This objective aspect demonstrates to parents the effect that any behavioral programs have on their child—especially helpful if the behavioral programs change the family's life-style. Lastly, the validity scales help me identify and understand test-taking biases.

TOVA/CPT and BASC: A good fit.

The TOVA (or other standardized continuous performance tests [CPTs]) are designed to provide an objective method for measuring sustained attention and impulse control. Behavioral rating scales do not as readily measure these hallmarks of ADHD. Rather, the behavioral rating scales reflect the behaviors of someone who may have problems with sustained attention and impulse control. Performance on the TOVA and other CPTs is affected by anything that might influence sustained attention. Anxiety and depression are two key factors that influence TOVA performance. The BASC provides a simple, reliable, and valid method for measuring both anxiety and depression. Parents and ADHD children can easily complete the tests in a short time. And the BASC has been demonstrated to be a useful diagnostic tool in the prediction of ADHD. The use of the BASC in conjunction with the TOVA increases the likelihood of making a correct diagnostic decision.

(continued)

INTERVIEW 7.3 *(continued)*

What do you like about the BASC?

Parents and children can complete the form in a short period of time. This may not sound like much, but it is. Parents and children (especially children with ADHD) do not want to complete lengthy tests. The shortness and relative ease of administration of the test does not come at the price of validity and reliability. I quickly get test data that I can depend upon to be accurate. This helps me with diagnostic and care decisions.

---

in the AAP COQI report and leads to serious problems with differential diagnosis.

Many disorders of childhood and adolescence can mimic ADHD as well as coexist with it. Prominent examples of disorders that can result in increased activity levels, impulsivity, and attention deficits in children include, but are not limited to, PTSD, generalized anxiety disorder, major depressive disorder, variations of bipolar disorder, and variations of pervasive developmental disorder not otherwise specified. The use of scales that focus solely on the core symptoms of ADHD, as recommended by the AAP COQI, is inappropriate and will result in misdiagnosis of children with the above and other disorders.

Narrow-band scales are useful on a postdiagnosis basis—after the diagnosis has been established and a treatment plan put into place. This principle includes the BASC ADHD Monitor scales, which are designed to identify, if present, the primary symptoms of ADHD emphasized in the DSM-IV, and which would fall under the AAP COQI guidelines for use in diagnosis. Yet, we view this recommendation as inappropriate.

The use of broad-band scales is imperative for reasons well stated in parts of the AAP COQI report but abandoned later. Broad-band scales, such as the BASC TRS and PRS, are necessary to identify comorbid conditions and to engage the process of differential diagnosis (e.g., Goldstein, 1999). Only by viewing the comprehensive symptom complex can an accurate diagnosis be reached. Narrow, focused assessment instruments do not tap into the symptom complex. Continuous performance tests (CPTs), for example, do an excellent job assessing the key components of an ADHD diagnosis: attention deficits and impulsive responding. However, there are many disorders that produce the same symptoms (see Riccio, Reynolds, & Lowe, 2001, for an extended review and discussion), and to base a diagnosis solely on the presence of these symptoms will result in many children with anxiety disorders, depression, variants of pervasive developmental disorder, psychotic symptoms, and other disorders incorrectly receiving a diagnosis of ADHD and improper, sometimes harmful, treatment.

Evidence (reviewed in Chapter 5; Ramsay, Reynolds, & Kamphaus [2002]; Reynolds & Kamphaus [1992]) supports the use of the BASC TRS and PRS specifically for diagnosis of ADHD. During the diagnostic process there is also the need to obtain self-reported information from the child. Children have much to tell us about their conditions, especially in the internal domain, and broad-based self-report scales such as the SRP are necessary to determining an accurate diagnosis. While we commend the AAP for recognizing the problems and issues involved in diagnosis of ADHD, especially the insights represented in the above quotes, the AAP COQI (2000) report fails in its recommendations for implementation.

EVALUATIONS OF CULTURAL/ETHNIC BIAS ON THE BASC

There are many differences in mean levels of performance, or scores, on the various BASC subscales associated with the gender of the child being rated. These differences are reported and discussed in the BASC manual (Reynolds & Kamphaus, 1992, especially Chapter 11 and Figures 11.2 and 11.3, pp. 95–96). Subsequent research has confirmed the presence of gender differences on some BASC subscales, even once the composite scores were used as a control variable (Dunbar, 1999). However, the relative reliability of the scales was constant across gender. Mean differences in scores do not provide evidence of bias. Rather, a detailed analysis of the question of test bias is required to understand the differences observed (e.g., see Reynolds et al., 1999).

During the development of the BASC, when the final items were being chosen, careful analyses of potential item bias were conducted by gender and ethnicity. Using item-plots, items that were found to function differently for boys and girls were eliminated from the BASC. A later study by Reynolds (1998) went back to the original BASC item pool and calculated common item statistics separately by gender. Applying a common set of item selection rules to choose items entirely on an objective basis resulted in essentially the same item-sets being selected, regardless of whether the underlying sample was male, female, or a combined male/female group.

These findings all support the use of the BASC scores and recommended interpretations for both boys and girls. The mean differences seen in BASC scores for boys and girls are consistent with gender differences generally reported in the scientific literature (e.g., Reynolds & Richmond, 1985; Reynolds,

Richmond, & Lowe, 2002) and cannot be attributed to gender bias in the BASC.

Ethnic differences are not reported or reviewed in the BASC manual; however, Knight (1996) undertook an extensive analysis of ethnic differences on the BASC for African Americans, Hispanics, and Caucasians. She reported no differences in mean scores (using multiple approaches to detection) at ages 4–5 years. At ages 6–11 years, Caucasians had higher overall scores on Aggression and Depression. At the 12–18-year-old levels, African Americans had higher scores on the Atypicality scale. A smaller-N study by Murphy (2000) compared the ratings of 77 Caucasian teachers and 10 African American teachers for a common group of 64 children (Caucasian and African American) participating in special education programs. Only one significant difference emerged; Caucasian teachers tended to rate Caucasian children as having more externalizing behavioral problems than did African American teachers rating the same children. At this point in the literature, few differences have been reported on the BASC as a function of the ethnicity of the teacher completing the TRS, but we consider this to be a ripe and necessary area for additional research.

As with the gender analyses of items, BASC items were also screened statistically for ethnic bias during the development of the BASC (see Reynolds & Kamphaus, 1992, Chapter 11). All items showing differential item functioning (DIF; see Reynolds et al., 1999, for an explanation and review) were eliminated. Postpublication of the BASC, Mayfield and Reynolds (1998) undertook an extensive analysis of potential ethnic bias on the BASC items, using methods similar to Reynolds (1998) but also conducting more extensive analyses. Common item-sets were found to be the best measures of the various BASC constructs across all ethnic groups. The care with which the initial items were selected, as well as follow-up research, indicate that ethnic group differences on the BASC, although relatively small, are real and not an artifact of bias. A common set of interpretations of scores on the various BASC subscales is supported across these ethnic groupings (African Americans, Hispanics, and Caucasians) and across gender.

Información sobre el BASC
para los padres

BASC es la sigla utilizada para denominar el Sistema Multidimensional de Evaluación de la Conducta de los Niños (En inglés: Behavioral Assessment System for Children). El BASC fue diseñado para facilitar el diagnóstico diferencial y la clasificación pedagógica de una variedad de desórdenes emocionales y comportamentales y para ayudar también en el diseño de planes de intervención. Se considera multidimensional porque mide numerosos aspectos del comportamiento y la personalidad, incluyendo dimensiones positivas (adaptativas) y negativas (clínicas). Los componentes del BASC son instrumentos confiables y muy sofisticados en términos psicométricos, si se usan individualmente proporcionan al clínico una variedad de información beneficiosa. Cuando el BASC se usa como sistema total proporciona información acerca de un niño desde distintas perspectivas, permitiendo así que quien lo utiliza obtenga el mejor conocimiento sobre el niño (Sandoval & Echandía, 1994).

CARACTERÍSTICAS DEL BASC

Esta escala mide una gran variedad de dimensiones. Además de evaluar problemas de personalidad, de comportamiento y trastornos emocionales, identifica atributos positivos que pueden ser aprovechados en el proceso de tratamiento.

El rango de dimensiones evaluadas ayuda a establecer un diagnóstico diferencial entre las categorías específicas del trastorno (tales como las anotadas en el DSM-IV) y categorías generales de otros problemas (tales como los descritos para la educación especial o "Individuals with Disabilitities Education Act" en los EE UU). El BASC cumple todos los requisitos gubernamentales relacionados con el diagnóstico de trastornos emocionales severos en los colegios (Flanagan, 1995).

Cada componente del BASC está diseñado para un ambiente específico o para el tipo de persona que lo contesta ya que algunos comportamientos son más importantes o tienen más valor en algunos ambientes que en otros. Las escalas del BASC son de gran valor interpretativo porque están construidas alrededor de situaciones o comportamientos claramente especificados. Ofrecen varios tipos de validez que permiten que el clínico mida la veracidad y la consistencia de los informantes (Kamphaus & Distefano, 2001)

La tabla A1 muestra las escalas clínicas y adaptativas de los cuestionarios de Padres (PRS) y Maestros (TRS). La tabla A2 muestra las escalas clínicas y adaptativas del cuestionario de Auto Informe.

ESCALAS DE LOS BASC TRS, PRS Y AUTO INFORME

TABLA A1. Las escalas clínicas y adaptativas de los cuestionarios de Padres (PRS) y Maestros (TRS)

Escalas clínicas

Hiperactividad. Tendencia a ser excesivamente activo, a precipitarse en el trabajo o en otras actividades y a actuar sin pensar.

Agresión. Tendencia a actuar de manera hostil (verbal o físicamente), amenazadora hacia los demás.

Problemas de conducta. Tendencia a un comportamiento antisocial, rompiendo las reglas, incluyendo la destrucción de propiedad privada (entre los 6 y los 18 años de edad).

Depresión. Sentimientos de infelicidad, tristeza y estrés que pueden ocasionar la incapacidad para llevar a cabo actividades cotidianas (síntomas neurovegetativos) o en pensamientos suicidas.

Somatización. Tendencia a ser demasiado sensible y a quejarse de pequeñas dolencias físicas.

Ansiedad. Tendencia a estar nervioso, con miedo y preocupado por problemas reales o imaginarios.

Problemas de atención. Tendencia a distraerse fácilmente e incapacidad de mantener la concentración.

Problemas del aprendizaje. Presencia de dificultades en el estudio, particularmente en la comprensión o realización de trabajo escolar.

Atipicidad. Tendencia a comportarse de manera inmadura, "extraña", conducta comúnmente asociada con la psicosis (como por ejemplo, alucinaciones visuales o auditivas).

Aislamiento. Tendencia a evadirse de los demás y a rechazar contacto Social.

Escalas adaptativas

Adaptabilidad. Habilidad de adaptarse a cambios ambientales (entre los 2,5 a los 11 años de edad).

Liderazgo. Habilidades asociadas con la consecución de metas académicas, sociales o comunitarias, en particular, habilidad de trabajar bien con los demás.

Habilidades sociales. Habilidades necesarias para interactuar eficazmente con compañeros y adultos en el hogar, la escuela y en la comunidad.

Habilidades en el estudio. Habilidades que conducen a resultados académicos positivos, incluyendo habilidad organizativa y buenos hábitos de estudio (TRS para las edades 6 a 11).

TABLA A2. Escala de Auto Informe

Ansiedad. Sensaciones de nerviosismo, preocupación y miedo; la tendencia a sentirse desbordado con problemas.

Actitud para el estudio/hacia la escuela. Sensaciones de alienación, hostilidad e insatisfacción con respecto a la escuela.

Actitud hacia los maestros. Sensaciones de resentimiento y antipatía hacia los maestros; piensa que los maestros son injustos, indiferentes y demasiado exigentes.

Atipicidad. Tendencia a tener fuertes cambios de humor, pensamientos extraños, experiencias subjetivas o pensamientos obsesivos y compulsivos frecuentemente considerados como "extraños".

Depresión. Sensaciones de infelicidad, tristeza y dejadez; el convencimiento de que nada sale bien.

Relaciones interpersonales. Percepción de tener buenas relaciones sociales y amistades con compañeros.

Lugar de control. Creencia de que los premios y los castigos están controlados por circunstancias externas y otras personas.

Relaciones con los padres. Consideración positiva hacia los padres y sensación de ser estimado por ellos.

Autoestima. Sensaciones de autoestima, autorespeto y autoaceptación.

Confianza en sí mismo/a. Confianza en la habilidad propia de resolver problemas; confianza personal y poder de decisión.

Búsqueda de sensaciones. Tendencia a arriesgarse, gusto por el ruido y búsqueda de emociones.

Sentimiento de falta de adecuación. Percepciones de estar fracasando en la escuela, incapacidad de conseguir las metas propias y sensación de inadecuación.

Estrés social. Sensaciones de estrés y tensión en las relaciones personales; sensación de ser excluido de las actividades sociales.

Somatización. Tendencia a ser demasiado sensible a la experiencia o quejas sobre molestias y problemas físicos de tipo menor.

Clasificación de los puntajes

Escalas clínicas. Puntajes T mayores de 70 evidencian problemas que necesitan evaluación clínica, tratamiento o intervención de algún tipo. Puntajes T entre 60 y 69 evidencian riesgo y los puntajes por debajo de 60 se consideran normales.

Escalas adaptativas. Puntajes T inferiores a 30 evidencian déficits en comportamientos adaptativos; puntajes T entre 31 y 40 evidencian déficits leves. Puntajes T por encima de 40 se consideran normales.

BASC Brief Overview
for Consumers

Behavior Assessment System for Children (BASC)
Cecil R. Reynolds and Randy W. Kamphaus
American Guidance Service, Inc. 1992

DESCRIPTION

Brief Description

The BASC is a multimethod, multidimensional approach to evaluating the behavior and self-perceptions of children. It has five components that can be used individually or in any combination. The three core components are Teacher Rating Scales (TRS), Parent Rating Scales (PRS), and Self-Report of Personality (SRP). Additional components include Structured Developmental History (SDH) and Student Observation System (SOS). The BASC measures positive (adaptive) as well as negative (clinical) dimensions of behavior and personality.

Primary Use/Purpose

The BASC facilitates differential diagnosis and educational classification of a variety of children's emotional and behavioral disorders and aids in the design of treatment plans.

Age/Grade Range Covered

4–18 years of age. The TRS and PRS each have three levels: preschool (4–5), child (6–11), and adolescent (12–18). The SRP has two levels: child (8–11) and adolescent (12–18).

Administration Time

Time varies for each component. TRS/PRS: 10–20 minutes; SRP: 30 minutes; SDH: Because this is a comprehensive history and background survey, it will vary from family to family; SOS: 15 minutes.

Individual versus Group

Individual

User Qualifications

Users are expected to have had formal training in the administration, scoring, and interpretation of behavioral rating scales and self-report personality scales. Clerical staff, with appropriate training, can administer and score various BASC components, but interpreting and applying the results require at least a graduate level of education.

CONTENT

Domains

The TRS, PRS, and SRP measure positive as well as negative dimensions of behavior and personality.

Scale Names

TRS/PRS Clinical scales include Aggression, Hyperactivity, Conduct Problems, Anxiety, Depression, Somatization, Attention Problems, Learning Problems, Atypicality, and Withdrawal. Adaptive scales include Adaptability, Leadership, Social Skills, and Study Skills.

SRP clinical scales include Anxiety, Atypicality, Locus of Control, Social Stress, Somatization, Attitude to School, Attitude to Teachers, Sensation Seeking, Depression, and Sense of Inadequacy. Adaptive scales include Relations with Parents, Interpersonal Relations, Self-Esteem, and Self-Reliance.

Composite Name

TRS/PRS composites include Externalizing Problems, Internalizing Problems, School Problems, Adaptive Skills, and a Behavioral Symptoms Index.

SRP composites include Clinical Maladjustment, School Maladjustment, Personal Adjustment, and an Emotional Symptoms Index.

Forms

The TRS, PRS, and SRP forms come in two formats: hand-scoring (carbonless) and computer entry.

SCORING INFORMATION

Items

Item Types

TRS/PRS items are descriptions of observable positive and negative behaviors. SRP items are descriptions of positive and negative personality traits, thoughts, attitudes, and feelings.

Response Format

The TRS/PRS rater circles N for Never, O for Often, S for Sometimes, and A for Almost always in response to behaviors observed. The SRP respondent circles T for True and F for False in response to personal thoughts and feelings experienced.

Item Scoring

Items are scored by scales. The N, O, S, and A responses correspond to 0, 1, 2, and 3 points. Adding the points for a particular scale yields a raw score, which can then be converted to a normative score.

Scoring Options

Forms can be hand-scored or scored by computer with the BASC Enhanced ASSIST or the BASC Plus software. Scanning software, utilizing as special response form, is also available.

Derived Scores Available

Scales

T scores and percentiles.

Composites

T scores and percentiles.

Domain

Norm Groups Available

General, gender-specific, and clinical.

Interpretive Features

1. Various validity indexes help identify forms that may be unusable because of an excessively negative or positive response set. In addition, the computer scoring programs provide indexes to detect random or patterned responding.
2. The record form provides information on the significance and rarity of differences between composite scores or between a scale score and the total score.
3. Both software programs provide an index of the similarity of two profiles. In addition, BASC Plus highlights items that are related to DSM-IV diagnostic categories.

Computerized Scoring

Available in the BASC Enhanced ASSIST and the BASC Plus software for DOS, Windows, and Macintosh. The BASC Plus includes online administration.

TECHNICAL INFORMATION

Standardization

Description

Goal was to collect samples representing population of U.S. children age 4–18, including representative sample of exceptional children.

Date

Fall 1988 through spring 1991.

Size

116 testing sites. TRS: $N = 2,401$; PRS: $N = 3,483$; SRP: $N = 9,861$. Based on U.S. census data in the year 1990.

Sample Controls

Samples were controlled for:

- Age: Yes.
- Gender: Yes.
- Race: Yes.
- Geographic region: Yes.
- SES/parent education: Yes.
- Community size: No,
- Special populations included: Yes.

Reliability

Internal Consistency

- TRS
  Scales: high .70s to low .90s
  Composites: low to mid .90s

- PRS
  Scales: .70s and .80s
  Composites: high .80s to low .90s

- SRP
  Scales: .70s and .80s
  Composites: high .80s to mid .90s

Test–Retest

- TRS
  Scales: most in high .70s to low .90s
  Composites: high .80s to mid .90s

- PRS
  Scales: most in .70s to low .90s
  Composites: .70s to low .90s

- SRP
  Scales: most in .70s and .80s
  Composites: high .70s to mid .80s

Interrater

- TRS
  Preschool: varied (.30s to .80s)
  Child: most in .50s to .80s (median = .71)

257

- PRS
  Preschool: .30s to .60s
  Child and adolescent: .50s to .70s

Validity

Intercorrelations

Structure of scales and composites was based on factor analyses of items and scales.

Content

Item content came from teachers, parents, and children; psychologists; and reference sources such as DSM and other instruments.

Construct

Concurrent

Groups of children with preexisting clinical diagnoses tend to show distinct BASC profiles.

Predictive

None.

Factor Analysis

See intercorrelations above.

Clinical Sample

Manual presents profiles for eight clinical groups.

Other Instruments Used in Correlation Studies

Note: BASC TRS and PRS scales correlate very highly with corresponding scales on the Achenbach (TRF and CBCL).

- TRS
  Teacher's Report Form (TRF; Achenbach)
  Revised Behavior Problem Checklist (RBPC; Quay & Peterson)
  Conners' Teacher Rating Scales (CTRS-39)
  Burks' Behavior Rating Scales (BBRS)
  Behavior Rating Profile (BRP; Brown & Hammill)

- PRS

  Child Behavior Checklist (CBCL; Achenbach)

  Personality Inventory for Children-Revised (PIC-R; Lachar)

  Conners' Parent Rating Scales (CPRS-93)

  Behavior Rating Profile (BRP; Brown & Hammill)

- SRP

  Minnesota Multiphasic Personality Inventory (MMPI; Hathaway & McKinley)

  Youth Self-Report (YSR; Achenbach)

  Behavior Rating Profile (BRP; Brown & Hammill)

  Children's Personality Questionnaire (CPQ; Porter & Cattell)

STRUCTURED DEVELOPMENTAL HISTORY

Special Features

- Easy to administer, quick to score.
- Assesses a wide range of distinctive dimensions (positive as well as negative).
- Aids in differential diagnosis of specific categories of disorders.
- Contains validity checks to gauge consistency of informant responses.
- Consistency of scales across gender and age levels and between teacher and parent forms.

Federal Mandates Met

- Differentiates between attention problems and hyperactivity (consistent with DSM-IV).
- Measures dimensions helpful for classification of severe emotional disorder (SED)

Adaptation of Special Needs

Audiocassettes of all levels of the PRS and SRP are available for those who have limited ability in reading English but a good understanding of spoken English.

Sensitivity to Other Cultures

Items were analyzed to see if they behaved the same way for both genders and for all minorities. Items that behaved differently by gender or race/ethnicity were dropped from the scales.

APPENDIX C

BASC Items by Scale

BASC

Teacher Rating Scales (TRS)

Items Belonging to Each Scale

Scale	Item Numbers TRS-P	TRS-C	TRS-A
Adaptability	1	1	
	11	38	
	28	75	
	38	89	
	55	112	
	65	126	
	82		
	92		
Aggression	2	2	2
	12	16	15
	21	29	28
	29	34	33
	39	39	37
	48	53	50
	56	66	63
	66	71	68
	75	76	72
	83	90	85
	93	103	98
	102	113	106
		127	119
		140	132
Anxiety	3	3	3
	13	17	16
	30	40	38
	40	54	51
	49	77	73
	57	91	86
	67	114	107
	76	128	120
	84		
	94		
	103		
Attention Problems	4	4	4
	31	18	39
	41	41	74
	58	55	87
	68	78	108
	85	92	121
	95	115	
		129	
Atypicality	5	5	5
	15	19	18
	23	30	29
	32	42	40
	42	56	53
	50	67	64
	59	79	75
	69	93	88
	77	104	99
	81	109	109
	86	116	122
	96	130	
	104	141	
	108	146	

Scale	Item Numbers TRS-P	TRS-C	TRS-A
Conduct Problems		6	6
		20	19
		31	30
		43	41
		68	54
		57	65
		80	76
		94	89
		117	100
		131	110
			123
			134
Depression	6	7	7
	16	21	20
	24	32	42
	33	44	55
	43	58	69
	51	69	77
	60	81	90
	70	95	111
	78	118	124
	87	132	
	97		
Hyperactivity	7	8	8
	17	22	21
	27	33	31
	34	35	34
	44	45	43
	54	59	56
	61	70	66
	71	82	78
	88	96	91
	98	107	101
		119	112
		133	125
		144	135
Leadership		9	9
		23	22
		46	44
		60	57
		83	79
		97	92
		120	113
		134	126
		145	137
Learning Problems		10	10
		24	23
		47	45
		61	58
		84	80
		98	93
		105	104
		121	114
		135	127

Scale	Item Numbers TRS-P	TRS-C	TRS-A
Social Skills	8	11	1
	18	25	14
	35	36	36
	45	48	49
	62	62	62
	72	73	71
	79	85	84
	80	99	97
	99	110	105
	106	122	118
		136	131
		147	
Somatization	9	12	11
	19	26	24
	36	49	46
	46	63	59
	53	86	81
	63	100	94
	73	123	115
	80	137	128
	90		
	100		
	107		
Study Skills		13	12
		27	25
		37	32
		50	47
		64	60
		74	67
		87	82
		101	95
		111	102
		124	116
		138	129
		148	136
			138
Withdrawal	10	14	13
	20	28	48
	37	51	61
	47	65	83
	64	88	96
	74	102	117
	91	125	130
	101	139	

Reprinted with permission from Reynolds and Kamphaus (1992).

Parent Rating Scales (PRS)
Items Belonging to Each Scale

Scale	PRS-P	PRS-C	PRS-A
Adaptability	1	1	
	12	36	
	34	48	
	45	71	
	67	83	
	78	105	
	88	117	
	100		
	111		
	121		
Aggression	2	2	2
	13	14	13
	23	25	24
	31	34	34
	35	37	45
	46	49	56
	56	60	66
	68	72	77
	79	84	88
	89	95	97
	101	106	108
	112	118	
	122	129	
Anxiety	3	3	3
	14	15	14
	24	38	25
	36	50	35
	47	61	46
	57	73	57
	69	85	67
	80	96	78
	90	107	98
	102	119	109
	113	130	
	123		
Attention Problems	4	4	4
	37	39	36
	48	51	47
	70	74	68
	81	86	79
	103	108	99
	114	120	110
Atypicality	5	5	5
	16	17	16
	25	27	37
	38	40	48
	49	52	58
	58	62	69
	71	75	80
	82	87	90
	91	97	100
	97	109	111
	104	121	121
	115	131	
	124		

Scale	PRS-P	PRS-C	PRS-A
Conduct Problems		6	6
		18	17
		28	27
		41	32
		53	38
		63	49
		76	59
		88	64
		98	70
		110	81
		122	91
			101
			112
			122
Depression	6	7	7
	17	19	18
	26	29	28
	39	42	39
	50	54	50
	59	64	60
	64	77	71
	72	89	82
	83	99	92
	92	111	102
	105	123	113
	116	133	
	125		
Hyperactivity	7	8	8
	18	20	19
	27	30	29
	32	43	40
	40	55	51
	51	65	61
	60	78	72
	65	90	83
	73	112	103
	84	124	114
	93		
	98		
	106		
	117		
	126		
	131		
Leadership		9	9
		21	20
		44	30
		56	41
		66	52
		79	62
		91	73
		101	84
		113	94
		125	104
		135	115
			125

Scale	PRS-P	PRS-C	PRS-A
Social Skills	8	10	1
	19	22	12
	28	32	23
	41	45	33
	52	57	44
	61	67	55
	74	80	65
	85	92	76
	94	102	87
	107	104	96
	118	114	107
	127	126	118
	130	136	
		138	
Somatization	9	11	10
	20	23	21
	29	33	31
	33	46	42
	42	58	53
	53	68	63
	62	70	74
	66	81	85
	75	93	95
	86	103	105
	95	115	116
	108	127	126
	119	137	
	128		
Withdrawal	10	12	11
	21	24	22
	43	47	43
	54	59	54
	63	82	75
	76	94	86
	87	116	106
	96	128	117
	109		
	120		
	129		

Self-Report of Personality (SRP)
Items Belonging to Each Scale

Scale	SRP-C	SRP-A
Anxiety	5	5
	16	19
	31	29
	42	36
	49	50
	57	60
	68	67
	75	81
	82	98
	93	112
	100	129
	107	143
	118	160
	125	174
	132	
	143	
	150	
Attitude to School	2	3
	15	18
	24	34
	28	49
	41	65
	54	80
	79	96
	104	111
	129	127
		158
Attitude to Teachers	9	12
	17	25
	26	43
	35	56
	43	74
	52	87
	61	105
	86	136
	111	167
	136	

Scale	SRP-C	SRP-A
Atypicality	7	11
	18	24
	25	42
	33	55
	44	61
	51	73
	59	86
	70	92
	84	104
	95	117
	109	123
	120	135
	134	148
	145	154
		166
		179
		185
Depression	45	7
	50	21
	60	38
	71	52
	76	69
	85	83
	96	100
	101	106
	110	114
	121	131
	126	145
	135	162
	146	176
	151	
Interpersonal Relations	4	1
	30	16
	56	32
	77	47
	81	63
	102	78
	106	91
	117	94
	131	109
	142	122
		125
		140
		153
		156
		171
		184

Scale	SRP-C	SRP-A
Locus of Control	3	2
	14	17
	22	33
	29	48
	40	57
	48	64
	55	79
	66	95
	74	110
	80	126
	91	141
	99	157
	105	172
	116	
	130	
	141	
Relations with Parents	6	10
	32	41
	58	72
	69	103
	83	134
	94	149
	108	165
	124	180
	133	
	149	
Self-Esteem	11	4
	37	35
	63	66
	88	97
	113	128
	138	142
		159
		173
Self-Reliance	1	31
	13	62
	27	93
	39	124
	53	155
	65	183
	78	186
	90	
	103	
	115	
	127	
	128	
	140	
	152	

Scale	SRP-C	SRP-A
Sensation Seeking		6
		13
		20
		30
		37
		51
		68
		82
		99
		113
		130
		144
		161
		175
Sense of Inadequacy	10	14
	20	27
	36	45
	46	58
	62	76
	72	89
	87	107
	97	118
	112	120
	122	138
	137	151
	147	169
		182
Social Stress	12	8
	21	22
	38	39
	47	53
	64	70
	73	84
	89	88
	98	101
	114	115
	123	132
	139	146
	148	163
		177
Somatization		15
		28
		46
		59
		77
		90
		108
		121
		139
		152
		170

BASC ADHD Monitor Sample Printout

BASC Monitor for ADHD: Sample Software Report

The BASC Monitor for ADHD software collects and organizes treatment and behavior information over an indefinite time period (months or years). Its primary purpose is to help the practitioner evaluate the effectiveness of treatments by showing how behavioral changes over time are related to changes in treatment.

Five categories of information may be input into the software:

1. Case information: Background information about the child, parents, school, physician, and other clinicians.

2. Treatment history: Descriptions of pharmacological and behavioral treatments, including dosages, schedules, and starting and ending dates.

3. Behavior ratings: Scores from the Teacher Monitor Ratings (TMR) and Parent Monitor Ratings (PMR) of the BASC Monitor, and relevant scales from the Teacher Rating Scales and Parent Rating Scales of the BASC. The BASC Monitor software scores TMR and PMR forms based on item responses.

4. Direct observations: Data from the BASC Student Observation System.

5. Other variables: The user may define and track any additional variables, such as continuous performance tests, other behavior rating scales, or school achievement.

The BASC Monitor software produces reports that can include tables and graphs showing the trend of behavior indicators over time. A sample report begins below. For some purposes, such as giving feedback to a physician, a shorter report may be produced. The user has many options for controlling the content and length of the report.

> For each BASC Monitor report, the user selects the information to be included. This sample report shows some of the report components that may be produced using the BASC Monitor Software.
> Click here to view all Basic Report and Optional Report Components

---

Reprinted with permission from Kamphaus and Reynolds (1998).

BASC Monitor for ADHD
by Randy W. Kamphaus and Cecil R. Reynolds

Basic case information is included in every report. Complete case information is an optional report component.

Child:	Jamison, Sara J	**School:**	AGS Elementary School
Age:	8	**Birth Date:**	01/10/1990
Grade:	2	**Sex:**	F

The Treatment History shows all pharmacological and other interventions logged for a child's treatment. Codes correspond with letters shown on Monitor Trend Graphs.

Treatment History

Code	Date Impl.	Medication	Dosage	Time(s)	Other Intervention	Time
A	01/25/1998	Methylphenidate	2.5 mg	7 a.m., 11 a.m.	Token system-home	NA
B	02/28/1998	Methylphenidate	5 mg	7 a.m., 11 a.m.	Token system-home	NA
C	04/15/1998	Methylphenidate	5 mg	7 a.m., 11 a.m.	Token system-home/school	NA
D	08/01/1998	Methylphenidate	10 mg	7 a.m., 11 a.m.	Social skills training	weekly

Behavior Monitor Ratings

T-score differences required for statisical significance are shown at the far right of the Ratings T-score Table.

T Scores (M=50, SD=10), Norm Group: General

Scale/Rater	01/14/98	01/22/98	02/06/98	02/24/98	03/12/98	04/14/98	05/12/98	05/27/98	SigDiff P<(.05/.10
Attention Problems	----------	----------	----------	----------	----------	----------	----------	----------	------------
1	61*	---	60	47	49	48*	---	49	15/13
2	58*	80	60	52	47	---	---	47	15/13
3	66*	---	---	59	58*	---	53	---	10/ 9

4	---	---	---	---	---	---	---	---	10/ 9
5	---	---	---	---	---	53*	---	62	9/ 8
6	66*	---	---	70	58*	---	---	---	10/ 9

Hyperactivity

1	57*	---	53	54	47	63*	---	47	15/13
2	63*	72	53	49	54	---	---	54	15/13
3	67*	---	---	68	57*	--	52	---	10/ 9
4	---	---	---	---	---	---	---	---	10/ 9
5	---	---	---	---	---	50*	---	55	8/ 7
6	67*	---	---	78	55*	---	---	---	10/ 9

Internalizing Problems

1	61*	---	49	44	49	47*	---	49	16/14
2	43*	55	49	49	44	---	---	44	16/14
3	41*	---	---	58	48*	---	50	---	13/ 11
4	---	---	---	---	---	---	---	---	13/ 11
5	---	---	---	---	---	45*	---	48	12/10
6	41*	---	---	56	53*	---	---	---	13/ 11

Adaptive Skills

1	25*	---	59	49	59	42*	---	59	12/10
2	46*	50	59	49	49	---	---	49	12/10
3	54*	---	---	47	53*	---	54	---	11/9
4	---	---	---	---	---	---	---	---	11/9
5	---	---	---	---	---	56*	---	51	10/ 9
6	54*	---	---	50	49*	---	---	---	11/9

* denotes
BASC rating

The Rating *T*-Score Table shows results from the 8 most recent BASC and BASC Monitor ratings entered for a child.

Rater Key	Name	Relationship
1	Dianne Jamison	Parent
2	Frank Jamison	Parent
3	Jonelle Sudan	Homeroom Teacher

4	Marti Sanchez	Reading Teacher
5	Sandy James	Resource Room Specialist
6	Franko Munoz	Math Teacher

The SOS Part B Table summarizes results from the Time Sampling of Behavior.

Student Observation System (SOS) Report of Time Sampling – Part B

Occurrences during 15-minute Observation Period

Behavior Category	01/10/98	02/12/98	02/20/98	03/29/98	04/21/98	05/10/98	06/13/
Response to Teacher/Lesson	2	2	2	3	3	3	---
Peer Interaction	1	1	3	2	3	2	---
Work on School Subjects	3	1	2	4	4	4	---
Transition Movement	0	2	0	0	1	0	---
Inappropriate Movement	9	4	6	2	8	2	---
Inattention	10	14	8	11	8	11	--
Inappropriate Vocalization	1	2	3	1	0	1	---
Somatization	0	0	0	0	0	0	---
Repetitive Motor Movements	2	3	4	6	2	6	---
Aggression	2	1	2	1	1	1	---
Self-Injurious Behavior	0	0	0	0	0	0	---
Inappropriate Sexual Behavior	0	0	0	0	0	0	---
Bowel/Bladder Problems	0	0	0	0	0	0	---

The Ratings Trend Graphs show *T*-scores for up to four raters across time. Treatment codes along the X-axis correspond to those shown in the Treatment History.

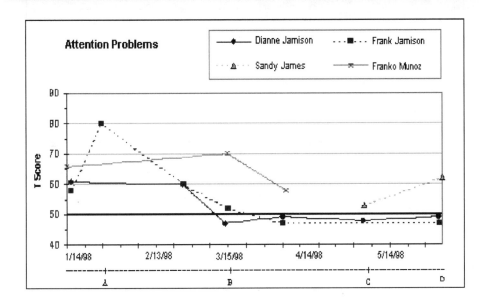

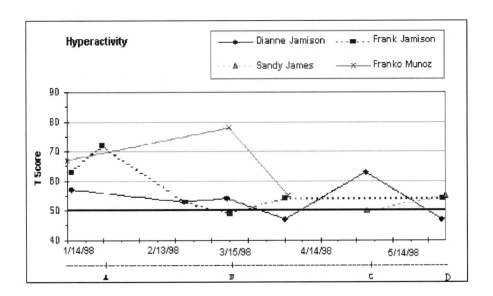

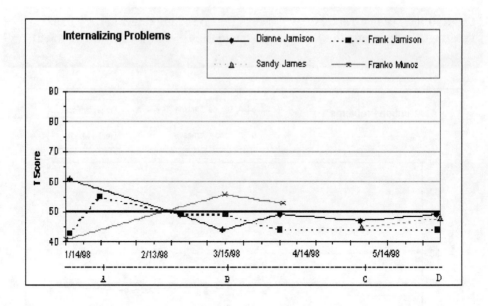

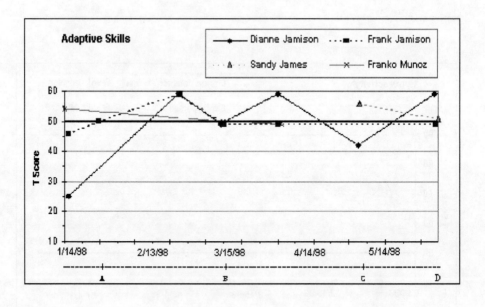

The SOS Part A and Part B Trend Graphs show observation results for any of the 13 SOS behavior categories, as well as for one optional user-defined category.

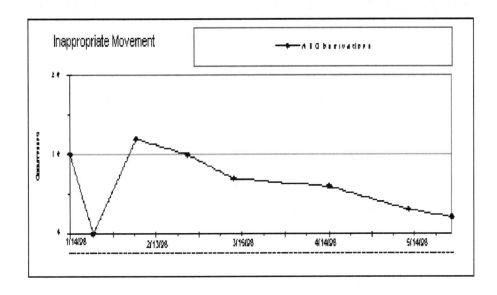

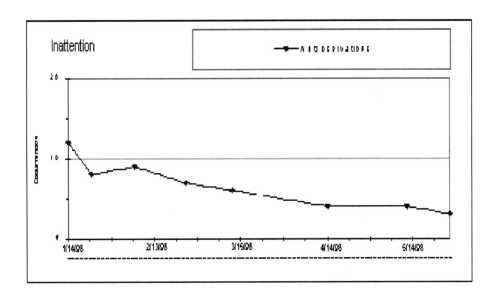

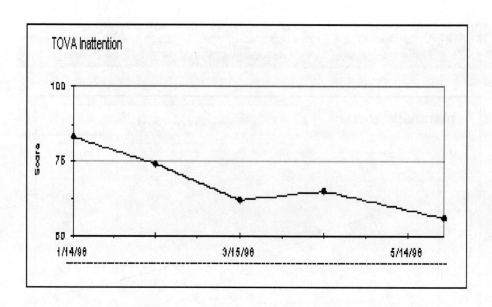

References

Adams, C. A., & Drabman, R. S. (1994). BASC: A critical review. *Child Assessment News, 4*, 1–5.

Alfonso, V. C., & Cancelli, A. A. (1997). The education of specialist-level school psychologists: An unanswered challenge. *Journal of Psychological Practice, 3*(3), 89–104.

Amaya-Jackson, L. (2000). Post traumatic stress disorder in children and adolescents. In B. Sadock & V. Sadock (Eds.), *Kaplan and Sadock's comprehensive textbook of psychiatry* (7th ed., pp. 2763–2769). Philadelphia: Lippincott, Williams & Wilkins.

American Academy of Pediatrics (2000, May 1). *AAP releases new guidelines for diagnosis of ADHD*. Online: *www.aap.org/advocacy/archives/mayadhd.htm*.

American Academy of Pediatrics Committee on Quality Improvement. (2000). Diagnosis and evaluation of the child with Attention-Deficit/Hyperactivity Disorder. *Pediatrics, 105*(5), 1158–1170.

American Psychiatric Association. (1994). *Diagnostic and statistical manual of mental disorders* (4th ed.). Washington, DC: Author.

Assing, R. (1998, August). *BASC Parent Rating Scale (Spanish translation): Validity study*. Paper presented at the annual meeting of the American Psychological Association, San Francisco.

August, G. J., McDonald, A. W., Realmuto, G. M., & Skare, S. S. (1996). Hyperactive and aggressive pathways: Effect of demographic, family, and child characteristics on children's adaptive functioning. *Journal of Clinical Child Psychology, 25,* 341–351.

Barringer, M. S. (2000). *Assessment of ADHD–hyperactive subtype using visual continuous performance, psychophysiological, and behavior measures*. Dissertation submitted to the Office of Graduate Studies, Texas A & M University.

Barringer, M. S., & Reynolds, C. R. (1995). *Behavior ratings of frontal lobe dysfunction*. Paper presented at the annual meeting of the National Academy of Neuropsychology.

Bender, W. N. (1997). Medical interventions and school monitoring. In W. N. Bender (Ed.), *Understanding ADHD: A practical guide for teachers and parents* (pp. 107–122). Upper Saddle River, NJ: Merrill.

Biederman, J., Wilens, T., & Mick, E, (1999). Pharmacotherapy of attention-deficit/ hyperactivity disorder reduces risk for substance use disorder. *Pediatrics, 104*(2), 20.

Binder, L. M., & Rohling, M. L. (1996). Money matters: A meta-analytic review of the effects of financial incentives on recovery after closed-head injury. *American Journal of Psychiatry, 153,* 7–10.

Bloomquist, M. L., August, G. J., Cohen, C., Doyle, A., & Everhart, K. (1997). Social problem solving in hyperactive–aggressive children: How and what they think in conditions of automatic and controlled processing. *Journal of Clinical Child Psychology, 26,* 172–180.

Bracken, B. A., Keith, L. K., & Walker, K. C. (1994). Assessment of preschool behavior and social–emotional functioning: A review of thirteen third-party instruments. *Assessment in Rehabilitation and Exceptionality, 1,* 331–346.

Bracken, B. A., Keith, L. K., & Walker, K. C. (1998). Assessment of preschool behavior and social–emotional functioning: A review of thirteen third-party instruments. *Journal of Psychoeducational Assessment, 16* (2), 153–169.

Brown, R. T., Reynolds, C. R., & Whitaker, J. (1999). Bias in mental testing since "Bias in mental testing. " *School Psychology Quarterly, 14,* 208–238.

Bunke, V. L. (1998). *Children's and adolescents' use of approach and avoidant coping strategies: The relationship with psychosocial adjustment*. Dissertation submitted to the Graduate Faculty, University of Georgia.

Butcher, J. N. (1990). *MMPI-2 in psychological treatment*. New York: Oxford University Press.

Butcher, J. N., Dahlstrom, G., Graham, J., Tellegen, A., & Kaemmer, B. (1989). *MMPI-2 manual for administration and scoring*. Minneapolis: University of Minnesota Press.

Cantwell, D. P. (1996). Classificiation of child and adolescent psychopathology. *Journal of Child Psychology and Psychiatry, 37,* 3–12.

Carter, S. P. (1999). The psychopathology of school violence. *Dissertation Abstracts International Section A: Humanities and Social Sciences, 59*(7–A), 2339.

Challinor, J. M. (1998). Behavioral performance of children with cancer: Assessment using the Behavioral Assessment System for Children. *Dissertation Abstracts International Section B: Sciences and Engineering, 58*(12-B), 6484.

Chelune, G., & Thompson, L. L. (1987). Evaluation of the general sensitivity of the Wisconsin Card Sorting Test among younger and older children. *Developmental Neuropsychology, 3,* 81–89.

Conoley, C. W., Graham, J. M., Neu, T., Craig, M. C., O'Pry, A., Cardin, S. A., Brossart,

D. F., & Parker, R. I. (2001, August). *The efficacy of solution focused family therapy with four aggressive and oppositional acting children*. Paper presented at the annual meeting of the American Psychological Association, San Francisco.

Cooper, D. (1993). *Developmental trends in children's depression inventory responses across age and gender*. Master's thesis, the University of Georgia.

Crijnen, A. A. M., Achenbach, T. M., & Verhulst, F. C. (1999). Problems reported by parents of children in multiple cultures: The Child Behavior Checklist syndrome constructs. *American Journal of Psychiatry, 156*(4), 569–574.

Dalton, J. E. (1996). Juvenile male sex offenders: Mean scores and the BASC self-report of personality. *Psychological Reports, 79,* 634.

Daniel, M. H. (1992, August). *Item-level covariance structure analysis for constructing personality/behavioral scales*. Paper presented at the annual meeting of the American Psychological Association, Washington, DC.

Daniel, M. H. (1993). *Diagnostic specificity of parents' vs. teachers' behavior ratings*. Paper presented at the annual meeting of the National Association of School Psychologists, Washington, DC.

Daubert v. Merrell Dow. (1993). 509 U. S. 579.

De La Torre, R. (1998). The utility of the Behavior Assessment System for Children with adolescent sexual offenders. *Dissertation Abstracts International Section B: Sciences and Engineering, 59*(6-B), 3053.

Doyle, A., Ostrander, R., Skare, S., Crosby, R. D., & August, G. (1997). Convergent and criterion-related validity of the Behavior Assessment System for Children—Parent Rating Scales. *Journal of Clinical Child Psychology, 26,* 276–284.

Dunbar, J. L. (1999). Differential item performance by gender on the externalizing scales of the Behavior Assessment System for Children. *Dissertation Abstracts International Section A: Humanities and Social Sciences, 60*(6-A), 1902.

DuPaul, G. J., Power, T. J., McGoey, K. E., & Ikeda, M. J. (1998). Reliability and validity of parent and teacher ratings of attention-deficit hyperactivity disorder symptoms. *Journal of Psychoeducational Assessment, 16,* 55–68.

Entwhistle, P., Kalinsky, R., & Toscano, L. (1997). *Neuropsychological assessment and the Behavior Assessment System for Children*. Paper presented at the annual meeting of the National Academy of Neuropschology, Las Vegas.

Erhardt, D., & Conners, C. K. (1996). Methodological and assessment issues in pediatric psychopharmacology. In J. M. Weiner (Ed.), *Diagnosis and psychopharmacology of childhood and adolescent disorders* (2nd ed.). New York: Wiley.

Faubel, G. (1998). An efficacy assessment of a school-based intervention program for emotionally handicapped students. *Dissertation Abstracts International Section A: Humanities and Social Sciences, 58*(11-A), 4183.

Flanagan, D. P., Alfonso, V. C., Primavera, L. H., Povall, L., & Higgins, D. (1996). Convergent validity of the BASC and SSRS: Implications for social skills assessment. *Psychology in the Schools, 33,* 13–23.

Flanagan, R. (1995). A review of the Behavior Assessment System for Children (BASC):

275

Assessment consistent with the requirements of the Individuals with Disabilities Education Act (IDEA). *Journal of School Psychology, 33*, 177–186.

Fletcher-Janzen, E., & Reynolds, C. R. (Eds.). (in press). *Reference manual of childhood disorders*. New York: Wiley.

Francis, D. J., Fletcher, J. M., Stuebing, K. K., Davidson, K. C., & Thompson, N. M. (1991). Analysis of change: Modeling individual growth. *Journal of Consulting and Clinical Psychology, 59*, 27–37.

Frick, P. J., Kamphaus, R. W., Lahey, B. B., Loeber, R., Christ, M. A. G., Hart, E. L., & Tannenbaum, L. E. (1991). Academic underachievement and the disruptive behavior disorders. *Journal of Consulting and Clinical Psychology, 59*, 289–294.

Gelman, C. F. (1998). Characteristics of a prenatally cocaine-exposed clinical population at school age. *Dissertation Abstracts International Section B: Sciences and Engineering, 58*(11-B), 6234.

Goldstein, S. (1999). Attention-deficit/hyperactivity disorder. In S. Goldstein & C. R. Reynolds (Eds.), *Handbook of neurodevelopmental and genetic disorders in children* (pp. 154–184). New York: Guilford Press.

Goldstein, S., & Reynolds, C. R. (Eds.) (1999). *Handbook of neurodevelopmental and genetic disorders in children*. New York: Guilford Press.

Graham, J. (2000). *MMPI-2: Assessing personality and psychopathology* (3rd ed.). New York: Oxford University Press.

Greenspoon, P. J., & Saklofske, D. H. (1997). Validity and reliability of the multidimensional students' life satisfaction scale with Canadian children. *Journal of Psychoeducational Assessment, 15*, 138–155.

Gresham, R. M., & Elliott, S. N. (1990). *Social skills rating system*. Circle Pines, MN: American Guidance Service.

Handfinger, A. S. (2001). The effects of behavior problems on the development of adaptive skills in children. *Dissertation Abstracts International, 61*, (9-B), 5027B.

Handwerk, M. L., Larzelere, R. E., Soper, S. H., & Friman, P. C. (1999). Parent and child discrepancies in reporting severity of problem behaviors in three out-of-home settings. *Psychological Assessment, 11*, 14–23.

Hartlage, L. C. (1989). Behavior *change inventory: Inventory of pre- versus postbehaviors with brain injury*. Burlington, VT: Clinical Psychology.

Hartley, M. M. M. (1999). The relationship among disruptive behaviors, attention, and academic achievement in a clinic referral sample. *Dissertation Abstracts International Section A: Humanities and Social Sciences, 60*(2-A), 0333.

Heaton, R. H. (1981). *Wisconsin Card Sorting Test Manual*. Odessa, FL: Psychological Assessment Resources.

Hechtman, L. T. (1999). ADHD and bipolar disorder. *ADHD Report, 7*(2), 1–4.

Henning-Stout, M. (1998). Assessing the behavior of girls: What we see and what we miss. *Journal of School Psychology, 36*(4), 433–455.

Hersen, M., & Bellak, A. (Eds.). (1998). *Comprehensive clinical psychology*. Oxford: Elsevier Science.

Hightower, A. D. (1986). The Teaher–Child Rating Scale: A brief objective measure of elementary children's school problem behaviors and competencies. *School Psychology Review, 15*(3), 393–409.

Hoover, H. V. A., Braver, S. L., Wolchik, S. A., & Sandler, I. N. (2000, August). Teacher's ratings of children's classroom behavior: Time of year effects? Paper presented at the annual meeting of the American Psychological Association, Washington, D.C.

Hoza, B. (1994). Reviews of the Behavior Assessment System for Children. *Child Assessment News, 4*(1), 5, 8–10.

Huberty, C. J., DiStefano, C. & Kamphaus, R. W. (1997). Behavioral clustering of school children. *Multivariate Behavioral Research, 32*, 105–143.

Hudziak, J. J., Heath, A. C., Madden, P. F., Reich, W., Bucholz, K. K., Slutske, W., Bierut, L. J., Neuman, R. J., & Todd, R. D. (1998). Latent class and factor analysis of DSM-IV ADHD: A twin study of female adolescents. *Journal of the American Academy of Child and Adolescent Psychiatry, 37*(8), 848–857.

Hudziak, J. J., Wadsworth, B. A., Heath, A. C., & Achenbach, T. M. (1999). Latent class analysis of child behavior checklist attention problems. *Journal of the American Academy of Child and Adolescent Psychiatry, 38*, 985–991.

Huebner, E. S., Funk III, B. A., & Gilman, R. (2000). Cross-sectional and longitudinal psychosocial correlates of adolescent life satisfaction reports. *Canadian Journal of School Psychology, 16*(1), 53–64.

Hughes, J. N. (1999). Child psychotherapy. In C. R. Reynolds & T. B. Gutkin (Eds.), *The handbook of school psychology* (3rd ed., pp. 745–763). New York: Wiley.

Hutchinson, K. T. (1999). The relationship between the affective processing capabilities and social skills functioning of children with attention deficit hyperactivity disorder. *Dissertation Abstracts International Section B: Sciences and Engineering, 59*(10-B), 5566.

James, E. M., Reynolds, C. R., & Dunbar, J. (1994). Self-report instruments. In T. H. Ollendick & N. J. King (Eds.), *International handbook of phobic and anxiety disorders in children and adolescents* (pp. 317–329). New York: Plenum Press.

Jones, K., & Witt, J. (1994). Rating the ratings of raters: A critique of the Behavior Assessment System for Children. *Child Assessment News, 4*(1), 10–11.

Kamphaus, R. W. (2001). *Clinical assessment of children's intelligence* (2nd ed.). Needham Heights, MA: Allyn & Bacon.

Kamphaus, R. W., & Frick, P. J. (2002). *Clinical assessment of child and adolescent personality and behavior* (2nd ed.). Needham Heights, MA: Allyn & Bacon.

Kamphaus, R. W., Huberty, C. J., Distefano, C., & Petoskey, M. D. (1997). A typology of teacher-rated child behavior for a national U. S. sample. *Journal of Abnormal Child Psychology, 25*, 453–463.

Kamphaus, R. W., Jiménez, M. E., Pineda, D. A., Rowe, E. W., Fleckenstein, L., Restrepo, M. A., Mora, O., Puerta, I. C., Jiménez, I., Sanchez, J. L., García, M., & Palacio, L. G. (2000). Análisis transcultural de un instrumento de dimensiones multiples en el diagnóstico del deficit de atención. *Revista de Neuropsicología, Neuropsyquiatría y Neurociencias, 2*, 51–63.

Kamphaus, R. W., Petoskey, M. D., Cody, A. H., Rowe, E. W., Huberty, C. J., & Reynolds, C. R. (1999). A typology of parent rated child behavior for a national U.S. sample. *Journal of Child Psychology and Psychiatry and Allied Disciplines, 40*, 1–10.

Kamphaus, R. W., & Reynolds, C. R. (1998). *BASC ADHD Monitor.* Circle Pines, MN: American Guidance Service.

Kaye, D. H., & Freedman, D. A. (2000). Reference guide on statistics. In Federal Judicial Center (Ed.), *Reference manual on scientific evidence* (2nd ed., pp. 83–178). Washington, DC: Federal Judicial Center.

Kline, R. B. (1994). Test review: New objective rating scales for child assessment, I. Parent- and teacher-informant inventories of the Behavior Assessment System for Children, the Child Behavior Checklist, and the Teacher Report Form. *Journal of Psychoeducational Assessment, 12*, 289–306.

Kline, R. B. (1995). Test review: New objective rating scales for child assessment, II. Self-report scales for children and adolescents: Self-Report of Personality of the Behavior Assessment System for Children, the Youth Self-Report, and the Personality Inventory for Youth. *Journal of Psychoeducational Assessment, 13*, 169–193.

Knight, L. W. (1996). The BASC parent rating scales: Patterns of behavior by gender, race, and socioeconomic status. *Dissertation Abstracts International Section A: Humanities and Social Sciences, 58*(1-A), 0084.

Kokko, K., & Pulkkinen, L. (2000). Prevention and treatment. *Aggression in childhood and long-term unemployment in adulthood: A cycle of maladaptation and some protective factors.* Washington, DC: American Psychological Association. Volume 3, Article 32.

Koppitz, E. M. (1982). Personality assessment in the schools. In C. R. Reynolds & T. B. Gutkin (Eds.), *The handbook of school psychology* (pp. 273–295). New York: Wiley.

Kratochwill, T., Sheridan, S., Carlson, J., & Lasecki, K. (1999). Advances in behavioral assessment. In C. R. Reynolds & T. B. Gutkin (Eds.), *The handbook of school psychology* (3rd ed., pp. 350–382). New York: Wiley.

Lahey, B. B., Applegate, B., McBurnett, K., Biederman, J., Greenhill, L., Hynd, G. W., Barkley, R. A., Newcorn, J., Jensen, P., Richters, J., Garfinkel, B., Kerdyck, L., Frick, P. J., Ollendick, T., Perez, D., Hart, E. L., Waldman, I., & Shaffer, D., (1994). DSM-IV field trials for Attention-Deficit Hyperactivity Disorder in children and adolescents. *American Journal of Psychiatry, 151*(11), 1673–1685.

Last, C. G. (1993). Introduction. In C. G. Last (Ed.), *Anxiety across the lifespan: A developmental perspective* (pp. 1–6). New York: Springer.

Leahy, R. L., & Holland, S. J. (2000). *Treatment plans and interventions for depression and anxiety disorders.* New York: Guilford Press.

Lett, N. J., & Kamphaus, R. W. (1997). Differential validity of the BASC Student Observation System and the BASC Teacher Rating Scales. *Canadian Journal of School Psychology, 13*, 1–14.

Lowman, M. G., Schwanz, K. A., & Kamphaus, R. W. (1996). WISC-III third factor: Critical measurement issues. *Canadian Journal of School Psychology, 12*, 15–22.

March, J. S., Mulle, K., Stallings, P., Erhardt, D., & Conners, C. K. (1995). Organizing an anxiety disorders clinic. In J. S. March, (Ed.), *Anxiety disorders in children and adolescents* (pp. 402–435). New York: Guilford Press.

Martens, B., Witt, J., Daly, E., & Vollmer, T. (1999). Behavior analysis: Theory and practice in educational settings. In C. R. Reynolds & T. B. Gutkin (Eds.), *The handbook of school psychology* (3rd ed., pp. 638–663). New York: Wiley.

Martin, R. P. (1988). *Assessment of personality and behavior problems: Infancy through adolescence*. New York: Guilford Press.

Matazow, G. S., & Kamphaus, R. W. (in press). Behavior assessment system for children (BASC): Toward accurate diagnosis and effective treatment. In J. J. W. Andrews, H. Janzen, & D. Saklofske (Eds.). *Ability, achievement, and behavior assessment: A practical handbook*. San Diego, CA: Academic Press.

Mayfield, J. W., & Reynolds, C. R. (1998). Are ethnic differences in diagnosis of childhood psychopathology an artifact of psychometric methods? An experimental evaluation of Harrington's hypothesis using parent-reported symptomatology. *Journal of School Psychology, 36*, 313–334.

McNamara, J. R., Hollmann, C., & Riegel, T. (1994). A preliminary study of the usefulness of the Behavior Assessment System for Children in the evaluation of mental health needs in a Head Start population. *Psychological Reports, 75*, 1195–1201.

Melton, G. B., Petrila, J., Poythress, N. G., & Slobogin, C. (1997). *Psychological evaluations for the courts* (2nd ed.). New York: Guilford Press.

Merenda, P. F. (1996). BASC: Behavior Assessment System for Children. *Measurement and Evaluation in Counseling and Development, 28*, 229–232.

Merydith, S. P. (2000). Aggression intervention skill training: Moral reasoning and moral emotions. *NASP Communique, 28*, 6–8.

Merydith, S. P., & Joyce, E. K. (1998, August). *Temporal stability and convergent validity of the BASC Parent and Teacher Rating Scales*. Paper presented at the annual meeting of the American Psychological Association, San Francisco.

Meyers, J., & Nastasi, B. K. (1999). Primary prevention in school settings. In C. R. Reynolds & T. B. Gutkin (Eds.), *The handbook of school psychology* (3rd ed., pp. 764–799). New York: Wiley.

Miller, D. C. (1994, Winter). Behavior Assessment System for Children (BASC): Test critique. *Texas Association of School Psychologists Newsletter*, 23–29.

Morgan, A. B. W. (1998). Childhood social withdrawal: The role of social skills in the relation of withdrawal and anxiety. *Dissertation Abstracts International Section B: Sciences and Engineering, 59*(6-B), 3097.

Murphy, S. B. (2000). The role of student and teacher ethnicity in the assessment of emotional and behavioral disorders: Examining ratings of student behavior on the Behavior Assessment System for Children (BASC). Unpublished manuscript.

Nail, J. M., & Evans, J. G. (1997). The emotional adjustment of gifted adolescents: A view of global functioning. *Roeper Review, 20*(1), 18–21.

Nathan, P. E., & Gorman, J. M. (2002). *A guide to treatments that work* (2nd ed.). New York: Oxford University Press.

Nelson, B., Martin, R. P., Hodge, S., Havill, V., & Kamphaus, R. (1999). Modeling the prediction of elementary school adjustment from preschool temperament. *Personality and Individual Differences, 26*, 687–700.

Neuman, R. J., Todd, R. D., Heath, A. C., Reich, W., Hudziak, J. J., Bucholz, K. K., Madden, P. A. F., Begleiter, H., Porjesz, B., Kuperman, S., Hesselbrock, V., & Reich, T. (1999). Evaluation of ADHD typology in three contrasting samples: A latent class approach. *Journal of the American Academy of Child and Adolescent Psychiatry, 38*(1), 25–33.

Oehler-Stinnett, J., & Stinnett, T. A. (1995). Teacher rating scales for attention deficit–hyperactivity: A comparative review. *Journal of Psychoeducational Assessment, Monograph Series, Special Issue on Assessment of Attention-Deficit/Hyperactivity Disorders.* Cordova, TN: Psychoeducational Corporation.

Olson, R., Mullins, L., Gillman, J., & Chaney, J. (Eds.). (1994). *The sourcebook of pediatric psychology.* Boston: Allyn & Bacon.

Ostrander, R., Weinfurt, K. P., Yarnold, P. R., & August, G. J. (1998). Diagnosing attention deficit disorders with the Behavioral Assessment System for Children and the Child Behavior Checklist: Test and construct validity analyses using optimal discriminant classification trees. *Journal of Consulting and Clinical Psychology, 66*, 660–672.

Pearson, D. A., & Aman, M. G. (1994). Ratings of hyperactivity and developmental indices: Should clinicians correct for developmental level? *Journal of Autism and Developmental Disorders, 24*(4), 395–411.

Ramsay, M., Reynolds, C. R., & Kamphaus, R. W. (2002). *Essentials of behavioral assessment.* New York: Wiley.

Rapoport, J. L. & Castellanos, F. X. (1996). Attention-deficit hyperactivity disorder. In J. M. Wiener (Ed.), *Diagnosis and psychopharmacology of childhood and adolescent disorders* (2nd. ed., pp. 265–292). New York: Wiley

Realmuto, G. M., August, G. J., Sieler, J. D., & Pessoa-Brandao, L. (1997). Peer assessment social reputation in community samples of disruptive and nondisruptive children: Utility of the Revised Class Play method. *Journal of Clinical Child Psychology, 26*, 67–76.

Reitan, R. M., & Wolfson, D. (2000). *Mild head injury: Cognitive, intellectual, and emotional consequences.* Tucson: Neuropsychology Press.

Reynolds, C. R. (1997). *Detection of malingering in head injury litigation.* New York: Kluwer Academic Press.

Reynolds, C. R. (1998). Need we measure anxiety differently for males and females? *Journal of Personality Assessment, 70*(2), 212–221.

Reynolds, C. R. (2001a). *Clinical assessment scales for the elderly: Professional manual.* Odessa, FL: Psychological Assessment Resources.

Reynolds, C. R. (2001b, October). *Forensic neuropsychological evaluation.* Workshop presented at the annual convention of the American Board of Forensic Examiners, Nashville.

Reynolds, C. R. (2001c, June). *Understanding and defending against the Daubert challenge to expert testimony.* Workshop presented at the annual convention of the American Psychological Society, Toronto.

Reynolds, C. R., & Bigler, E. D. (1994). *Test of memory and learning.* Austin, TX: PRO-ED publishing.

Reynolds, C. R., & Fletcher-Janzen, E. F. (Eds.) (1997). *Handbook of clinical child neuropsychology* (2nd ed.). New York: Kluwer Academic Press.

Reynolds, C. R., & Kamphaus, R. W. (1992). *Behavior Assessment System for Children.* Circle Pines, MN: American Guidance Service.

Reynolds, C. R., Lowe, P. A., & Saenz, A. (1999). The problem of bias in psychological assessment. In C. R. Reynolds & T. B. Gutkin (Eds.), *The handbook of school psychology* (3rd ed., pp. 549–596). New York: Wiley.

Reynolds, C. R., & Mayfield, J. W. (1999). Neuropsychological assessment in genetically linked neurodevelopmental disorders. In S. Goldstein & C. R. Reynolds (Eds.), *Handbook of neurodevelopmental and genetic disorders in children* (pp. 9–37). New York: Guilford Press.

Reynolds, C. R., & Richmond, B. O. (1985). *Manual for the revised Children's Manifest Anxiety scale.* Los Angeles: Western Psychological Services.

Reynolds, C. R., Richmond, B. O., & Lowe, P. A. (2002). *Manual for the Adult Manifest Anxiety scale.* Los Angeles: Western Psychological Services.

Riccio, C. A., Hall, J., Morgan, A., Hynd, G. W., Gonzalez, J. J., & Marshall, R. M. (1994). Executive function and the Wisconsin Card Sorting Test: Relationship with behavioral ratings and cognitive ability. *Developmental Neuropsychology, 10,* 215–229.

Riccio, C. A., Reynolds, C. R., & Lowe, P. A. (2001). *Clinical and research applications of continuous performance tests: Measuring attention and impulsive responding.* New York: Wiley.

Rosenthal, G. (1996). The Behavior Assessment System for Children: Locus of Control scale. *Child Assessment News, 5*(5), 1–5, 12.

Rowe, E. W., Circle, E. L., Reynolds, C. R., & Kamphaus, R. W. (1998). Behavior Assessment System for Children (BASC) Monitor for ADHD: An introduction to applications in practice. *The ADHD Report, 6*(6), 113–129.

Sandoval, J. (1998). Review of the Behavior Assessment System for Children. In J. C. Impara & B. S. Plake (Eds.), *Thirteenth Mental Measurements Yearbook* (pp. 128–131). Lincoln, NE: Buros Institute of Mental Measurements.

Sandoval, J., & Echandia, A. (1994). Behavior Assessment System for Children. *Journal of School Psychology, 32,* 419–425.

Sattler, J. M. (1998). *Clinical and forensic interviewing of children and families.* San Diego: Author.

Scahill, L., Schwab-Stone, M., Merikangas, K. R., Leckman, J. F., Zhang, H., & Kasl, S. (1999). Psychosocial and clinical correlates of ADHD in a community sample of school-age children. *Journal of the American Academy of Child and Adolescent Psychiatry, 38*(8), 976–984.

4

References

Schwanz, K. A. (2001). *Disruptive behavior problems associated with adaptability, social, and study skill deficits in school-age children.* Dissertation submitted to the University of Georgia.

Schwanz, K. A., & Kamphaus, R. W. (1997). Assessment and diagnosis of ADHD. In W. N. Bender (Ed.), *Understanding ADHD: A practical guide for parents and teachers.* Upper Saddle River, NJ: Merrill/Prentice Hall.

Schwean, V. L., Burt, K., & Saklofske, D. H. (1999). Correlates of mother- and teacher-ratings of hyperactivity–impulsivity and inattention in children with AD/HD. *Canadian Journal of School Psychology, 15*(1), 43–62.

Shelby, M. D. (1999). Risk and resistance factors affecting the psychosocial adjustment of child survivors of cancer. *Dissertation Abstracts International Section B: Sciences and Engineering, 59*(7-B), 3740.

Shelby, M. D., Nagle, R. J., Barnett-Queen, L. L., Quattlebaum, PD., & Wuori, D. F. (1998). Parental reports of psychosocial adjustment and social competence in child survivors of acute lymphocytic leukemia. *Children's Health Care, 27*(2), 113–129.

Sorneson, E., & Johnson, E. (1996). Subtypes of incarcerated delinquents constructed via cluster analysis. *Journal of Child Psychology, 37*, 293–303.

Stein, M. A., Szmowski, E., Blondis, T. A., Roizen, N. J. (1995). Adaptive skills dysfunction in ADD and SDHD children. *Journal of Child Psychology, 36*, 663–670.

Stowers-Wright, L. E. (2000). *A behavioral cluster analysis of male juvenile defenders.* Dissertation submitted to the graduate faculty of University of Georgia.

Strayhorn, J. M. (1993). Statistical case puzzle: The case of the agreeable raters. *Journal of the American Academy of Child and Adolescent Psychiatry, 32*(6), 1301–1303.

Thorpe, Kamphaus, R. W., Rowe, & Fleckenstein, (2000, August). *Longitudinal effects of child adaptive competencies and internalizing problems on behavioral and academic outcomes.* Paper presented at the annual meeting of the American Psychological Association, Washington, DC.

Tsoubris, K. T. (1998). Relationship between prenatal cocaine exposure and behavioral patterns among preschool children with disabilities. *Dissertation Abstracts International Section B: Sciences and Engineering, 59*(5-B), 2441.

Valdez, G. M., & McNamara, J. R. (1994). Matching to prevent adoption disruption. *Child & Adolescent Social Work Journal, 11*(5), 391–403.

Vaughn, M. L, Riccio, C. A., Hynd, G. W., & Hall, J. (1997). Diagnosing ADHD (predominantly inattentive and combined type subtypes): Discriminant validity of the Behavior Assessment System for Children (BASC) and the Achenbach Parent and Teacher Rating Scales. *Journal of Clinical Child Psychology, 26*(4), 349–357.

Verhulst, F. C., Koot, H. M., & Van der Ende, J. (1994). Differential predictive value of parents' and teachers' reports of children's problem behaviors: A longitudinal study. *Journal of Abnormal Child Psychology, 22*, 531–546.

Volkmar, F. R., Sparrow, S. S., Goudreau, D., & Cicchetti, D. V. (1987). Social deficits in autism: An operational approach using the Vineland Adaptive Behavior Scales.

282

Journal of the American Academy of Child and Adolescent Psychiatry, 26(2), 156–161.

Wang, J. -J. (1992, April). *An analytical approach to generating norms for skewed normative distributions.* Paper presented at the annual meeting of the American Educational Research Association, San Francisco.

Wasielewski, S. M., Gridley, B. J., & Hall, J. (1998, April). *Construct validity of the Behavior Assessment System for Children with the Personality Inventory for Children—Revised with a clinical sample.* Paper presented at the annual meeting of the National Association of School Psychologists. Orlando, FL.

Whelan, T., & Walker, M. (1997). Coping and adjustment of children with neurological disorder. In C. R. Reynolds & E. Fletcher-Janzen (Eds.), *Handbook of clinical child neuropsychology* (2nd ed., pp. 68–711). New York: Plenum.

Williford, A. P., Ryan, E. E., & Shelton, T. L. (2000). *Kindergarten readiness in an at-risk population: Child and family factors.*

Williford, A. P., Woods, J. E., & Shelton, T. L. (2000, August). *Project Mastery: A family-centered intervention for preschoolers with behavior problems.* Paper presented at the annual meeting of the American Psychological Association, Washington, DC.

Witt, J. C., & Jones, K. M. (1998). Review of the Behavior Assessment System for Children. In J. C. Impara & B. S. Plake (Eds.), *The Thirteenth Mental Measurements Yearbook* (pp. 131–133). Lincoln, NE: Buros Institute of Mental Measurements.

Woodin, M. F. (1999). Screening for the interface between attention, executive functioning, and working memory: A cluster and profile analytic study. *Dissertation Abstracts International Section B: Sciences and Engineering, 59*(10-B), 5590.

Wootten, S. A. (1999). Attention-deficit/hyperactivity disorder. *Dissertation Abstracts International Section B: Sciences & Engineering, 60*(1-B), 0380.

Wutzke, T. M. (1999). An examination of factors associated with resiliency in siblings of children with juvenile rheumatoid arthritis: A family systems perspective. *Dissertation Abstracts International Section B: Sciences and Engineering, 60*(1-B), 0380.

Youssef, S. (1999). Students with juvenile rheumatoid arthritis: Psychosocial and health perceptions in relation to the implementation of school interventions. *Dissertation Abstracts International Section B: Sciences and Engineering, 59*(10-B), 5591.

Index